# DUNBLANE
## NEVER FORGET

This book is especially for Sophie

It is also dedicated to the memory of Sophie's classmates
Victoria Clydesdale, Emma Crozier, Melissa Currie,
Charlotte Dunn, Kevin Hasell, Ross Irvine,
David Kerr, Mhairi MacBeath, Brett McKinnon,
Abigail McLennan, Emily Morton, John Petrie,
Joanna Ross, Hannah Scott and Megan Turner,
her teacher Gwen Mayor
and her mum Barbara Lockwood

# DUNBLANE
## NEVER FORGET

Mick North

MAINSTREAM
PUBLISHING

EDINBURGH AND LONDON

Copyright © Mick North, 2000

All rights reserved

The moral right of the author has been asserted

First published in Great Britain in 2000 by

MAINSTREAM PUBLISHING COMPANY (EDINBURGH) LTD

7 Albany Street

Edinburgh EH1 3UG

ISBN 1 84018 300 4

A catalogue record for this book is available from the British Library

Typeset in Allise and Van Djick

Printed and bound in Great Britain by Creative Print and Design Wales

# Contents

# Preface

On 13 March 1996, described by some as Scotland's blackest day, I was suddenly plunged into an unimaginable situation beyond my worst fears. This book is the outcome of my wish to record and analyse the events of that day and to try to understand what led up to them and what happened in the aftermath. I am certain there will be a few who won't want the book to have been written. It is, if I've achieved my aim, a vivid reminder of the horror and trauma experienced by a small Perthshire town. But it's more than that, for in describing the Dunblane massacre I've raised and resurrected many difficult issues. Some of them may be too sensitive for those people who would like the tragedy to be placed firmly and irretrievably in the past. Like these people I would much rather there'd been no need to write a book that has such a dreadful crime at its heart. Unlike them, I believe that it's essential to learn lessons from tragedy – even when that involves the hard task of facing up to the reality of what happened and how individuals, communities and organisations responded.

Why should I want to write a book that concerns my daughter's murder? Should I not have left it to a more detached observer, someone who undoubtedly would not have found it so draining? I've had to relive the most difficult and painful days of my life and have found that neither the research nor the writing were cathartic exercises. Only time will tell whether I feel better or worse for having gone through these processes.

Two reasons for writing *Dunblane: Never Forget* were foremost. First, I was in a position to observe events from the inside. I know how things were actually handled and my perspective as one of the Dunblane victims' parents affords unique insights into the motivations and motives of others who were involved. My second reason is indicated by the title. I don't want what happened in Dunblane to be forgotten. I've no desire for it to dominate people's lives, but unless it remains a part of everyone's consciousness, essential lessons won't be learnt. For many of us whose children died in the Primary School gymnasium, there's been a drive to do as much as we can to ensure that others never have to go through the experiences we have faced. Only by listening to victims and their families will it be possible to ensure that necessary changes in practice and attitude are put in train. Equally, only by recognising the positive things that can happen after a tragedy will provision for these be incorporated into post-disaster strategies.

In my career as an academic I was accustomed to objective analysis backed by substantial and rigorous proof. I recognise, therefore, that this book is tempered with more subjective thoughts. Nevertheless I believe I have balanced these with an equitable examination of what happened. I've been critical of certain agencies, groups and individuals; but the book is not my attempt to fulfil, as one local newspaper editor once put it, 'a need to find people to blame, to seek out scapegoats for a crime which defied the comprehension of normal people'. His attitude effectively says that, because of the enormity of the criminal act, everybody else may be excused his or her shortcomings and insensitivity. I try to explain why it would be wrong to dismiss, as that editor did, the shortcomings and insensitivity by saying 'any perceived errors in judgment were magnified out of all proportion because of the scale of the tragedy'.

The massacre and its aftermath raised questions about a number of important issues: firearms legislation; police operations; the response of the emergency services (especially the police) to disasters; public inquiries; the community response to tragedy; disaster funds; counselling and victim support; bereavement; the ability of victims and their families to recover from traumatic events; and the rights of those whose lives are shattered by a much-reported crime. These are not trivial matters and discussion must never be suppressed because of oversensitivity towards distressing circumstances.

At the book's core is that horrendous day, the Thirteenth of March 1996. The early chapters describe how a little girl came to grow up in Dunblane. It is a family story touched with joy and sadness. There is also a contemporaneous account of episodes from the life of a man I never met. Regrettably he was too much a part of the story to ignore, for the lives of that man and the little girl eventually collided with the most dreadful consequences. Afterwards another story begins, one involving a different family, an extended family of people brought together by a tragic event that had devastated all their lives. It describes the magnificent response to their plight, but also how they had to watch and respond as self-interest sometimes masqueraded as 'freedom', the 'custodian of law and order', the 'legislature' or the 'caring community'. I hope that the book will prompt readers to revisit some of the issues. I look forward to it stimulating some genuine and serious debate on topics that, up until now, have not always been fully explored.

The idea of writing a book about Dunblane took seed during the autumn of 1996. I knew then that it would take time to complete the task. As sub-sequent events unfolded and more lessons appeared to go unlearnt, the imperative for writing it increased. It was never my intention to record and discuss every Dunblane-related event and issue and my purpose has been to focus on those events and issues that, to my mind, are most significant. Over the last four years I've kept notes and attempted to stay in touch with all the relevant issues. To supplement my personal recollections I have relied on the evidence I heard while attending the Cullen Inquiry, Lord Cullen's Report, various other reports such as those of the Home Affairs Select Committee, the Dunblane Fund and the Dunblane Support Centre, the accounts of parliamentary debates published in Hansard, press cuttings and video recordings of television news coverage and documentaries. I know from my own experience that it's easy to find oneself misquoted in the press. I have tried to limit quotes to those that appear authentic, because they are consis-tent with other statements or quotes from the same person. A bibliography is provided that includes my sources and details of other books mentioned.

It is difficult to envisage how I could have embarked on writing this book, let alone completed it, without the help and support of many others. The sympathetic and sensitive way in which the vast majority of the media reporters dealt with what I had to say reassured me that it was appropriate to write a book about Dunblane. The colleagues I've met through gun-control movements both in the UK and abroad have given me inspiration. Many people have provided practical help and information. I'm particularly grateful to Keith Brown, Tim Bugler, Jenny Booth, Alan Williams and Lord Ewing of Kirkford. My special thanks go to Phil Scraton for discussing many of the key issues with me and for his encouragement throughout. I am indebted to everyone at Mainstream Publishing who ensured that my original outline was transformed into a published book.

Since the Dunblane massacre I've found support among many friends and family. I'd particularly like to thank my mum and my sisters, Elspeth Cameron, John Goodfellow, Sharon Kelly, Olwen and Jim Lawson, Alison McRae, Alison and Jeremy Mottram, Kay and Bob Nicol, Sheena and Stuart Ogg, Lewis and Evelyn Stevens and Sandra Uttley. I would also like to thank Sandra for her comments on the manuscript and for keeping a check on press articles.

The families of Sophie's classmates have always looked out for me and I can't thank all the members of the Thursday group enough. I am especially grateful to John Crozier, Barbara and Martyn Dunn, Liz McLennan, Les Morton, Pam and Kenny Ross, David Scott and Isobel Wilson for their help during the final stages of the preparation of the book.

When the going got tough I took time off with my Australian friends. I am grateful to Denise Warner and Bruce Allen for their help with one of the chapters. It is a pleasure to thank Fran Gale and Michael Dudley for their hospitality, care and invaluable help with the manuscript. Fran's encouragement in particular ensured that I got my life going again and instilled in me the belief that 'all my projects will be successful'.

*Mick North*
*Perthshire*
*September 2000*

# INTRODUCTION

## 6 JUNE 1996

Dunblane, 5 miles north of Stirling, will for many years to come be associated
with the horrific massacre that took place in the primary school in 1996

*LONELY PLANET GUIDE TO BRITAIN, 1999*

# Running Away
## 6 June 1996

'And what is your address?'

It was a Thursday afternoon. I was driving alone along the M74, the motorway that connects the central belt of Scotland to England. I'd spent the whole morning sitting in the Albert Hall, the main public arena in Stirling, listening attentively to a number of police officers giving evidence about a man whose name had meant nothing to me three months earlier. I had been listening to an assortment of people give evidence about him for over a week and by that Thursday had just about had enough. After lunch I had to get away.

At that time of year I might have been off on holiday. Had I been working, all my teaching duties as a biochemistry lecturer at the University of Stirling would have been over. Early June had always been a good time to take a holiday. That day I was prepared to travel anywhere, in fact I hadn't a clue where I would end up. After lunch I had paid a quick visit to the cemetery, then got into the car and drove south. I was running away.

The route runs through the Southern Uplands, a thinly populated area of farmland, moor and forest. During the years I'd lived in Scotland the road had been upgraded and now most of it was motorway. When I'd moved from England in 1975 the M74's predecessor, the A74, was notorious for accidents, but in 1988 it wasn't the road that had brought disaster. On 21 December a bomb explosion shattered a Pan Am Boeing 747 flying 31,000 feet above southern Scotland. Everyone on board was killed. Part of the plane crashed into the Dumfriesshire town of Lockerbie, killing eleven people on the ground, and ending up beside the A74. Barbara and I had been planning to drive to relatives in England that evening, but Barbara had a Christmas party at her work, and we'd decided to leave a day later. We'd avoided being close to one of those tragedies that have punctuated Scottish life in recent decades. Lockerbie had joined a group of towns whose names are forever linked with tragedy. For many weeks after the Lockerbie tragedy the physical scars left by the crashed jumbo could be seen from the road, a manifestation of the inhumanity present within the human race.

Lockerbie was on a very familiar route for a 'white settler' living in Scotland. Although I could not qualify as a native Scot (my London accent gave me away, anyway), I had been proud that Sophie, Barbara's and my only child, was Scottish by birth. By 1996 she'd become a bright, keen and alert five-year-old, an integral member of Primary One Class 1/13 since starting school the previous August.

My car sped past Lockerbie, where new housing has now been built on the site of the crater left by Pan Am's *Maid of the Seas*. I switched the stereo from tapes to radio, as news bulletins came on, then back to tapes again. I played the music from Disney's *Lion King* (bought two years earlier at Disneyland, California) and listened to a compilation called *For Our Children* (sold by Disney to raise money for the Pediatric AIDS Foundation), a set of songs so evocative of other times when I'd been on long drives. Now the songs prompted streams of tears. Music so often did. But it was important for me to cry; I had to release some of the emotion.

It was the poignant songs that affected me most: 'Child of Mine' by Carole King, 'Gartan Mother's Lullaby' sung by Meryl Streep, and 'A Child is Born' by Barbra Streisand. On another tape I listened to Sting's song 'Fragile' with the lyrics 'like tears from a star' and 'how fragile we are'. Then it was Everything But The Girl. First, 'The Night I Heard

Caruso Sing' with the sad line, 'I've thought of having children but I've gone and changed my mind – it's hard enough to watch the news let alone explain it to a child'. Then their version of 'I Don't Want to Talk About It', with its opening line, 'I can tell by your eyes that you've probably been crying for ever'. It certainly felt like it.

The news included regular reports regarding a detective chief inspector from Central Scotland Police. DCI Paul Hughes had been answering questions about a report he'd made five years earlier. It concerned a local man who'd been the subject of a number of investigations relating to his dubious activities at various boys' clubs and summer camps. Hughes, then in charge of the Child Protection Unit, had grave reservations about this man. One of his concerns was that he had a firearms licence, and in unequivocal language Hughes's report had spelt out – no, shouted out – that the man was an unsuitable person to possess guns. Hughes felt his firearm certificate should have been revoked. Yet Hughes's superiors had ignored his advice, something that in March 1996 was to prove devastatingly costly.

I still didn't know where I was going. I was now in England, driving along the M6. Nobody knew where I was. I couldn't face phoning anyone before I left. I passed Carlisle and Penrith, the Pennines looming on my left and the hills of the Lake District on my right. For the first few years of Sophie's life we'd gone to a time-share in the Lake District during the university's winter break. That year I'd decided not to go, as it would have meant taking Sophie out of school for a week. Her schooling was very important to me and I was glad that her school had become important to her. After Penrith the M6 climbs over the bleak Shap Fell before dropping down into the Lune Gorge at Tebay. In March the previous year, during a snowstorm, I'd stayed at a hotel here. It had been comfortable, and as I'd now been driving for over three hours I thought it was time to stop. But the hotel was full and I returned to the car, back to the tapes and the radio, and continued heading south.

The motorway emerges from the hills near Morecambe and then passes Lancaster. Beyond is the Forton Service Area, so familiar from earlier journeys. Once when Sophie and I had stopped there for lunch, we'd bought a little foil balloon that held the all-time record for staying inflated. Two and a half years later it was in the living-room, still as puffed up as the day it was bought. Another time I'd had to buy some ointment while driving a very itchy Sophie back from a holiday. Here at Forton I decided to make another attempt to break my flight from Scotland.

The motel looked okay. I was going to need a decent-sized room, as I'd brought with me a number of brightly coloured plastic boxes, the toy boxes you can buy at B&Q. They were full of papers, letters I'd received from all over the world and various statements relating to a series of incidents that had taken place in central Scotland during the last twenty years or more. I also had a recently acquired copy of the report on the shootings that had taken place at Hungerford, Berkshire, in August 1987. Hungerford, another town name synonymous with tragedy. I was going to read some of these things while I was away. It was going to be a difficult, almost unbearable task. A massive burden.

That day I felt extremely overburdened. For three months I'd lived in a haze, trying to function, to take in everything that had happened, to cope with my emotions and hope there was something left over to share with my friends. But sometimes, as now, when my head was too clogged up, I had to be on my own. I had to be away from the phone, away from the house, away from people asking me how I was. Away so that I could try to start putting my life together again.

I walked into the motel. At the desk the receptionist confirmed they had a room and asked me my name. No problem. And then I had to give my address, to say it out loud. I started, '1, Bridgend –' then hesitated. For the first time in three months I was going to have to tell a stranger where I came from. Before 13 March 1996 there had been no difficulty. I wasn't ashamed of my Perthshire hometown, and it's quite possible that a motel receptionist in Lancashire wouldn't have known it. But that had all changed one cold March day. I couldn't lie about my address, so it had to come out: 'DUNBLANE'. The latest of those tragedy town names. Dunblane was where I was running away from, the city where thirteen weeks earlier Sophie, my beautiful five-year-old daughter, had been gunned down by Thomas Hamilton.

Back in the Albert Hall in Stirling, DCI Paul Hughes's evidence had completed the seventh day of the Public Inquiry into the Shootings at Dunblane Primary School on 13 March 1996 — the Cullen Inquiry. Sixteen children and their teacher had been killed; three teachers and eleven other children had been injured. Dunblane had joined the roll-call of Scottish tragedies, and although many fewer lives had been lost than at the Ibrox soccer ground in 1971, on the Piper Alpha oil platform in 1988 or at Lockerbie, the massacre had rendered the country numb. It was such a callous and needless destruction of young and innocent lives, decades and decades of life never to be lived. It was something that nobody would ever want to forget. Or would they?

# PART ONE

## 1975–1996

My constant thought when reading this was, 'This man could have been stopped, this man should have been stopped, I need never have had to know who he was'

MICK NORTH, *SCOTLAND ON SUNDAY*, 20 OCTOBER 1996

# CHAPTER ONE

# Before Dunblane

## 1975–1989

'I have pleasure in offering you the post of Lecturer in the Department of Biochemistry'

The job was advertised in the scientific magazine *Nature* on 27 February 1975.

> University of Stirling, Lectureship in Biochemistry. Applicants should have teaching experience and research interests, preferably in the field of membrane biochemistry, control mechanisms or enzymology.

I worked on enzymes. Throughout my short career one of my main interests had been in the mechanisms involved in the control of complex biochemical processes within living cells. I'd gained sufficient teaching experience to know that lecturing was something I was good at, enjoyed and wanted to do. Indeed the job seemed to suit me perfectly and I hoped that, in turn, I might suit the University of Stirling.

The official guide to Stirling told me that 'Despite the promise of James VI of Scotland to the town of Stirling in 1617 to found a "free college", the new University of Stirling has only come into existence as recently as 1967, three hundred and fifty years later'. Stirling was

Scotland's only brand-new university in the expansion of higher education that occurred in the 1960s. Its modern buildings were located in the Airthrey Estate, two miles northwest of the centre of Stirling, and were close to the attractive little town of Bridge of Allan. The campus had gained a reputation as the most beautiful university site in Britain.

I was delighted when, a few weeks later, I was invited for an interview. Academic posts, especially permanent ones, were then (as now) not easy to get. I was twenty-seven years old and on a two-year fellowship that terminated in the autumn. Without another post, my career in academia might be about to terminate as well. After gaining my PhD in 1973 I'd gone to work in the Biochemistry Department at the University of Leicester, studying a tiny soil amoeba – a cellular slime mould called *Dictyostelium discoideum* that was proving extremely useful in investigations of some of the most fundamental processes of developmental biology. Even before I'd started at Leicester, however, my new boss had been appointed to a post at Essex University; a few months later Lyn, my first wife, and I had to move again, this time to Colchester. That upheaval had made me determined to find a more permanent job. I wanted to continue my research work and I wanted to teach, so a tenured post as a university lecturer was exactly what I was looking for. If it were in a good location, so much the better.

I travelled to Stirling for the interview on a warm, sunny day in early May and was immediately struck by the scenery. That day the epithet of 'most beautiful campus' was more than justified. The university grounds sit below the slopes of the Ochil Hills, which rise dramatically on the northern side of the Forth Valley. To the east of the campus is the wooded outcrop of Abbey Craig on top of which perches the idiosyncratic but impressive Wallace Monument, built to commemorate William Wallace, the historic Scottish hero and patriot featured in the movie *Braveheart*. Two decades later it was a landmark Sophie could spot from all over central Scotland. 'It's Daddy's work!' Well, not quite, but it was very close by and I could certainly see it from my office window.

The night before the interview I stayed at the Royal Hotel in Bridge of Allan. Next day, on the short walk back to the campus, I looked across to the western horizon and saw the peaks of Ben Lomond and Ben Ledi, still capped with snow in spite of the warm spring weather. Behind Ben Lomond would be Loch Lomond, Scotland's largest lake, its southern end studded with little islands. Everything looked beautiful; Stirling was indeed a good location for a new job.

I thought the interview had gone well, but as it was my first formal job interview I wasn't certain. I needed to leave immediately afterwards, as I had a train to catch to return to Northumberland, where I was staying overnight with a friend. I'd left my home phone number with Lewis Stevens, the head of Biochemistry, and should he need to contact me Lyn would be able to take a message. That evening she called me to say that I was being offered the post. If I wasn't back in Colchester before the university switchboard closed next day, I was to phone Lewis at his home in Dunblane. DUNBLANE. That was the first time I heard the name.

Back in Colchester I looked up Dunblane in my road atlas. I realised that we'd driven through the town in 1971, although I hadn't remembered much about it – only that we'd crawled along the A9 at a point, just north of Stirling, where the road became a single carriageway for a mile or so. That first encounter had been on a very wet and dismal summer's day. Now there was a chance to see Dunblane again, this time in spring sunshine. After I'd accepted the job Lewis and his wife Evelyn invited us to stay during our house-hunting expedition. Their Victorian house was in Doune Road, just up the road from the local primary school.

The City of Dunblane lies six miles north of Stirling on one of the main road and rail routes between central Scotland and the north. A burgh since 1442, it was named after St Blane who, in the seventh century, had founded a church beside the Allan Water, a tributary of the River Forth. Its cathedral had been laid out in 1233 by Bishop Clement. After the Reformation the building was neglected, but a series of restorations ensured that Dunblane in the late twentieth century had a fine cathedral at its centre. Until April 1975 Dunblane burgh had been part of Perthshire, administered from Perth, thirty miles away. That month, local government changes brought in a new two-tier system and Dunblane became part of Stirling District, one of the three districts that constituted the new Central Region.

The town itself had expanded significantly during the early 1970s with the proliferation of new housing estates. The increased population had necessitated the building of the new Dunblane High School in 1974, which allowed all secondary pupils to be educated within Dunblane. The existing Dunblane Burgh School, built in 1962, was originally used for both primary and junior secondary pupils. With the opening of the High School it became Dunblane Primary School, exclusively for younger pupils.

The population of Dunblane, calculated to be 5,222 in June 1973 and increasing to nearly 8,000 by 1996, was made up of many who had been born and bred in the town, but included a significant proportion of incomers. In 1992 the Community Council found that 44 per cent of the townspeople surveyed had lived in the town for less than five years and 68 per cent for ten years or under. That same survey showed over two thirds of those in employment worked outside the town, using the good road and rail connections to commute to Edinburgh, Glasgow and elsewhere in the central belt.

It would be another fifteen years before I lived in Dunblane. Lyn and I bought a house in Easter Cornton, an area closer to the university campus, and in September 1975 I started my new job in the Biochemistry Laboratories. Over the years, if things weren't going well I would look through my office window towards the Ochils or the Wallace Monument and think, 'Things could be a lot worse.'

★

Two years earlier, in July 1973, Thomas Watt Hamilton, a twenty-one-year-old Stirling man who ran a DIY shop called 'Woodcraft' in the town's Cowane Street, was appointed Assistant Scout Leader of the 4th/6th Stirling Scout Troop. Later that year he became leader of the 24th Stirlingshire troop at Bannockburn. However, although he was said to have been very keen and willing, it wasn't long before a number of complaints were made about his leadership.

At the beginning of 1974 Hamilton had on two occasions taken parties of his troop to Aviemore in the Scottish Highlands. Instead of arranging accommodation in a hostel, as he claimed to have done, Hamilton made the boys in his charge sleep in the cold in his van. On the second occasion the boys' clothing had already been very wet. Complaints were made and, because of his lack of preparation and planning for these adventure holidays, the County and District Commissioners decided that Hamilton should resign. On 13 May 1974, one year to the day before I accepted the lectureship at Stirling, the District Commissioner wrote to Hamilton requesting the return of his warrant book; he was being asked to leave the Scouts.

There is evidence that problems with Thomas Hamilton pre-dated his ill-planned trips to Aviemore and expulsion from the Scouts in 1974. Indeed Dunblane appears to have been involved at a very early stage. Harry Ewing, now Lord Ewing of Kirkford, was Labour MP for Stirling during the 1970s. In a 1997 debate on the Firearms (Amendment) Bill, Lord Ewing told the House of Lords how he remembered Thomas Hamilton from as early as 1971 as a youth club worker in Dunblane, which then had its own town council. He told how a horrendous argument broke out in the town, one half of the community wanting to be rid of Thomas Hamilton and the other half wanting to retain his services:

> For 12 years I was Thomas Hamilton's Member of Parliament. Every Saturday morning when I held a surgery in Stirling, the first person to turn up was Thomas Hamilton. So no one knows, understands or tries to understand Thomas Hamilton more than I do.
>
> Hamilton came to see me, complaining about his perceived problems there [Dunblane]. I sent him to see Sir Alec [the Stirling constituency didn't then include Dunblane, whose MP until 1974 was ex-prime minister Sir Alec Douglas-Home], who explained to him that he did not become involved in disputes between two factions in a community for the simple reason that one could not win.

Following the return of his warrant card in 1974 Thomas Hamilton made a number of attempts to return to scouting, but because of their previous experience of him the Scouts blocked any further involvement. In April 1977 he wrote that he was discontinuing the thought of holding a warrant 'as I do not want my good name to be part of this so-called organisation in this district'. Yet in 1978 he offered his services as a scout leader in another district. Turned down again, he developed an unfounded grudge against the District Commissioner concerned, a Dunblane resident. Hamilton's concerns about his good name were raised frequently, and he would always refer back to his rejection by the Scouts.

Hamilton had shown a keen interest in guns since he was sixteen. Stories in the media and at the Cullen Inquiry confirmed that he was using air guns in the early 1970s. He would invite boys into the back of his shop, which was set up as an improvised firing range. A neighbouring shop owner had been concerned about the guns he had at the shop, and had had a 'quiet word' with the police about the number of boys who were hanging around Hamilton's shop.

His interest in guns was given official sanction in 1977 when he was granted his first firearm certificate. This authorised him to purchase or acquire a .22 target pistol. His certificate indicated that he would be shooting at Callander Shooting Club or other suitable clubs and ranges. During the next two years he purchased a number of guns and his arsenal gradually expanded. In August 1977 a variation to his firearm certificate authorised him to purchase or acquire a .22 rifle and a .22 semi-automatic pistol. This he duly did. A further variation in 1979 allowed the purchase or acquisition of a .357 revolver and a .270 rifle, and with each variation he was allowed to increase the amount of ammunition he could hold. The Cullen Report records that in the period from 1977 to 1979 he purchased no fewer than 13,300 rounds of ammunition of .22 calibre. He named a number of gun clubs he was using or would use, including the full-bore target shooting range at Dunblane. Full-bore shooting involves larger-calibre and more powerful weapons.

★

The year 1979 marked a watershed in British politics. Since 1974 Labour had been in power, first under Harold Wilson and then James Callaghan. A significant feature of that parliament was the record eleven seats held by the Scottish National Party (SNP). The Government's majority was tiny, which dictated that it had to pay special attention to Scottish matters. Home rule had been at the top of the agenda and the 1978

Scotland Act paved the way for a referendum on devolution. But devolution was delayed. In the referendum held on 1 March 1979 the number of votes cast in favour of devolution fell short of the required 40 per cent of those entitled to vote. In the fallout the Government lost a vote of no confidence and a general election was called for 3 May. When all the votes had been counted the United Kingdom had its first woman prime minister, Margaret Thatcher, the leader of the Conservative Party. The Tories would remain in power until 1997.

In 1979 Lyn and I moved to a cottage in Bridge of Allan, where we lived together until we split up in 1985. I had spent my first years in Stirling working hard, combining my teaching and supervision of students with a developing and expanding research programme. I'm sure I became a workaholic. In 1980 I took sabbatical leave, a period when academics are allowed time off from their teaching duties to focus on other aspects of their work, usually research.

Towards the end of my sabbatical, in January 1981, I arranged a short European tour to give talks on my work in Paris, Munich and Zurich. The trip was overshadowed by the news that my father had become very ill and needed a heart valve replacement. Every day I would phone my mum to check that everything was all right. When Lyn and I returned to England we visited my dad, now recovering from his operation in Papworth Hospital, and were relieved that the operation appeared to have been successful. Less than two weeks later my heart sank as I heard the phone ring in the early morning. My elder sister Christine was calling to tell me that my dad had collapsed and died.

I recall being calm on the outside but very stressed inside. I felt guilty that I hadn't known my dad better, especially in recent years. I was also scared. My father had died a few days before his sixtieth birthday, a few days before he was due to take early retirement. That wasn't the way things were supposed to happen. He had died at a much younger age than anyone else to whom I'd been close. I'd never been to a funeral and was worried about how I would cope with that. I bottled up too many things, because I didn't want to have to think about them. I wanted to get on with my career and do well and, of course, stay as healthy as possible myself.

I continued to throw myself into work. As a result of meeting Graham

Coombs, a lecturer at the University of Glasgow, I'd recently embarked on a new area of research, the biochemistry of parasites. Graham and I shared an interest in a group of enzymes that digest proteins (proteinases), and began a collaboration that lasted until I retired. We published three important research papers from our initial joint efforts, but the work had to be subsidised from our other projects and its progress was limited. To remedy this we submitted a successful application to the Medical Research Council for a grant to study a parasite called *Trichomonas vaginalis*, the causative agent of trichomoniasis, a widespread sexually-transmitted disease. In the summer of 1983 we appointed two research assistants. Alison Bremner joined Graham in Glasgow and Barbara Lockwood came to work in my laboratory at Stirling.

In June 1983 the political map of Stirling changed significantly. Following boundary changes, there was a new Stirling constituency that now included all of the northern and western parts of Central Region. As well as the town of Stirling it took in the rural areas of the Forth Valley and reached out to Ben Lomond, Ben Ledi and beyond. It had also acquired both Bridge of Allan and Dunblane. These changes had turned Stirling into a marginal seat, though Conservative new-boy Michael Forsyth swept to victory with a majority of 5,133, as his party notched up a thumping majority of 144 seats at Westminster. Forsyth went on to become Chairman of the Scottish Conservatives and to hold ministerial posts at the Scottish Office, the Department of Employment and the Home Office. In 1995 he was appointed to John Major's cabinet as Secretary of State for Scotland. Like his predecessor Harry Ewing, Stirling's new MP was to have many dealings with his constituent Thomas Hamilton.

★

During the early 1980s Hamilton started his own boys' clubs in Dunblane and Bannockburn. Later he set up others elsewhere. He obtained support largely by sending leaflets to houses and primary schools, although headteachers tried to stop their schools being used to promote these clubs. He always believed he was doing something worth while, giving the boys discipline and keeping them off the streets, and there is no doubt that many parents agreed. But the way the clubs were being run raised concerns among others. The clubs were considered to be over-regimented and militaristic and people came to think that his motivation was to dominate the boys in his charge. There were worries that the exercises Hamilton made the boys do were over-strenuous. The concerns were raised independently by various sets of parents whose boys attended different clubs.

Hamilton took photographs of the boys posing in ill-fitting swimming trunks, which he insisted the boys wear. He had his favourites, showing unusual interest in certain of the boys. Many years later there were a number of suggestions that Hamilton had committed acts of indecency. At the 1996 Public Inquiry only one such incident was given any credence by Lord Cullen: a witness described how, when he was twelve years old, Hamilton had rubbed him on the inside of his leg at the Dunblane Rovers Group. The authorities would always claim that in the absence of appropriate evidence of criminal activity they were never able to act against him at the time.

Many of the boys' clubs were run in premises belonging to Central Regional Council, including the gymnasium of Dunblane High School. In spite of the hostility towards Dunblane that Harry Ewing had noted in the early '70s, Hamilton seemed to be drawn back to the town. By the summer of 1983 there were complaints about his Dunblane Rovers Group. Dunblane parents had split into two groups, those concerned about the clubs and those who found no evidence of wrongdoing. One of the concerned Dunblane parents was George Robertson, MP, who was later to become Labour's Shadow Scottish Secretary. He'd visited the club after Hamilton had demanded an explanation from his son about his absence. Immediately after seeing how the club was run – it reminded him of the Hitler Youth – George Robertson and another parent decided that their sons would not be returning. Robertson communicated his unease about Hamilton to his fellow MP Michael Forsyth.

The growing concerns were discussed at a meeting of Central Regional Council's Further Education and General Purposes Sub-committee. Use of the name 'Rovers' meant that the club was confused with the Scout Movement, giving it a status it didn't possess. Some parents thought, incorrectly, that the clubs had official support because they were held on Council property or promoted through schools. There were rumours circulating that Hamilton had been removed from the Scouts for homosexual tendencies. The Sub-committee decided to cancel Hamilton's lets of Bannockburn and Dunblane High Schools.

In October 1983 Hamilton complained about the cancellation to the local government Ombudsman, the Commissioner for Local Administration in Scotland. In his complaint he was supported by letters he'd collected, a petition signed by Dunblane residents, and by his Regional Councillor, Robert Ball. He made a fresh application for a let of Dunblane High School, but the Sub-committee delayed its decision until the Ombudsman had reported.

In November 1984 the Ombudsman found in favour of Hamilton, concluding that there had been maladministration on the part of Central Regional Council – a decision that was criticised in the Cullen Report. As a result, and in spite of all the concerns, Hamilton was allowed to let Council facilities again. His MP, Michael Forsyth, wrote to him expressing his congratulations. According to the Cullen Report, Hamilton was convinced that his problems with Council lets could be laid at the feet of Scout officials and he confronted two of them during the succeeding months.

Hamilton went on to run a series of boys' clubs across central Scotland. His official-looking headed notepaper, his largely fictitious committees and false claims of support from well-known local people disguised the fact that his organisation was effectively a one-man band and that he was under-qualified for the role he'd taken on.

All the while Hamilton maintained an interest in guns. Boys from the Dunblane Rovers Group were taken to Dunblane Pistol and Rifle Club for tuition in the use of air rifles and air pistols. Every three years his firearm certificate was routinely renewed. Another variation in 1984 allowed him to obtain a 9 mm pistol and a .223 rifle, and in 1986, he was permitted a second 9 mm pistol and a 7.62 mm rifle (he never bought the latter). The justification for the ownership of these weapons was always target shooting, each gun supposedly to be used for a separate discipline. Questions were raised by the police about the need for a second 9 mm pistol, but he was still allowed it.

★

Shortly after a merger between the departments of Biochemistry and Biology, I took charge of the biochemistry teaching and examinations. It was a busy and productive time. My research group worked hard, the research was well funded from various grants and we were publishing plenty of papers. In 1985 I was promoted to Senior Lecturer.

Since her arrival at Stirling, in October 1983, Barbara Lockwood had made a big impact on the work and life of the department. A bright and outgoing young woman, she was proving herself to be a first-class research scientist. There was a feisty side to her too – typically Yorkshire, some would say. Barbara and I began a relationship and from the summer of 1986 shared a flat in Bridge of Allan. Our first dinner guests were Karen and David Scott. Karen had recently joined the department as a technician and was then working in my laboratory. Barbara and Karen became close friends, working together and socialising together and retaining close links through the years.

In the autumn of 1986 Barbara and I bought a time-share week in the Lake District. We spent our first week at The Lakeland Village in January 1987, just before I went on sabbatical leave again. For five months I worked at the Imperial Cancer Research Fund Laboratories (ICRF) at South Mimms, to the north of London and not far from Barnet where I grew up during my schooldays. It was a nostalgic time, but at that time London and the Southeast were too busy and crowded for me. I drove myself hard enough as it was; I didn't need the place where I lived to be putting too much pressure on me as well. My stay convinced me that I preferred to be in central Scotland. It seemed a more comfortable and safer place. I returned to Bridge of Allan. Barbara had gained her PhD while I'd been away and, having taken up a post of Postdoctoral Research Assistant with Graham Coombs, had moved to Glasgow for the time being. I was soon off on my travels again, completing my sabbatical leave at the University of Windsor in Canada, on my first visit to North America.

Windsor is an industrial town in the southwest of Ontario, a relaxed city where I could walk downtown from my campus accommodation in safety. One route took me alongside the Detroit River. Close by on the other bank was the United States of America and the city of Detroit, Michigan. Detroit to me meant the home of Motown records and the Detroit Tigers baseball team, but it was also somewhere that seemed dangerous, not a place where I would have strolled leisurely to the downtown area. When work colleagues took me for an evening meal in Detroit, driving me through the tunnel under the river on my first-ever visit to the USA, the differences between Detroit and Windsor were dramatic: there were many more police on duty and it was obvious they were armed. Recent statistics have revealed that during one year (1997) in which Windsor had only four firearm homicides, Detroit, a city only five times larger, had 354. The USA's love affair with the gun, especially the handgun, had helped to make these neighbouring towns different worlds in terms of risks from gun violence.

That summer, however, you didn't have to be in the USA to witness the damage wrought by guns. The world's eyes turned on Hungerford, an archetypal English market town. I learned from my Canadian newspaper that on 19 August Michael Ryan, a twenty-seven-year-old local man armed with legally held guns, had killed sixteen people and injured fifteen others in and around Hungerford. The carnage had ended when he shot himself in the John o'Gaunt School where he'd been holed up for a few hours. Not for the only time people would be asking themselves 'How could something like that happen in such a quiet place?' But too often that is what happens. Massacres by lone gunmen don't take place in high-crime areas, they take place where you least expect them.

Lives are lost in many horrible ways. All premature death is tragic. Three days before Ryan went on his shooting spree, a North West Airlines DC9 crashed during take-off at Detroit's Wayne County Metropolitan Airport, a few miles from where I was staying. A total of 156 people died. That was awful, but I experienced a greater chill when I read about Hungerford later in the week. There is something particularly disgusting about a gun massacre. For someone to point a gun so many times at innocent victims and then deliberately pull the trigger is cold, calculating and inhuman.

Despite the loss of life at Hungerford and the worries about firearms ownership, no public inquiry was held. Was there going to be any hope of checking a growing gun culture in the UK? In June 1987 Margaret Thatcher had won her third general election in a row. Support for the Conservatives remained strong and, in spite of a leftward swing in Scotland, Michael Forsyth held on to the Stirling seat. This government, with its large majority, didn't have to be too concerned about opposing views. Many of its members were the shooters' friends and they certainly paid them special attention. Changes to the law were minimal. The Firearms (Amendment) Act of 1988 resulted in the banning of semi-automatic rifles such as the Kalashnikov with which Ryan had murdered eight of his victims; but the handgun he used to kill the others remained legal.

One family didn't leave the matter there. Tony and Judith Hill, whose twenty-one-year-old daughter Sandra was Ryan's youngest victim, tried hard to get people to listen to their concerns about gun ownership. The response was minimal, until we all came to meet up nine years later.

★

Thomas Hamilton also owned a semi-automatic rifle and resented having to surrender the .223 Browning. He complained about the compensation he received and was still moaning about this in 1996. By 1987 he also owned a .357 Smith and Wesson revolver, and two pistols (a 9 mm Browning and a 9 mm Beretta). He'd originally purchased lower-calibre weapons, but it was the more powerful, high-calibre weapons that were to make up his arsenal from now on – an arsenal he could keep at home, quite lawfully. At the Cullen Inquiry one witness inadvertently betrayed his fellow shooters who claim the sport is just about skill and concentration by revealing that some of them want the buzz they get from these more powerful weapons. Low-calibre weapons are sissy.

★

The next summer Scotland was rocked by disaster. On 6 July 1988 the Piper Alpha offshore oil platform, located in the North Sea 110 miles northeast of Aberdeen, exploded. Of those on board, 165 were killed, along with two members of the crew of a fast-rescue craft. Secretary of State for Energy Cecil Parkinson ordered a Public Inquiry into the circumstances of the accident and its cause. It was conducted by a Senator of the College of Justice, the Honourable Lord Douglas Cullen, a senior Scottish judge. For Cullen's report, the praise from politicians and journalists was fulsome; and the oil industry seemed content with it, even though it recommended wholesale changes in the practices of the offshore oil companies. It was on this basis that I was assured of Cullen's qualities and his appropriateness for the 1996 Dunblane Inquiry. However I now know that these views weren't universally held. He had, perhaps, been what the Government wanted most: a safe pair of hands.

★

During the late 1980s a number of incidents involving Hamilton should have had warning bells clanging throughout central Scotland. They undoubtedly did, but those in authority did not or could not take appropriate action.

One such incident, in July 1988, was at a summer camp organised by Thomas Hamilton on Inchmoan Island, one of the small islands in Loch Lomond. Complaints about the camp came to the attention of Strathclyde Police, who informed Central Scotland Police. Two of the latter's PCs visited the island. The campsite was a mess. The thirteen boys there were cold and inadequately dressed. They had not been allowed to wear trousers. There were allegations of slapping of one or two boys. No charges were brought, but parents were contacted and some boys were taken home. In later precognition statements several boys described being struck by Hamilton, but no criminal proceedings were instituted. However the Procurator Fiscal did indicate that the police should take these matters up with the social work department, the Reporter to the Children's Panel and the education authorities that let the schools used by the boys' clubs involved.

Hamilton's response to all this was to make an informal complaint about the police officers. The complaint was rejected, but Hamilton made it official. It was investigated by Insp. Keenan, on behalf of the Deputy Chief Constable of Central Scotland Police, Douglas McMurdo. Lord Cullen writes in his report that 'a barrage of letters from Thomas Hamilton continued, becoming personalised and critical of the competence and professionalism of the police'. Keenan found the complaint unfounded and exonerated the officers concerned.

DCC McMurdo submitted a report to his counterpart in Strathclyde Police, and the matter was eventually referred to the Regional Procurator Fiscal in Paisley. The incident, like others, shows that during a period when Central

Scotland Police kept renewing Hamilton's firearm certificate, senior officers were well aware of his activities. These officers included DCC McMurdo, the man ultimately responsible for issuing firearm certificates.

One parent whose son had attended the camp was Doreen Hagger from Linlithgow, a town in Lothian Region midway between Stirling and Edinburgh. She was extremely opposed to Hamilton's activities. Her son had told the police how Hamilton had got boys to rub suntan oil all over his body. In an attempt to ensure that the remaining boys were properly fed, she and a friend assisted at the 1988 camp but eventually left, threatened by Hamilton or other men camping with him.

In May 1989 Hagger's concerns about Hamilton led her to make a premeditated assault on him as he was leaving Linlithgow Academy, where he had a let from Lothian Regional Council to run Linlithgow Boys' Club. The attack was witnessed by a local reporter. Doreen Hagger wanted the Council to revoke the let to prevent Hamilton organising another summer camp that year. She hoped to be taken to court for the assault to ensure that Hamilton was investigated, but he refused to make a complaint. Her actions did lead to Lothian Council becoming aware of the police investigations into the boys' camp at Inchmoan and the let was suspended. As usual Hamilton complained, this time to the Ombudsman, but no investigation was carried out. Unlike their counterparts at Central Region, Lothian Regional Council had been able to stop the let.

There is evidence that during the mid-1980s Hamilton showed off his firearms by taking them to the homes of other people. In 1988 he took two handguns and his semi-automatic rifle to the home of boys from his Linlithgow club. The parents didn't complain, but said later that they had not been at ease with someone bringing guns into their house and that 'a firearm certificate holder should not behave in that way'. The matter was investigated by Lothian Police, who passed on the statements to Central Scotland Police. In June 1989 a memorandum from Chief Supt Gunn stated, 'It may be a quite harmless display of weapons, but nevertheless an action which leaves a lot to be desired.' The memo was addressed to DCC McMurdo, who decided not to issue a warning.

On 14 February 1989, McMurdo had renewed Thomas Hamilton's firearm certificate.

Britain in the late '80s was beset by disasters: the capsize of the *Herald of Free Enterprise*, Hungerford, the fire at King's Cross underground station, Piper Alpha, the Clapham rail crash, Lockerbie and then Hillsborough. On 15 April 1989, at the Hillsborough football stadium in Sheffield, the FA Cup semi-final between Liverpool and Nottingham Forest was only a few minutes old when hundreds of Liverpool fans were crushed after too many people had been allowed into a section of the ground behind the Leppings Lane end. Ninety-six people lost their lives.

Like others, I learned about this disaster while listening to the match commentary on the radio. What we didn't know then was that this was no accident and was certainly not the fault of the fans. At first the talk was of drunken Liverpool fans being responsible by breaking into the ground. But over time the truth has come out. It was the police who had ordered the gates to be opened, allowing too many fans into one small area. Not only had they made an error, but they also lied and tried to cover it up, deflecting blame on to the fans. Their later treatment of victims' families was appalling. Even a Public Inquiry chaired by Lord Justice Taylor failed to get to the whole truth. This was a shameful episode, one that we hoped would never be repeated. But that would have required a change of attitude among senior police officers, which appears to have been too difficult for some.

By 1989 I had been promoted to the position of Reader. I took this as an endorsement of my approach to work, a combination of good research, good teaching and efficient administration. Barbara was doing well at her job in Glasgow, but decided that she would prefer to be living back in Bridge of Allan and commuting by car or train. She joined a group of friends in a keep-fit group led by Karen Scott. She was active, healthy and leading a full and fulfilling life.

During the summer of 1989 Barbara and I both went to North America, she to do research in Cleveland, Ohio, while I worked again in Windsor, Ontario. We met up in Cleveland – as hospitable, welcoming and friendly as any American city. Yet we feared walking the streets, especially close to the hostel where Barbara was staying, not far from downtown Cleveland. Later that summer we had the same feeling when we visited friends in Washington, DC, and when we drove through a run down area of Trenton, New Jersey, after taking a wrong turning. Behind our fears was the thought that there were too many guns out there.

Barbara returned to Scotland before me. She had been offered an academic post in Cleveland, but by the time I got back she'd already decided not to accept the job and to continue working in Glasgow. Meanwhile Graham and I were about to get two big research grants, there would be two new research staff joining me at Stirling, and we were organising a big international conference. And most important of all, within four months of deciding to stay in Scotland, Barbara was pregnant.

CHAPTER TWO

# Dunblane

## January 1990–October 1993

'Willowbank House, Bridgend, Dunblane. A spacious, Victorian
cottage-style property built in stone with slated roof'

At first Barbara's pregnancy took me by surprise, though I should have taken all those earlier hints more seriously: the unnecessary detours down supermarket aisles past the disposable nappies, the lingering outside Mothercare in Stirling's Thistle Centre. This was going to be a big change. I was just coming up to my forty-second birthday. Some men have become grandfathers by then. I was apprehensive about the prospect of parenthood, unsure if I could make the necessary adjustments to my life. But soon I became very positive and once that had happened I started to look forward to being a dad like nothing else before in my life.

I knew from the start that the baby was a girl. I have no idea why, perhaps just wishful thinking. Barbara felt the same and during the next nine months we thought only of girls' names. Sophie was beginning to grow and develop: all those biochemical controls that I explained to students and tried to understand from my research were working perfectly to turn a tiny fertilized egg into a complex little human being.

Barbara's pregnancy remained a secret for a few weeks, though there were hints that friends might have spotted. One described our new grey

Renault 9 as a *family car*. The best clue came one evening in March when we had gone to the Westerton Arms, our local in Bridge of Allan, with Karen and David Scott, Morag, my PhD student, and her partner Michael. Uncharacteristically, Barbara wasn't drinking, but then neither was Karen. A few days later during one of the sessions at a parasitology meeting in Aberdeen, one of Barbara's colleagues got her to confess. She'd given him one evasive answer too many about why she'd quit smoking again and wasn't drinking alcohol. Morag, sitting close by, heard the news and confirmed that Karen too was pregnant.

Barbara and I had already given a lot of thought to where we were going to live with our baby. We couldn't stay in Bridge of Allan. The house was suitable for two adults, but there wasn't really enough room for a child as well. A larger house in Bridge of Allan would be too expensive. So what about Dunblane? Friends like Karen and David were already there. Dunblane, with its railway station for Barbara's commuting. Dunblane, the pleasant quiet town, with its good schools, suitable for bringing up children.

After a failed attempt to buy a house in Doune Road we put in an offer for Willowbank House in Bridgend. It was close to the Primary School and very convenient for the station. We were told that the house, now a hundred years old, had once been occupied by the station-master. If so, it would have allowed him to keep a close check on the comings and goings at his station and the sidings that once occupied the far side of the tracks. Though it ceased to be a junction in the 1960s, Dunblane station remained busy and was the terminus for regular trains to and from Glasgow and Edinburgh.

The front and side of the house were finished in a pink wash. To some it was the 'Pink House'. Inside there was a comfortable living-room at the front and a large kitchen at the back with ample wall space for future displays of artwork from nursery or school. Upstairs were two large bedrooms with another, smaller, room at the front. The front bedroom had a unique bowed window with a view over the station. During her first months our baby would be sleeping in the small room, where we could get to her quickly in the night. The back room, in need of decoration, served as the spare bedroom until one day it became a little girl's room. Through the windows was a fine view of Dunblane Cathedral. Up another flight of stairs was a converted loft whose large window overlooked the Allan Water and the town centre. It was supposed to be a study, but I never did get much work done up there. Later it was used more as a playroom.

The house stood at the end of one of Dunblane's oldest streets. Bridgend was the first suburb of Dunblane and probably dated back to the building of the bridge over the Allan Water in 1409. It had once been a crowded area. In 1841, well before Willowbank House was built, as many as 300 people lived there: most were hand-loom weavers of wool and cotton. A number of the old houses had been demolished when the railway arrived and by 1990 there were many fewer residents. The road came to an abrupt end by our house, closed off in 1866 when a footbridge to Doune Road replaced a level crossing over the railway. Another footpath led from the end of Bridgend. It descended towards the Allan Water and ran beside the river past the Memorial Park and on to the Laighills Park with its swings, slides and sandpit.

In a survey conducted in 1992 Dunblane's residents considered that its best features were its central location and access to rail and road; that it was small, friendly and quiet; and that it was rural. The worst things were the lack of facilities, especially for young people and for shopping. Its image was not helped by the gloomy appearance of the High Street where too many shops stood empty. Sometimes it had the feel of a town that hadn't quite taken enough care of itself.

The year moved on as our baby, briefly called Twinkle and then Prawn, grew inside Barbara. On Friday, 13 July we collected the keys for Willowbank House and moved our belongings the next day. It was not the best day for moving, a summer Saturday with a large amount of holiday traffic. The journey up the hill from Bridge of Allan to Dunblane can be made in less than ten minutes, but that day some journeys in the rental van were taking half an hour or more. The Dunblane stretch of the A9 had been a bottleneck for years – relieved in December 1990 when Michael Forsyth, then transport minister at the Scottish Office, opened a bypass.

Any thoughts that Dunblane would be a quiet town were quickly dispelled. Our house stood at a diagonal crossroads formed by the two footpaths at the end of Bridgend, Bridgend itself and Station Road, which leads down to the station. It was a gathering point, especially in the late evening, and too often our sleep was disturbed by loud conversations and worse. There were frequent acts of petty vandalism, the damage minor, but wilful and annoying. Within weeks one of the cars had been broken into and a number of audiotapes stolen. After that I lost count of the number of times my car was damaged or the TV aerial cable ripped from the outside wall. There were also problems with young drivers who used Bridgend and Station Road as a racetrack and screeched around the hairpin corner between the two streets. This was a town with a youth problem. Reflecting this, the Community Council reported that fear of young people was one of the major reasons for an almost unanimous belief that more policing was necessary in Dunblane: there was 'a problem with gangs of youths hanging around the High Street and Station Road which was not only irritating but also intimidating'.

Our baby wasn't due until September and, with Barbara's pregnancy going well, we could take our time settling into the house. We were going to ante-natal classes, having started out with Karen and David Scott. Graham and I were busy organising the meeting on 'Biochemical Protozoology as a Basis for Drug Design' that we were hosting at Stirling in late August. My autumn semester started in mid-September and I began teaching again, but whatever I was doing now, whether it was at the university or away from Stirling, I made sure I'd be able to get home quickly.

The due date was past and it was now October. There had been a number of false alarms and so, on the morning of the Second, when Barbara again thought she might have had contractions in the night, we couldn't be sure whether they were the real thing. We decided that I should still go to work. Sometime around eleven o'clock I got a call from Barbara. She'd already phoned the hospital to say she was on her way, as indeed was the baby. I asked Morag to tell my students that I wasn't going to be giving the afternoon lecture, and left. At the ante-natal classes we'd been told to prepare food in anticipation of a long period of labour, and once home I dutifully made the Marmite sandwiches and collected up some crisps, chocolate and biscuits.

At the hospital it became apparent that Barbara was well into labour. Very soon, a few days late but earlier than expected on the day, Sophie Jane arrived. She was born at Stirling Royal Infirmary at 2.41 p.m. on Tuesday, 2 October, weighing in at 3,170g (7lb). 'Tuesday's child is full of grace' and she was. And why the name Sophie? I'm not entirely sure, but to me it was a name that evoked a mix of charm and sophistication, what we might call Sophiecation. It turned out to be the perfect name for her. Sophie means 'wisdom' and wise she would be. Her birth was registered on 17 October 1990 at Dunblane Registry Office.

Sophie was taken away for checks and Barbara and I ate our Marmite sandwiches. With Barbara needing some rest, I decided to go back to work to pass on our news. What the hospital staff didn't tell me was that Sophie had a problem. Before it was realised how imminent the birth was, Barbara had been given painkillers. The drugs had affected Sophie. During delivery she'd taken in some fluid and had developed breathing problems. The staff had taken her to the special care unit and when I returned she was lying in an incubator being fed by tube. It was just a precaution, but this wasn't what we'd anticipated and it emphasised our child's vulnerability. We would have to make sure we took extra special care of her.

In the end Sophie was fine and after two days she and Barbara were together in the ward. They might even be home at the weekend. I was running behind schedule with decorating Sophie's room when I got a call on Saturday morning asking me to fetch them that afternoon. I was able to smooth down the last piece of wallpaper just before I set off for the hospital. Then, very carefully, I drove Sophie and her mum back to Dunblane, back to the house that was to be Sophie's home.

I kept some newspapers from the day Sophie was born, recorded the early evening programmes on BBC1 and bought the Number One single, 'Show Me Heaven' by Maria McKee. As well as the BBC's news programmes, I'd captured a mixed bag of *Telly Addicts*, *EastEnders*, *May to December* and *On the Up*. What was happening in the world that day? *The Times* had reported friction in the Labour Shadow Cabinet (under Neil Kinnock) and *The Guardian* led with 'LABOUR FACES HURDLE OVER £4 BN

FOR PENSIONERS'. The *Glasgow Herald* reported an opinion poll showing an upsurge in support for the Scottish National Party. The main sports headline was that Grand Prix driver Nigel Mansell was to continue driving in Formula One.

On the previous day the fatal accident inquiry into the Lockerbie air crash had opened. The *Evening Times* reported the tragic news that Michael Hughes, one of the lawyers representing families of Lockerbie victims, had been killed that night in an accident on the M74. This was also reported on BBC Scotland's *Reporting Scotland*. But it was two other news items that made me shudder when I watched the videotape years later. One, the lead story, is about the sentencing of the murderer of a young Glasgow girl. The other is a report on another fatal accident inquiry. It is brief, but chilling. On 18 March a gun-club member, Alan Parkhill, had shot dead a nineteen-year-old student teacher, Thomas McIntyre, in Glasgow's Renfield Street. He had then shot himself. On the day that Sophie was born, Elizabeth Munro, leading the evidence at the inquiry, urged that the case be referred to a special committee on firearms. I'm sure it never was. Thomas McIntyre and Sophie would both be remembered during a debate at the Labour Party Conference six years later.

The 1990 Labour Party Conference was the main item on BBC's *Nine o'Clock News*, although the most momentous world event was yet to come. At midnight West Germany and East Germany reunited. This was the time of the New World Order: a more optimistic era had supposedly begun. In Britain it was still the Thatcher era, though only just. By the end of November a fractious Conservative party dumped Margaret Thatcher and replaced her with John Major. Neither did the optimism last long. Iraq had already invaded Kuwait and a war in the Gulf was looming. Operation Desert Storm began in January and this, perhaps more than any other event, signified the dawn of another era, the age of global live news broadcasts. From now on we could expect television cameras to swoop into any location in the world, immediately covering horrific stories as they unfolded.

Five weeks after Sophie's birth Karen and David Scott had a baby daughter, Hannah Louise. Photos taken at the end of the year show the two baby girls lying side by side on our living-room carpet. Barbara and Karen would sit breastfeeding the girls together. Hannah and Sophie would be seeing each other at nursery and at lots of parties. They would eventually be in the same class when they started school.

After a quiet Christmas spent in Dunblane, Barbara prepared to go back to work in the New Year, her maternity leave over. The previous June, when I'd been away at a conference in America, she had told me that she'd been awarded a prestigious Royal Society Fellowship. This would allow her to continue her research work at Glasgow for at least another five years and give her more independence. During that same transatlantic conversation she'd described her visit to Arnhall Nursery, where Sophie would start at the beginning of the year.

Sophie was the first new baby Arnhall Nursery had ever taken. It had recently opened in premises on the Keir Estate, a mile south of Dunblane and well away from any roads. The only traffic would be the comings and goings of the parents and the occasional farm vehicle. Surrounded by trees and estate land, it was in an almost perfect setting. As part of a nursery promotion, the *Stirling Observer* published a lovely photograph of a group of Arnhall children, cute little Sophie being held by Kris, one of the nursery staff. This was a few weeks after Sophie had started. Nowadays I read far too much into dates and give pure coincidences a significance they don't have, but when I retrieved the cutting from my filing cabinet I was horrified to discover that it was dated Wednesday, 13 March.

Parenthood had started so well, but now there were problems. Because of soreness and swelling of her left breast, Barbara had given up breastfeeding early. She was treated for mastitis and told that there was nothing to worry about. Some symptoms persisted, however, and she was eventually sent for a mammogram at Stirling Royal Infirmary. The results were inconclusive and she was asked to go back in June.

I would be abroad again by then. I'd been invited to give a talk at the Second Conference on Proteolysis at Brdo, just outside Ljubljana in the then Yugoslav republic of Slovenia. It was not the best time to go. By June 1991 various factors had precipitated a crisis in Yugoslavia, Slovenia was about to make a declaration of independence and Croatia would follow suit. I really wanted to be at this meeting and set off for Ljubljana by train. My companions for part of this journey were Montenegrins to whom I talked about the political situation. They were critical of the Slovenian threats to leave Yugoslavia and thought they wouldn't actually go through with it.

The first few days were much as I'd expected, scientists talking to one another, enthusing about their own work, providing advice to others and planning collaborative projects. Away from the science, the organiser, Vito Turk, was very excited about Slovenian independence and knew it was going to happen. On our last evening, Thursday, 27 June, we were taken into Ljubljana by coach to attend the independence ceremony. We entered the square to the applause of the crowd. We were special guests, an international group of scientists given a front-row view. A ceremony of speeches, fireworks, local singers and dancers culminated in the raising of the Slovenian flag. That evening I sent a postcard to Sophie telling her that, although she'd not understand just now, I had witnessed a new country being born.

By the time we got back to the conference centre there was already news of trouble in the Yugoslav capital, Belgrade; and by the morning we'd learnt that Ljubljana airport, not far from where we were staying, had been bombed. No one could leave by plane, and Slovenia's land borders were being closed by Yugoslav federal troops. Vito Turk began to make arrangements to get his international guests out of his new country. In stoical academic fashion, the last session of the meeting went on. Even after a convoy of vehicles had been organised, there were still a few enthusiastic colleagues who wanted to make comments about the talks. Incredibly, we delayed our departure with a question-and-answer session.

I was in a minibus, eventually to be the last vehicle of fifteen in the convoy. We set off on back roads, up through lush alpine meadows, past roadblocks manned by heavily armed Slovene local militia. We crossed over a flyover above the main road to Austria, blocked solid with traffic, back on to another major road and through the town of Jesenice. All the time, federal army helicopters were buzzing above us, heading up the valley in the same direction as ourselves. I read sometime later that these were transporting supplies to their men closer to the border, but for all we knew they were armed and could have prevented any movement of traffic by firing at the vehicles. A day later a Turkish truck driver was killed south of Ljubljana in a similar situation.

At one village the main road was completely blocked by wooden barriers and we had to go down a sidetrack and across an almost derelict bridge. Bringing up the rear of the convoy, we wondered if the bridge would have any strength left as we went across. We were getting close to the Austrian border when our Slovene driver realised we were running out of fuel. Amazingly, we came to an open filling station and because no other traffic had got through, there weren't any vehicles to queue behind. But as we waited a column of federal troops passed by, going in our direction. We started again, turned off the main road and began to ascend a steep hill. Around one hairpin bend we were confronted by a frantic Vito Turk urging us to make haste and join the others who'd crossed into Austria. At the border the troops were parking their vehicles. Some Slovene border guards had barricaded themselves into a roadside café, but the one guard on duty let us through without delay. Safely into Austria, we looked back to see that the Yugoslav troops were closing the border. Had we been a minute later our party might have been stuck in Slovenia.

Most of the people in the convoy headed for Munich to catch flights home. I had a train ticket: if my original train were still departing from Trieste, I might even have been able to catch up with it somewhere in Italy. Three of us were dropped off in Villach, where I learned that I could get a train to Venice in time for my Paris connection. That, however, wasn't the end of it, for the train broke down at Udine. By some miracle I did make it to Venice, though with less than a minute to spare, and literally leaped on to the overnight train to France. The attendant, who'd given up on me when the train left Trieste, was able to give me a compartment to myself.

The Montenegrins I'd met on the outward journey had warned me that thieves board night trains in northern Italy, stealing from sleeping passengers and slipping off the train again before anyone misses anything. They'd shown me how to secure the door using curtain ties from the compartment. Acting on this advice, I locked myself in and slept soundly and undisturbed.

This was never going to be a simple journey. In Paris there was a Métro strike and available taxis were scarce, so I had to trek the long distance from the Gare de Lyon to the Gare du Nord on foot. When I got on the train for Calais I heard an English couple moaning about some mishap they'd had on their previous journey. After all I'd been through, I wanted to scream at them, 'You think you've had problems!' A ferry and another train ride later, I arrived in London, exhausted. At Euston station I told the sleeping-car attendant about my eventful journey and he, too, was kind enough to give me a compartment to myself. I would soon be home.

When people describe an experience as their worst nightmare it often turns out, with hindsight, to have been something trivial. But I really did believe I'd gone through my 'worst nightmare' on that journey out of Slovenia. If only.

I'd phoned Barbara from Villach, not knowing whether anyone in Scotland would be aware of the situation in what had now become 'the former Yugoslavia'. Barbara wasn't at work; and then I remembered about her hospital appointment and phoned home. She told me that the doctors were still unable to give her good news. There were continuing worries. She was to go back again in six weeks' time.

In six weeks, on 9 August, Barbara and I were getting married. Barbara had to go back to the hospital the day before the wedding. She didn't want me to go with her, but as her parents were in Dunblane, she asked her dad to drive her. Afterwards she breezed into the house, saying immediately that everything was fine. But it hadn't been. A little later, she came upstairs and told me that the news wasn't good: she needed an exploratory operation that might result in a mastectomy. For the moment, she didn't want anyone to know, she didn't want the news to spoil other people's enjoyment of our wedding. She'd asked the consultant whether she could go ahead with the trip we'd planned. He'd said that she could delay having the operation for three weeks, but no longer.

Barbara sailed through the wedding as if nothing were wrong. In the morning she mentioned to Olwen, the nursery deputy, that we'd be collecting Sophie at lunchtime. Asked if it was for anything special, Barbara casually replied, 'Oh, we're getting married.' By the time I collected Sophie, our clever ten-month-old had 'made' us special cards. We'd invited a handful of family and friends to the wedding ceremony in the upstairs room of the Dunblane Burgh Chambers, above the Registry Office. Afterwards we took photos in the garden at the Cross, by the small roundabout at the end of the High Street. In the evening we hosted a party at Willowbank House and by Monday morning we were on our way to the USA.

It was Sophie's first plane journey and I'm sure that, like all parents, Barbara and I were over-anxious about the possibility of leaving vital things behind. We seemed to have packed everything she might need – toys, books, food, formula, bottles, sterilising tablets, etc. etc. Sophie signalled that she would always be a great traveller: she fell asleep in the departure lounge at Glasgow Airport and didn't wake again until we were high over the Atlantic. The trip was to include ten days' touring around the Pacific Northwest states of Washington and Oregon and then a week in Vancouver, British Columbia, where I was participating in a slime mould conference. After arriving at Seattle we stayed two nights in Tacoma, Washington, before driving to Portland, Oregon, to stay with a colleague and his family. As they drove us around Oregon Mike and Terry played the Pediatric AIDS Foundation tape that included the songs by Carole King, Meryl Streep and Barbra Streisand which brought tears to my eyes years later.

I gave a research talk at the Vancouver meeting, but my mind wasn't really on slime moulds. Sophie sparkled and made people smile wherever we went. Barbara was struggling, especially during those hours when I was at the conference. Even Sophie's sparkle couldn't always make her feel better. Around others Barbara never showed any apprehension and I still don't know that I ever appreciated all the feelings she had to cope with. After a last couple of days in a rainy Seattle, the trip was over. We arrived back on a Saturday. By the Monday morning, Barbara was in hospital awaiting surgery and an uncertain prognosis.

★

Two weeks before the wedding DS Paul Hughes of the Child Protection Unit at Bannockburn had visited a boys' summer camp at Mullarochy Bay on Loch Lomond. Hughes's visit followed another, two days earlier, by a Central Scotland detective constable and a social worker. The reason for both visits was to look at a camp that Thomas Hamilton was running. There had been more complaints about assault, photographs and videotaping of boys. Hamilton admitted the assault and sought to justify it. The nature of the photographs had been of particular concern, as the boys were wearing only swimming trunks. One child had been forced to lie in cold water against his will as the photos were taken.

Hughes was uneasy about a lot of things, including the lack of supervision of the boys, and it became clear that Hamilton was lying about the photographs. Denying at first that he'd taken any still photographs, Hamilton later responded to a request from the police and handed over a number of slides and prints. It seems certain that he withheld other photos.

In September DS Hughes took a report to the Procurator Fiscal. It listed ten draft charges, but by November the authorities had decided to take no action. Yet again a Procurator Fiscal's office said there was insufficient evidence of criminality. We'll never know the detail of the Hughes report: it is unavailable to the public. After the Inquiry in 1996 Lord Cullen decided it should be put away with a hundred-year time seal.

★

Barbara was diagnosed with breast cancer, and her operation resulted in a mastectomy. She took the consequences in her stride. Her main concern was her prognosis and whether the mastectomy had improved her prospects. She wanted to be able to do all the things she'd planned for herself as a mother and a scientist. She read avidly, bought medical books, healthcare books and willpower books, and slipped off to the Glasgow University library to consult the books and journals there. She also wanted to help promote research on breast cancer.

Shortly after she was diagnosed, a new charity was launched. Breakthrough Breast Cancer's aim was to provide dedicated laboratory facilities for breast cancer research. It encouraged its supporters to be Challengers, each of whom aimed to raise £1,000. If 15,000 people met the challenge this would provide the £15 million needed to build the laboratory. The number was significant as around 15,000 women die in Britain each year of breast cancer. Barbara signed up and Breakthrough's purple crocus symbol became a familiar sight around the house.

Even at the best of times life rarely runs smoothly, but there are occasions when problems couldn't be worse timed. The implications of Barbara's condition were brutally rammed home within days of her operation. We'd received an enquiry from our building society about the life cover linked to the mortgage. As part of the mortgage deal we'd arranged extra life insurance. However, the forms hadn't been processed and for over a year this had gone unnoticed. When I went to the building society office I was told that there would be no problem: all we had to do was reapply, fill out the forms again. But in fact there was a problem, a huge problem, because Barbara could no longer take out life insurance. After a brief investigation the building society accepted responsibility for the error and made an arrangement that would not leave me with financial difficulties in the event of Barbara's death. We were very grateful for this, but the episode had accentuated the changed parameters of our lives.

Sophie, almost at the walking stage, kept us going. October arrived and so did Sophie's first birthday. Anyone seeing us that evening, out for a meal with Sophie's granny (my mum), wouldn't have known that anything was wrong, and as much as possible that's how we wanted it to be. But Barbara's optimistic outlook was soon challenged. After she got in from work one Friday she discovered lumps under her left arm. There was little doubt that the mastectomy had failed to prevent the spread of malignant cells to her lymph nodes. Next Monday, 11 November, at the clinic in Bridge of Allan, the doctor confirmed Barbara's fears and another hospital appointment was arranged. As neither of us could face going back to work, we collected Sophie from nursery and drove north into a golden Perthshire autumn day, to Killin for lunch and Pitlochry for tea. In any other circumstances it would have been a lovely day out, an unplanned escape from work. That golden day, however, was edged with black.

★

The same day was one of the most significant in the continuing history of Central Scotland Police's dealings with Thomas Hamilton. DS Hughes had discovered that Hamilton had a firearms licence and wrote a memo in which he requested that serious consideration be given to its withdrawal:

> I am firmly of the opinion that Hamilton is an unsavoury character and unstable personality . . .
>
> I respectfully request that serious consideration is given to withdrawing this man's firearms certificate as a precautionary measure, as it is my opinion that he is a scheming, devious and deceitful individual who is not to be trusted.

The request, and the obvious warning it contained, were dismissed by Central Scotland Police's hierarchy. DCC McMurdo stamped Hughes's request 'no action'. The material relating to Hughes's concerns wasn't placed in Hamilton's firearms file, nor was it recorded in Criminal Intelligence.

★

Barbara had more surgery, with a number of lymph nodes removed, but she could no longer avoid having treatment and so started courses of both chemotherapy and radiotherapy. It would be wrong to say that Barbara's first period of treatment went well, but it wasn't nearly as debilitating as she'd anticipated. At monthly intervals she had six sessions of chemotherapy at the Beatson Oncology Centre at Glasgow's Western Infirmary. After the first session she was very nauseous, but next time was switched to a newer and more effective anti-nausea drug she insisted on being given after a pharmacologist friend had told her about it. She'd have chemotherapy one day, recover for a day or two and then go back into work. The Western was close to Barbara's department and for her radiotherapy sessions she would go there as part of a normal workday.

We got through Christmas, spent with Barbara's family in Dunblane, and began to relax more during the time-share week in January. By spring Barbara's treatment was over. Her work had hardly suffered: she was lecturing, doing her research and had submitted a successful research grant application. Around Easter we went to more conferences, travelling back to Dunblane on the day of the April general election. During the campaign Sophie and I had walked past our MP, Michael Forsyth, on the stump in Dunblane High Street. For some reason Sophie called out 'bye bye'. But it wasn't 'bye bye' and against most expectations, and a significant shift to Labour elsewhere, Scotland swung marginally to the Conservatives. Stirling's MP held his seat by 236 votes. Prime Minister John Major's soapbox campaign had ultimately succeeded. The Conservatives remained in power, albeit with a much-reduced majority of twenty-one.

★

As 1992 continued Thomas Hamilton was pursuing his complaints. He protested to the Ombudsman about the conduct of Central Scotland Police and about DS Paul Hughes, and to the Social Work Department about harassment and disruption of his activities. Yet with all this going on, his firearm certificate was renewed on 17 February 1992, this time by Chief Supt Adamson, in DCC McMurdo's absence.

Trouble continued. In the summer of 1992 Hamilton ran a sports training course at Dunblane High School. On 29 June three young boys from the camp, wearing only pyjamas, were found by the local police wandering the streets of Dunblane. A few days later another complaint about lack of supervision was received from a parent. The Child Protection Unit became involved and sent a report to their colleagues in Fife, where the boys lived. Mr Somerville, Senior Assistant Director of Education of Fife Regional Council, wrote: 'I feel that the events of 29 June 1992 in Dunblane in a sense serve as a warning . . . I fear that a tragedy to a child or children is almost waiting to happen.'

He had meant this in the context of the boys' club, but with hindsight these words are so prophetic. But who was responding to these warnings? Certainly not the Procurators Fiscal. In their view Hamilton's behaviour had never crossed the border into obvious criminality. To protect children, would the authorities act only once a crime had been committed?

★

We went out a lot that summer – excursions in Scotland and trips to England. Later in the year there was a more ambitious expedition, for in December we flew to Australia with Sophie's nan and grandad (Barbara's parents). I was taking up a long-standing invitation to work with a colleague at Macquarie University in Sydney and Barbara was participating in a meeting in Fremantle, near Perth. She, Sophie and Nan and Grandad stayed for a week in Perth, with Barbara's aunt and uncle, while I got on with my research on the other side of the country. After a week they joined me in Sydney. Barbara's parents returned to England in time for Christmas, but with my research work completed, the three of us stayed on to spend our Christmas under the warm sun of New South Wales. Australia was fantastic. We went sightseeing around Sydney, relaxed at the beaches, drove to Canberra and Newcastle, went wine tasting in the Hunter Valley and had picnics – the best one being on Christmas Day on one of Sydney's northern beaches, Whale Beach. Although it rained, and we had to eat our picnic in the car, it was Christmas Day at the beach. We returned to a cold Manchester Airport on New Year's Eve and drove home to Dunblane through dismal rain. That set the scene for 1993.

In Australia Barbara had suffered slight backache, but she thought it might be strained from carrying Sophie. The previous year I'd had to spend a week in bed with sciatica brought on by lifting Sophie awkwardly. But Barbara's back got worse. She had a bone scan at the beginning of February, but nothing showed up. A week later, after visiting our friends Jeremy and Alison in Glasgow, Barbara seized up as she got into the car. She was in agony for a few minutes. Anxious not to get stranded in Glasgow, she asked me to drive her to the Accident and Emergency department at Stirling. There the casualty doctor told her that her back problem had nothing to do with cancer. Reassured, we drove back to Dunblane and after a few days' rest Barbara felt better and returned to work.

One Monday morning in mid-March Barbara slipped and fell at the bottom of the stairs as she was about to leave for work. She was seizing up again. She tried to take heart from the negative bone scan; but within days she couldn't move, was confined to bed and became totally dependent on me. There was also another worrying symptom, Bell's palsy, facial distortion due to a lesion of the facial nerve. In Barbara's case the most likely cause was a brain tumour.

Few people other than close friends knew about Barbara's cancer, although it was never something she wanted to hide. She mentioned it on a need-to-know basis. In October 1992 she'd told Olwen at nursery about her mastectomy and how at one time she hadn't expected to live to see Sophie's second birthday. Olwen had said then that if we ever needed help, we had only to ask. Now we needed that help. On 28 March Barbara was admitted to Stirling Royal Infirmary again. A CAT scan revealed bone tumours. Barbara needed drastic chemo- and radiotherapy and was transferred to Glasgow Western Infirmary. At Stirling she had been fortunate enough to have a room of her own, but at the Western she was put into a conventional ward, the oncology ward, and this had an immediate effect on her. Her will evaporated, even before the therapy started. She slept a lot and, for a while, had little interest in what was going on around her.

I drove the thirty-five miles between Dunblane and Glasgow every day. Sophie came with me on some evenings and for weekend visiting, otherwise I would collect her from Olwen's when I got home. The ward provided toys for her, or we would read stories together. She'd adjusted well to her mum's illness and would simply tell people, 'My Mummy is in hospital because she's got a bad back.' She was so good with me at home. After I'd picked her up from Olwen's, we'd go home and have especially long storytimes. Winnie-the-Pooh was a particular favourite around this time.

Barbara's parents visited at the weekends, but she was reluctant to see other people. She communicated with the world through me. I'm not sure friends fully understood, when I told them that Barbara didn't want visitors, that she didn't want to be seen. She wanted them to think of her as she'd been before she became ill.

The prognosis wasn't good. Not long after being admitted to the Western, Barbara was told that she may have only two years to live. By then she was very weak and perhaps unable to take in the full impact of this news. We had to do things about the future. What would happen to Sophie if anything happened to me as well? It had to be something Barbara and I both agreed on: we had to sort that out now. I still feel guilty about having to prompt these discussions and the letters we wrote instructing our solicitor, planning things for a time when Barbara would no longer be alive.

Barbara wanted to be looked after at home and emphatically ruled out going to a hospice. It was going to be tough. There were times I would be able to leave her for a short while, checking back frequently by phone, but it was inevitable that my work would have to be adjusted and reorganised to allow me to care for Barbara and Sophie. Infections delayed Barbara's return home once the radiotherapy course was complete and necessitated her transfer to an isolation ward. A few days after getting back to Dunblane, Barbara had to return to the Western for a week when her temperature rose again. This became a pattern for the forthcoming weeks. Four of her five chemotherapy sessions were followed a week or so later by problems.

Barbara moved into the back bedroom. Her inactive weeks in bed had taken their toll on her muscles and tendons and, unable to manipulate one of her ankles, she couldn't walk unaided. She was provided with a wheelchair, but this was no help around the house. She needed physiotherapy and very gradually learned to walk again using a stick – a long and arduous process that took most of the will and energy she possessed. But her fighting spirit began to come back. She became very determined, stubborn even, only accepting help if absolutely necessary.

Nothing was easy. Barbara drifted in and out of sleep and was frequently sick. She could no longer wear contact lenses and needed new glasses. She lost her hair and was given a strange-looking wig that she preferred not to wear. I searched the shops in Perth for a suitable turban. There was a daily drug regime involving up to eight different sorts of medication. I hated to see her so weak and frustrated that she couldn't do everything she wanted to. Our GP, on his first visit after Barbara's discharge from the Western, had handed me a disability living allowance application form. This would provide financial support to allow me or somebody else to care for Barbara at home. The award would be automatic. When I checked the form I realised that one of the few automatic categories was for terminally ill patients who had a maximum life expectancy of six months. So that was it, then. Just six months.

I endeavoured not to let anyone down at the university that spring and summer. I bought a fax machine and a personal computer to make it easier to work at home and communicate with my colleagues. I felt isolated from the department. Of the senior staff, only Lewis reached out and showed concern for the effect this could have on the students' courses and the longer-term damage it might do to my career.

★

Another report on Thomas Hamilton was submitted to the Procurator Fiscal on 9 June 1993, this time in relation to complaints about his conduct at three clubs in Central Region premises, Denny High School, Stirling High School and Dunblane High School. The problems again involved photographs of boys and the swimming trunks he asked them to wear. By now the police had also become aware of Hamilton's previous problems with the Scouts. The Family Unit, as the Child Protection Unit was now known, dealt with the complaints. The Unit's DC Gordon Taylor visited the Procurator Fiscal's office to ask for a warrant to search Hamilton's flat for photographs. The request was refused on 10 September 1993. A report was sent to DCC McMurdo, who by that stage was well aware of a catalogue of complaints. Indeed he was involved in correspondence with the Scottish Office about Hamilton and had on occasion become exasperated by it. The complaints continued, another from the summer camp at Dunblane High School and one from Balfron Boys Club. Central Regional Council had been investigating his activities all year.

★

Nan and Grandad often stayed at the weekends when Sophie and I had a particular routine. On Saturday mornings we made the half-hour drive to Perth, went shopping and then ate at McDonalds (a burger for me, a Happy Meal with its free toy for Sophie: Aladdin characters that summer). I chose a longer route home to give Sophie a chance to sleep. Sometimes we were able to do other things: visiting the farm life centre, getting our hair cut, or having a special treat like going to Morag and Michael's wedding. And as we drove together Sophie and I became closer and closer. We were becoming the team.

Home life oscillated between calm and crisis. Twice Barbara had to be admitted to Stirling Royal for blood transfusions. On the first occasion she collapsed as I helped her downstairs and, for a few moments, I thought she had died. Everything was pointing to the fact that the chemotherapy was killing her. She was too weak to deal with all the side effects. It had to stop, but there would be nothing now to check the growth of the tumours. There were bone tumours, almost certainly a brain tumour and now confirmation of liver tumours as well.

Once the chemotherapy finished, Barbara began to feel a lot better and her quality of life improved. She moved back into the front bedroom. Now able to walk more freely, and with the wheelchair in the car, she could venture out. First, we all went to Pizzaland in Stirling for an evening meal and then, a couple of weeks later, to Dunblane's India Gate where, before her mum's illness, Sophie had been a big favourite. Barbara joined us on one of our Saturday runs to Perth and we all ate at McDonalds. We visited the Blair Drummond Safari Park. Eventually we dared to go away for a night, driving to North Berwick, where we walked around for a while and sat on the beach before booking into a hotel. It was good to know we could still take trips.

It was time to get Sophie's new bedroom ready. When Barbara had been in the Western she'd chosen a yellow-and-blue colour scheme and we'd already bought a bedspread and matching bedclothes from a Marks and Spencer catalogue. Barbara came with me to choose the wallpaper and furniture. Sophie would have yellow-and-white striped wallpaper, with a bright sunny frieze, and a light blue carpet. Going out was never without its difficulties, but we were able to get some things done, especially if these were for Sophie.

We decided to try to do more special things and booked a longer time away, a long weekend in Inverness. Barbara sat by the hotel swimming pool as Sophie splashed happily in the water. On the Sunday we drove to Skye on another of those sunny autumn days. The car filled with the sound of children's songs from a new tape that we played as we headed west. It began to rain as we approached Skye, but the weather couldn't hide the island's splendour. It was a day I wanted to relive with Sophie one day.

We spent the Monday on the Moray Firth coast at Nairn, and further east at Findhorn and Lossiemouth. Sophie and I played on the beaches for a while, but we couldn't leave Barbara alone in the car for long. We had a lengthy drive home the next day, punctuated by stops when Barbara felt sick. If the journey were okay we might be able to consider travelling to Leeds for her brother's wedding in three weeks' time.

The following weekend we went out for Sunday lunch to the pub at Rowardennan on the east side of Loch Lomond. As Barbara stood up to leave, her legs gave way beneath her. This was the first time for weeks that she'd been unable to support herself. It was a bad day.

When we got home I precipitated a crisis. Sophie's room had been decorated that week, the carpet had been laid and all the new furniture was in place. As part of the makeover, an old washbasin had been removed and the pipes sealed, but the remaining pipes knocked together when the bathroom taps were run. I tried to adjust their position very slightly. I succeeded only in breaking the mains pipe, and water gushed out over Sophie's new room. I stuck my finger in the pipe to stem the flow. We had no way of turning off the water, as there was no stopcock in the house. I couldn't move from the pipe and Barbara was downstairs, virtually immobilised. I shouted downstairs and Sophie tried to come up to see what was happening. I didn't want her to witness the deluge and told her not to come in. This upset her. Through her tears she went and told her mum and Barbara tried to phone the plumber. The first plumber wasn't in, but she persevered and managed to contact another. I found two bowls and spent nearly an hour rushing between the bedroom and bathroom emptying one as the other filled.

By the time the plumber arrived and saved Sophie's room, I was devastated – not so much by what had happened, but by the fact that after all this time, after all the stress, I hadn't coped. I'd stood there with my finger in the pipe yelling at myself. For months we had done so well, but this accident had exposed our limitations.

By the next Sunday Barbara was back in bed, her body weaker and her mind now affected. Her last conversation was with her brother Matt when she summoned up the strength to apologise over the phone for not being able to get to his wedding that day. Slowly her words, often slurred, deserted her and once again she became entirely dependent on me. She was slipping away and I wanted to make everything as comfortable as I possibly could. I'd given my first lecture of the semester but was ordered by our doctor, quite rightly, to sign off work. This, I was surprised to find, left the teaching arrangements in some disarray as no contingency plans had been made.

Sophie's third birthday arrived at the beginning of October. During the week, while Nan and Grandad were staying, I went shopping for her presents and showed them to Barbara when I got home. She could hardly acknowledge what was happening. Sophie, thrilled with the gifts on her birthday, wanted her mum to see them, but by now Barbara was unable to convey any feeling. It was so hard trying to make this a happy day for Sophie. I took her for lunch at Burger King in Stirling and in the afternoon she went to a birthday party at the Spiers Centre in Alloa, the first she'd ever been to. Sophie was so excited, but I found it heartbreaking taking her to and from that party.

Barbara's last few days were calm. For a while she'd been very restless, but on the day after Sophie's birthday she settled, drifting in and out of consciousness. Changes in medication and special care from the nurses from the health centre and hospice had helped. By the Thursday there was little hope that Barbara would live for more than a few days. I was awake most of the night, scared that Barbara might die whilst I was asleep. At seven in the morning I heard her breathing change. I phoned the doctor. During the night Sophie had crept into bed and had squeezed between us. Now she wanted to go to the loo and I rushed her to the bathroom. When we got back Barbara was still with us, but within minutes her breathing had stopped. She died at 7.20 a.m. on Friday, 8 October, aged thirty-one.

I had to go back to Dunblane Registry Office, where the registrar was devastated by the news. A birth, a marriage and a death, all within three years. I prepared for Barbara's funeral and arranged it at Falkirk Crematorium for the following week, for Wednesday the Thirteenth.

# CHAPTER THREE

# Single Parenthood

## October 1993–March 1996

'Don't cry Daddy, it'll be all right'

How do you cope when you find you have sole responsibility for a young child? For some mothers it's an immediate reality, for other parents it happens after the break up of a relationship. It can be sudden, but I'd had time to prepare and I'd effectively had total responsibility for Sophie for the six months before Barbara died. The need to make sure Sophie's life was as little affected as possible predominated and it probably led to my overlooking myself.

It is impossible to see how I would have managed single parenthood entirely on my own. I didn't have to: I had Arnhall Nursery. There were never any regrets about sending Sophie to nursery so early in her life. Indeed, in view of what happened it was one of the best decisions we could have made. By the time Barbara became seriously ill, Sophie had spent over two years at Arnhall, and while things were changing daily at home, nursery provided her with stability in the company of caring and loving people. It was an extension of our family. During the period before and after Barbara's death, Sophie was prepared by reading her books written especially for children experiencing bereavement. At home we read *When Uncle Bob Died* by Althea over and over again. 'It's very sad when someone dies' it said on the back cover. 'Reading this story may make it easier to talk about and understand our feelings.' At nursery the children played a board game called *All About Me*, devised to help children through traumatic events. I borrowed it to play at home.

In quick succession Sophie's friends were having birthday parties for the first time. It is painful to record that the next party she went to was a joint one for her future classmates Hannah Scott and Megan Turner. Like many parties, it was held at the Cowane Centre, a favourite venue in Stirling. The kids would spend the first hour romping around the Soft Room – filled with coloured foam blocks of various sizes and shapes – and the second hour in the adjacent room where food and drink were served and games played. I'd thought I'd be able to leave Sophie with her pals while I went to see friends for an hour. I'd had little opportunity to visit people on my own. But Sophie clung to me and wouldn't let me leave. How could I desert this vulnerable three-year-old at a time like that? I stayed. Years later, Kareen Turner gave me a photo from the party showing Sophie in a pink dress sitting on the floor with me beside her looking somewhat lost.

We were frequent customers at Torags, the local toyshop, choosing birthday presents for Sophie's friends. Parties could also be emotional occasions. At one point during her illness Barbara became very upset because she was not going to be able to take Sophie to parties, something she had really looked forward to. The thought of Barbara's sadness hit me particularly hard after I'd dropped off Sophie at a party in Dunblane in January 1994. The party was for Fleur, daughter of another nursery mum, Ann Pearston.

I gradually sorted out Barbara's things. Going through the contents of her office in Glasgow was particularly painful. This was her private place and it was so hard to comprehend how this successful career woman was no longer here. I had a first experience of an I-don't-want-to-have-to-explain-this-to-you situation, when confronted by an officious University of Glasgow security man who asked me to move my car as it didn't have a permit. 'I'm just here to clear out my late wife's office.'

Sophie and I went away a lot, sometimes because of my work, but not always. Wherever we went we'd sing with The Singing Kettle: we had a sticker in the back window of the car to prove it. The Singing Kettle – Cilla, Artie and Gary (and now Jane) – do more than sing. Theirs is a very slick and popular children's entertainment. I'd heard them for the first time in October when Olwen had lent Sophie the *Singing Kettle 2* video. Right from the start, with 'The Bear went Over the Mountain', the show oozed fun and enjoyment. It was difficult to get their songs out of my head. The audiotapes I'd bought for the car included more traditional songs and I realised that some of them mentioned tricky topics such as death and heaven. How was I going to be able to explain what these were? I'd attempted to provide Sophie with some explanation of what had happened to her mum, but didn't have all the answers. At that stage I worried too much, as the questions didn't come immediately.

I was trying to work from home. Sharon, who worked as a research assistant in the department, had acted as my postie for months, allowing me to deal with all my work mail promptly. I kept in close touch with my research staff and students, but my future research plans were not in good shape. Months of neglect of the recent scientific literature had left me in danger of being out of touch. My inability to prepare any research grant applications meant that I had no new major research projects in my laboratory. All things considered, my best option was to take sabbatical leave as soon as possible, next autumn. I'd not be able to go away from Dunblane. It would have been inconceivable to destabilise Sophie's life by removing her from nursery and taking her off somewhere else where I couldn't care for her full time. Neither did I want anybody else looking after her. I concluded that I would need to revive my research at Stirling. To do this I needed to have a few months free of teaching duties as soon as possible in a supportive environment. My biochemistry colleagues were okay about this, but my head of department vetoed the idea. I would have to wait – other things and other people in the department had higher priority. I was devastated. This would make it so much harder to get going again and restrict my ability to compete for limited research funding.

By January 1994 I was back working on campus and started lecturing again when the semester began in February. I've found that one consequence of bereavement is a massive loss of confidence. I was very nervous giving those first lectures. Fortunately I was teaching two groups of students who knew me well and helped me get through those initial steps back into work.

Before Barbara had died I'd hardly met any of the other nursery parents. We were nodding acquaintances at best. I started meeting them more as Sophie's social life took off; in fact I rarely went out without Sophie. Sophie's best friend at nursery was Rosie. The confidence Sophie had gained in her time there was infectious. It had rubbed off on Rosie and had helped her settle in when she arrived at Arnhall. Not long after Barbara's death, Rosie's mum Sheena wrote to me inviting Sophie round to tea at their house in Gargunnock. After that we went on a number of outings with Rosie's family. It wasn't until I went back to work that I tried to resurrect an independent social life by making a weekly standing order for a babysitter with the nursery staff. However, apart from those Wednesday evenings out, usually for a quiet drink in the local pub, I rarely did anything without Sophie. In April a whole gang of us went to the MacRobert Centre at the university for our first Singing Kettle concert, 'The Time Machine'.

The next month Sophie and Rosie enrolled in Jumpin' Beans, a weekly club run by Stirling District Council for pre-school children, where the children ran around doing exercises and playing games. The first Jumpin' Beans session was on 12 May. Just before I left my office to collect Sophie from Gargunnock, I heard that John Smith, the Leader of the Opposition, had died of a heart attack. Supporters and opponents alike mourned the loss of a sincere man and able politician. His death heralded the beginning of the 'New' era for Labour with the election of Tony Blair as leader.

In July Sophie caught chicken-pox. We were returning from a trip to England when she became itchy on the journey (the time I stopped at Forton services for ointment). I crumpled – a combination of my general emotional state, thoughts of the extra care Sophie would need and that lack of confidence from which I was still suffering. I did manage to get through the worst of it and my mum came and stayed with us for a couple of weeks while I sorted myself out. I desperately wanted to cope with everything, do as much as possible on my own, but this had warned me that sometimes I couldn't.

Sophie and I were about to leave for America on a big adventure. At the end of July we flew from Glasgow to San Francisco. Sophie was near perfect on the flights, playing quietly, reading books, or sleeping – and helping the cabin crew by checking on the other passengers, getting very concerned if tray tables were down or seat backs not in the upright position during take-off and landing. I started to relax as I realised that everything was going well. I hired a car in San Francisco and we headed north to stay with our friends in Portland, Oregon. Sophie was excellent company in the car. There was just one problem. She would never let me play anything on the stereo system except her music or stories. We listened to The Little Mermaid, Pinocchio, Postman Pat and, of course, the Singing Kettle, over and over again. We drove through the Cascade Mountains, where my three-year-old companion tolerated the visits to lava fields and crater lakes. It was a trade-off: she got to go to McDonalds and Denny's and to collect all the colouring books and toys they handed out with the meals; I got to see the volcanoes.

There was a work reason for going back to the West Coast. I had another slime mould conference to go to and when our visit to Portland was over I drove south. After several hundred miles of freeways, numerous scenic views and countless burgers, we arrived in San Diego in Southern California. I was only able to go to the conference if someone could look after Sophie while I was at the sessions. Sharon had volunteered and, a day after our arrival in Southern California, she flew in to join us in our apartment.

The conference went well. Sophie came to my poster session when I talked to people about my research: it had been a while since I'd spoken to anyone at length about slime moulds. While I went to the talks, Sharon and Sophie had fun together in the apartment or at the beach. After the conference was over we had some spare days to do a few extra things. Sophie got first choice, Disneyland. She loved it, though was somewhat wary of all the people dressed up as Disney characters, especially Mickey

Mouse (and we'd queued for ages to see him!). We watched the impressive *Lion King* parade, and went off to the store and bought the audiotape of the music. As we drove north out of Los Angeles the sounds of Africa boomed through the car. At last we'd found a tape that was our music, something we'd both listen to. When we got home Sophie's friends were really impressed that she knew all about a new Disney movie that hadn't arrived in Britain. After Disneyland we had a grown-ups' visit to Yosemite. It was difficult to know what a little girl made of all these scenic wonders, though there were always plenty of questions. She had reached the stage when she continuously wanted to know 'why?' and 'how?'.

After we got back from California our household doubled in number with the arrival of two kittens from the Cats Protection League. Sophie chose their names. Kit Kat was a grey, Rosie was a tortoiseshell. Sophie's friend Rosie had a cat called Sophie and now she had a cat called Rosie, and the two girls took immense pleasure in this symmetry of names. It was Kit Kat whom she chose to smother with love. There was a gentle awkwardness to Sophie's cuddles at first, but the kitten got used to them.

Sophie finally moved into her new bedroom. She'd been reluctant to be far from me after her mum died, but I gently nudged her into thinking that she should start to sleep in her special room. After the move it was so comfortable reading stories on her new bed, and when they were over and Sophie had fallen asleep, I was tempted to nod off as well.

Soon it was October again and Sophie's fourth birthday. I wanted to give her a party, but it had to be different, not just another Soft Room bash. I held it at home. There were eleven girls, including Sophie, and six boys. Although I say it myself, it went amazingly well. I surpassed my previous drawing attempts by producing an Eeyore lookalike for 'Pin the Tail on the Donkey' and managed to rig the 'Pass the Parcel' to avoid any disappointments around the circle. Even Sophie's choice of cake, a horribly pink Mr Blobby, tasted good. A gold star for Dad that day, I thought.

Sophie's birthday was always followed quickly by the anniversary of

Barbara's death. That first year I visited Falkirk Crematorium on my own.

I was about to spend my longest time away from Sophie. The parasitology meeting in Izmir, Turkey, was an important occasion for me, a chance to meet colleagues and discuss joint projects that would help get my research launched again. Sophie, staying at Olwen's, got daily calls from me as I ran up a one-million-Turkish-lire phone bill. She did well, but became quite tearful by the end of the week. At least I'd remembered to leave her sooky this time. Once there were four sookies, Sophie's comforters, the tops and bottoms of two pairs of Barbara's pyjamas. She needed one as an almost constant companion and I knew the dire consequences of losing them. It had happened in Sydney and in the Asda store in Perth, and by the autumn of 1994 we were down to the last one. On a previous occasion I'd gone to a weekend meeting in rural Perthshire, only to realise I still had Sophie's sooky in the car. I just about got away with that – but never again, and not for a week.

Just before Christmas 1994 my colleagues and I were shocked by news of the death of Michael Meenaghan. Spike, as we knew him, had been a biochemistry student at Stirling and had stayed on to complete a masters degree with one of my colleagues. We had got to know him well and had been pleased to see how his research career had developed after he left Stirling. Spike had been shot dead at his flat in Oxford. As far as I know the murder has never been solved. Guns can do such awful damage.

★

In February 1995 Thomas Hamilton's firearm certificate was due for renewal. A young police constable, Anne Anderson, went to Hamilton's home in Stirling. It was the first firearm certificate renewal she had ever checked and she had a strange feeling about the man. She felt he was gloating when he showed her one of his guns. When she checked the criminal intelligence file she found only three lines on Hamilton – a 'glaring deficiency', according to Lord Cullen. She reported her misgivings to her superior, but was told that the force knew all about Hamilton and not to be concerned about it. So in spite of her feelings and everything else that would have been known to Central Scotland Police, Hamilton's firearm certificate was renewed on 28 February by DCC McMurdo. From what he said at the Cullen Inquiry, it transpired that he took no more than a few minutes to stamp it 'Approved'.

Hamilton's other activities were still a cause for anxiety among a number of people whose children became involved in his boys' club. On 10 December 1994 two men had visited Hamilton's flat, demanding the return of photographs that he'd taken of a boy at one of his clubs. The police were called because of the disturbance the men caused. After explaining the situation, they were told to leave things in the hands of the police. It seems that everyone was being told to put their trust in Central Scotland Police because they knew all about Hamilton.

★

In March Sophie and I made another trip to the USA. I wanted to spend time discussing collaborative research with American colleagues I'd met in Turkey. When we arrived in San Francisco, northern California was suffering from heavy rain and floods. As I had some spare time I decided to go and find some sun in Arizona. We drove southeast through Salinas and Bakersfield, ending the day in the desert town of Barstow, California. The next morning, 13 March 1995, we went east to Nevada and Arizona. Along the old Route 66 the scenery is magnificent: you can literally see for miles and miles and miles. Eventually we reached Williams, Arizona, the terminus of a steam railway to the Grand Canyon. This was a must and I booked us into a motel for three nights.

The Grand Canyon is an awesome, magnificent place. No matter how many photographs I'd seen of it, nothing had prepared me for its scale and grandeur. Sophie had become apprehensive on the train when I told her we were going to see an enormous hole in the ground. I shall never know whether this was going to be something that remained in her memory. Sadly, though, she probably remembered something else from that day, something that still haunts me.

The train ride took about ninety minutes in each direction. Entertainment was provided. Two musicians came and sang in each carriage on the outward journey. On the return trip the train was stopped by a band of 'outlaws' on horseback. They were firing guns. The 'outlaws' got on board and walked through the train scaring the passengers. Sophie was terrified and hid under my jumper, squealing every so often as the 'outlaws' approached. Unfortunately one of them spotted her and made a comment, at which she screamed. Eventually one of the others told him to 'leave off and stop frightening the kid'. The drama ended with the arrival of a 'sheriff', but it had been too scary an experience for Sophie from the time she first heard the gunfire. She told her friends all about it when we got home, but what impression had it left on her? How was she going to feel if she ever heard gunfire again?

I'd never been to America without having some apprehension about guns. On our return from Yosemite the previous summer I had worried when I'd pulled up sharply at traffic lights in rural California and the driver behind gesticulated violently from the cab of his pick-up truck. He might have a gun, I thought, don't react, don't let his road-rage turn into something worse. This wasn't fanciful. A recent survey has revealed that one in eight motorists in the state of Arizona has driven with a gun in the car and that three-quarters of them reported their weapons were always loaded. People have been shot as a result of road-rage. Little incidents can escalate so easily when lethal weapons are readily available.

Back in Scotland that spring, preparations were under way for the next year's local government reorganisation. This would introduce unitary authorities throughout Scotland. A new Stirling Council was to replace the Labour-run Central Regional Council and Tory-controlled Stirling District Council. The Conservatives had won control of the latter on a cut of the cards after the voters had elected ten Labour and ten Tory councillors in May 1992. Dunblane West's Patricia Greenhill had cut the ace of spades, which not only determined who ran the council but also ensured that she became Provost of Stirling (the equivalent of the mayor). To allow time for the new council to bed in, its councillors were being elected a year early. Labour gained a majority of four. Pat Greenhill lost to Labour's Arthur

Ironside, but would remain Provost until the end of March 1996. My ward, Dunblane East, would continue to be represented by Anne Dickson for the Conservatives.

The summer of 1995 was the barbecue summer. In all our years in the house, Sophie had never been down to the bottom of the garden. I'd neglected it since we'd moved in, there had been too many things happening. Our house stood at the top of a bank that sloped down to the Allan Water. Immediately behind the house was the only garden Sophie knew, a paved yard. A flight of steps led down from there, between trees and bushes, to the lower and main part of the garden. One day I hacked my way through the overgrown foliage with Sophie following behind. At the bottom of the steps, shrouded by tall trees, was a paved patio area, perfect for barbecues. I tidied up the garden and the barbecues commenced. In the autumn Sophie helped me plant bulbs in our garden: purple crocuses to remember her mum, bright yellow daffodils and narcissi, and some of those pure white innocent flowers that would bloom before the others, snowdrops. They should look beautiful when spring arrived in 1996.

As the months passed Sophie never lost her attachment to her mum. She always wanted to see photographs of her. Most poignantly, she would look at a porcelain trinket pot decorated with purple crocuses that I'd bought for her from Breakthrough Breast Cancer. She knew it was linked to her mum's illness. 'It helps me remember Mummy.'

Life was almost hectic. We still had our shopping trips to Perth and I'd become an expert at buying girls' clothes. There was another Singing Kettle concert – Sophie dressed as a pirate with an eye patch and a parrot on her shoulder. Sophie had plenty of parties to go to. In late June she and Rosie went to one for Emily Morton, another of Sophie's special Arnhall friends. Later in the summer we joined Rosie's family at St Andrews where Sophie and I spent two nights in a tent. In August I celebrated twenty years at Stirling by climbing to the top of the Wallace Monument. There had been a number of ups and downs in that time, but right now I seemed to be doing all right again.

There had been a warning, though, not that I would have recognised it as such. One afternoon I came home to find a flier, dated 18 August, on the doormat. It was about boys' clubs and was asking for recruits for one in Dunblane. But it wasn't a straightforward advertisement for the club. The writer sang his own praises, describing how successful his clubs had been in the past. He wrote about his problems, about how he'd been badly treated by the Scouts. As promotion for a boys' club this was a strange document. Like countless others, I'm sure, I thought it had no relevance to me and I binned it.

It had been written by a man named Thomas Hamilton, a man I knew nothing about. Unbeknown to me he was also a man with a firearm certificate who was, in his own words, about to return to his guns.

———————

In August Sophie left nursery to embark on the next phase of her life: schooldays. I was somewhat apprehensive about her going to school. Part of it was my fear, largely irrational, that I was handing my child over to an institution that I hardly knew, a loss of control over my family's life. I didn't have any fears, however, about the wider problems that Sophie might encounter in a world away from nursery, for it never occurred to me – nor would it to anyone – that she would be in danger at primary school.

I didn't know a great deal about Dunblane Primary School. I knew it had a good reputation and that it was big, with the largest school roll in Central Region, over 640 pupils. I'd been to two school fêtes where I'd gained the impression of an active school with plenty of parental involvement. The buildings, though, were a shock, sprawling over a large site, with lots of entrances. A number of classrooms were housed in huts away from the main building. It was not a purpose-built primary school and it showed.

Sophie and I had made a preliminary visit to the school in June. Others from Arnhall were there, too, and as they walked up the stairs to the classrooms, Sophie, Emily and John Petrie, another friend from nursery, held hands. The deputy head, in charge of the infant years, spotted them and remarked that she would have to make sure they were in the same class. They were. All were placed in Mrs Mayor's Primary Class 1/13.

The intake into the Primary One classes was so large – about ninety pupils that year – that their start of term was staggered. Divided among three classes, the children began on Tuesday, Wednesday or Thursday according to their birthdays. Emily began on Tuesday; Sophie started on the Wednesday, 23 August. After her first day Emily came back to nursery to show off her school uniform. Her mum Kathryn took photographs of the two girls on that last afternoon at Arnhall. Next day I walked Sophie to school. Outside the main entrance I met Karen Scott. It was Hannah's first day too. We went with the children up to Mrs Mayor's classroom. The children received a warm welcome and were told to go and play. Karen and I hesitated for a moment, just enough time for the girls to start ignoring us, and then we slipped away. School life had begun.

From then on my contact with the school itself was rather limited, my link was with the Dunblane Kids Club. This was a pre- and after-school club in which the children did a variety of activities under the guidance of Eddie, a neighbour of ours in Bridgend. It was a great relief to know that there was somewhere safe and reliable for Sophie to go outside school hours while I was at work. A number of Sophie's ex-Arnhall friends, including Emily, were there. Kids Club ran until six o'clock. I was never sure whether Sophie wanted me to arrive early or late, it seemed to vary, but whether she was ready or not I was always greeted with her special brand of affection. If she were playing outside, she would run and jump into my arms. Sometimes as I walked past the gym I saw the children playing in there, but within seconds Sophie would be outside with a welcoming cuddle. If I were lucky I might get a pancake they'd just cooked. I carried home pieces of craftwork, paintings, models and computing drawings. Sophie had quickly become the Kids Club expert on Microsoft's Fine Artist program.

Kids Club always seemed a very happy place, often giving the impression of 'organised anarchy'. I'm sure Sophie treated it as a continuation of nursery, which just happened to have some school lessons sandwiched between the morning and afternoon sessions. Sometimes I saw other parents as I collected Sophie, the same kind of nodding acquaintanceships I'd had at nursery. Emily's dad, Les Morton, and I have often remarked on the fact that this was exactly the way we knew each other then.

At the end of Sophie's first school week I held a nursery-leaving party when all her Arnhall pals, children, parents and staff came to the house. She had been a special child there and I wanted to do something to thank everyone who had helped to make her feel so happy and secure. The afternoon ended with Sophie and Emily playing on the computer. I'd upgraded my home computer to provide things that Sophie could use — an encyclopaedia and interactive stories. I bought a colour printer and made the computer speak. One message, from the day of the party in August, was still on the hard disk years later:

> Good morning Sophie/ I always say that don't I?/ What is the weather like today?/ I hope your party goes well/ Take care/ Bye/ Speak to you later.

Sophie loved everything to do with offices. When she came with me to work, which she often had to do at weekends, she was quite happy drawing on the board in my office, making things with sellotape and staples or stamping things.

We eagerly awaited the class photo that was eventually published in the *Stirling Observer* on 20 September. Unlike almost all of her classmates, Sophie, a girl who claimed she never felt the cold, wasn't wearing a sweatshirt or cardigan. Perhaps that's why I always thought she stood out in that now much-seen photograph. Or was that just the biased view of a very biased dad?

★

By September 1995 Thomas Hamilton was taking a keen interest in guns again. DCC McMurdo's approval of his licence in February 1995 had ensured that for three more years Hamilton would be able to hold and purchase the guns on his certificate without anyone in authority checking, whatever changes might occur in his personality or mental state. His fitness to use firearms could only be judged by fellow shooters, and none of them did anything. On 11 September he had purchased a second Browning 9 mm pistol, the first gun he'd acquired for nine years. Eleven days later he began to buy ammunition, apparently for the first time since October 1987.

Three of Hamilton's boys' clubs had ended in March 1995, but he'd now started another at Bishopbriggs on the outskirts of Glasgow. Strathclyde Regional Council contacted Central Regional Council about his application for a let for this club. Regional Councillor Robert Ball, then convener of the Education Committee, had given Hamilton a reference that included the required phrase, 'The leaders are known to me and are worthy of support'. Given Hamilton's history with Central Regional Council, it is incredible that this reference was ever signed, especially as in August 1995 the Council had held a meeting with the specific aim of protecting children by finding ways of stopping Hamilton's activities in their own area. There was no follow-up meeting.

★

When I'd completed Sophie's school registration form, I'd added a paragraph explaining our situation as I was anxious that the staff were aware that I was her sole parent. One episode reinforced my anxiety. Sophie brought home a letter, I can't remember what it was about, addressed to Mrs North. Setting aside the presumptuousness to assume that only a mother would be concerned about a child's school life, it was apparent that my comments about our home situation had not been noted. I wrote back asking them to ensure that the information was properly recorded. I received a very apologetic phone call from a school secretary. At least someone was paying attention. I assumed that all this information would be readily available on Sophie's record card.

That term I met Gwen Mayor for the first time at a parents' evening. Sophie was getting on so well that there seemed little to discuss. I think I checked whether being left-handed, like her dad, was hindering her in any way (which it wasn't). At another meeting in November, Gwen told me that everything was fine, Sophie couldn't be getting on better. What could she say about her? Apart from that and a larger meeting in

September about the *Oxford Reading Tree*, those were my only links with Sophie's schoolwork. She had a home book, in which she practised writing. She'd bring home reading books as well. I enjoyed the role reversal as she read me the stories about Kipper, Biff and Chip. She was making great strides with her reading. I didn't see the other things she did in class until March.

I wasn't interested in joining the PTA or the School Board. In fact, the very existence of the latter had passed me by. Only later did I realise that I'd received notification of a forthcoming election in October. As far as I know, no election took place, and so I assume that the two new Board members had been appointed unopposed. I don't remember being informed about this and didn't recognise the names when they appeared in the papers next spring.

On 1 October a well-respected university colleague died. Murray MacBeath had been at Stirling since 1972 in the Philosophy and Religious Studies departments. I didn't know him well, but I'd done some work for him many years before when he was writing a paper entitled 'Who was Doctor Who's Father?' in which Murray considered the possibility of a time traveller being his own father. I'd been asked to look at the question of whether this was feasible genetically. The university newsletter said:

> For Murray's friends, colleagues and students, past and present, his loss is a source of desolation. But we know who has lost most. Isabel, so brave and so strong, little Mhairi, five next month, and also that child whose arrival in December is so keenly awaited.

I didn't know it then, but Mhairi MacBeath and Sophie were classmates. In February 1996 university staff received a letter inviting them to a meeting to commemorate Murray's life and work. The meeting was set for the afternoon of 13 March.

On the second anniversary of Barbara's death I took Sophie to see the Book of Remembrance at Falkirk Crematorium and read her the words I'd written for her mum.

A week later I spent some of the most precious days I ever had with

Sophie. The school had a week's break during October and I needed some time away from work. My initial plan was to visit friends in Nova Scotia, a tentative plan that was immediately scrapped when I realised that the first Sunday of the holiday was Rosie's birthday. There were, of course, more important things than trips to North America. Rosie would be having a party and Sophie couldn't miss it, especially as she and Rosie had seen less of one another now that they went to different schools. But I still wanted to get away, even though we would have two fewer days for a holiday, and decided on some European driving therapy.

The day after Rosie's party, we drove to Hull to board the ferry to Zeebrugge. From there we headed for Denmark. On the first night we stopped in a small town in Schleswig-Holstein and in my increasingly desperate German I tried to explain that the 'zwei' who wanted a room were Sophie and myself. The owner was looking for another adult. So often people assumed that Sophie's mother would be there. It was good for Sophie to know that other languages were spoken. We had a beginners' French tape in the car and now she found out that she wouldn't always be able to understand what people said when we went away. Being a smart cookie, she had spotted the 'funny letters' – the 'o's with diagonal lines and the 'a's with little circles on the top – as we drove through Danish towns like Oksbøl and Åbenrå.

Our destination was Billund, the home of Legoland. It was a treat. There were models made from Lego and Duplo and an exhibition on the history of Lego. We, and I do mean we, played in huge troughs of Lego. We spent two nights in Denmark in a spacious chalet near the West Jutland coast where we played football on a windy beach. In the evening we made the new Lego models Sophie had bought and wrote postcards; and when Sophie was asleep I watched soccer on TV. I was away from work and having a peaceful time with my wonderful daughter.

Sophie was leading a busy social life, with parties every other week. We began to spend time with Jenny, one of her nursery friends, and her mum Jane. I'd still not met many of Sophie's new school friends. I heard some of their names when she was playing pretend school games with her soft toys: if I'd listened more carefully I would have learned more about what these children were like, but assumed I would get to meet them in time. When Christmas came there were cards from some of them. Another card was from Miss Young who, Sophie explained, was a teacher. Jacqui Young was a trainee working with Gwen Mayor. She has been able to tell me what Sophie was like in the classroom and confirms that she was a livewire and a real treasure.

I saw Gwen Mayor for the last time on 15 January. Sophie was going to see the school dentist and I wanted to be there too. Emily went at the same time, and I agreed to take the girls back to the classroom. There was absolutely no need. They knew their way back and ran off ahead of me. By the time I got to room 1/13 they were already sitting listening to a story. I gave Gwen a self-conscious wave and left.

★

On 23 January Thomas Hamilton purchased a second .357 Smith and Wesson revolver. During the five months since September 1995 he had bought thousands of rounds of ammunition, much of it from Crockarts in King Street in the centre of Stirling.

His boys' clubs were attracting less and less support. On 26 January he wrote a 'private and confidential' letter to Cllr Ball, which he nevertheless copied to a number of primary school headteachers and the Scouts. He complained about rumours being spread by staff of primary schools and the malicious attitude of Scout Leaders. 'Teachers at Dunblane Primary School have contaminated all the older boys with this poison.' He mentioned how even former cleaners and dinner ladies at Dunblane Primary School had been told he was a pervert. 'I have no criminal record nor have I ever been accused of sexual child abuse by any child and I am not a pervert.'

On 11 February Hamilton wrote to his MP Michael Forsyth, again complaining about malicious gossip circulated by certain Scout officials. He added that the long-term effect 'has been a death blow to my already difficult work in providing sports and leisure activities to local children as well as my public standing in the community'. Around this time there had been a disturbing incident at Hamilton's house involving James Gillespie, up until then a frequent visitor. Hamilton had pointed a 9 mm pistol at him and pulled the trigger because Gillespie had told him that if he had kids he wouldn't send them to one of Hamilton's clubs. The chamber was empty and Gillespie didn't report the incident.

★

At the beginning of February we had a special family party for my mum's seventy-fifth birthday, at her home in Hitchin. Everybody was so impressed with how grown-up Sophie was. I was certainly very proud of her. I felt the same when, on a sunny Sunday afternoon at the beginning of March, I took Sophie, Jenny, Rosie and Rosie's younger sister Hannah to the play parks in Dunblane's town centre and at the Laighills. I took plenty of photographs of the girls playing on the swings, slides and roundabouts. Every time I took Sophie out I came back feeling good about how well we were doing as a team.

★

Hamilton was shooting at the Whiteston range in Dunblane and went to a competition in Largs. His shooting style was unorthodox, which should have been of concern to those who witnessed it. He fired rapidly, was not interested in competing and would put pieces of paper on to the standard targets. One of those who travelled with him to Largs said of Hamilton, 'That is a right weirdo, that one. He talks about guns as though they were babies.'

Hamilton's assistant at some of his boys' clubs had noticed that he no longer spoke about his interest in cameras. He talked about guns. Hamilton had also started shooting at the Callander Rifle and Pistol Club. On Wednesday, 6 March he insisted that another member try out one of his Browning pistols and made him feel very uneasy. The same man was persuaded to give Hamilton a lift to Dunblane station and felt unsettled by his presence in the car.

Earlier that day he'd been on the phone to a photography acquaintance, but had hardly spoken. The last thing he'd said before he rang off was, 'I'm going back to my guns.' He had also phoned the Scottish Scouts Headquarters to find out who their patron was. Next day he wrote to the Queen, complaining about his treatment at the hands of the Scouts and asking her, as patron, for some kind of intervention to help him restore his reputation in the community. Copies of this letter were sent to Cllr Robert Ball, Michael Forsyth, the Scout Association and to the headteachers of Bannockburn and Dunblane Primary Schools.

Sometime towards the end of that first week in March Hamilton met an ex-policeman in the Debenhams store in the Thistle Centre in Stirling. During a fifteen-minute conversation he told this man how much the authorities were against him. He talked about Michael Ryan and the Hungerford shootings and about a firearms incident at nearby Cowie. He quizzed the man about whether police involved at Cowie had been armed or not and how quickly a firearms response unit could get to the scene of an incident.

Thomas Hamilton spent the morning of Monday, 11 March in Stirling in the library, talking with acquaintances and collecting a trophy from a shop in Upper Craigs. In the evening, as he left one of his boys' clubs, he said to his assistant, 'Thanks very much, Ian. See you next Monday.'

★

My mum was staying with us at the beginning of that week. The two of us collected Sophie from Kids Club on the Monday evening and because Granny was leaving in the morning, we went out for a meal in Stirling. Sophie didn't eat much, distracted by the fun of climbing on a large model elephant. On Tuesday, 12 March my mum left by train to go home (via my sister Christine's on Teesside). In the evening Sophie gave me some chocolates that the children had been making at Kids Club. I put them in my coat pocket, where they stayed for days. They remain uneaten, stored in the Breakthrough porcelain trinket box that used to remind Sophie of her mum.

★

Two hours after my mum had caught her train from Dunblane, Thomas Hamilton was at Dunblane station catching a train to Stirling. We don't know when he'd arrived in the town, nor what he did that morning. In Stirling he went to hire a white van. Later he visited his mother for six hours, had a bath and something to eat, and chatted with her. She found nothing unusual in his manner. In the evening he had a phone conversation with an acquaintance in Aberdeen, who thought he sounded down.

★

Sophie and I were settling down for a quiet evening when Jane phoned to ask if I'd look after Jenny for a short while. The girls played on the computer, making Fine Artist pictures. After Jenny had gone home, Sophie completed one last picture. The file's properties tell me it was finished at 20:37:30 on 12 March 1996. I read her a story, a favourite one from her *Playdays 1996 Annual*. 'A Picture for Aunt Helen' was about a girl called Josie who painted a picture at school that consisted of a big, thick, bright yellow blob. No one knew what it was. But when she showed it to her aunt, Josie realised it was bananas and custard, which they then had for tea. Sophie fell asleep and I did a little work before going to bed myself. I'd been tired during the day. After one of my lectures I had nodded off while a candidate for a new lecturing post was giving a talk. I wasn't going to be teaching the next day, but I wanted to be more alert.

★

Thomas Hamilton was in debt. After he'd sold his Woodcraft shop in the mid-1980s, he'd registered as unemployed, but made money from a number of ventures including trading in photographic equipment. He'd fallen foul of Trading Standards and the magazine *Amateur Photographer* and had just lost a dispute with them. His photographic business was 'down the tubes'. He apparently ran the boys' clubs and camps at a loss. In February a summary warrant had been granted as a result of continued non-payment of council tax arrears. The enforcement had been delayed for two weeks, but the date due for the money to be paid was 13 March.

★

I might have been tired, but I knew that there were plenty of things about being a parent that I thoroughly enjoyed. It had become fashionable to write articles about single dads. I still have a copy of one entitled 'Do fathers make good mothers?' It included a piece about John, who had twin daughters and whose wife had died of cancer. He said he found the overwhelming responsibility was lightened by the joy of their close relationship. His most awful moment as a single parent had been when his daughter had fallen over and had to have her head X-rayed. John had feared the worst and visiting the hospital had brought back to him the pain of his wife's illness. Happily, his daughter recovered.

My own happiness was about to be shattered.

# PART TWO

## MARCH 1996

Sixteen children went happily to school this morning, tonight they have not come home

*SCOTLAND TODAY*, 13 MARCH 1996

# CHAPTER FOUR

# The Thirteenth of March

## 13 March 1996–22 March 1996

'Bye Soph, see you this evening'

I've thought, talked and written about that cold grey Wednesday so many times. The events are etched into my very being. The day had started so normally. For Sophie and me it was at around 7.30 a.m. Sophie dressed herself, slipping on her blue polo shirt, grey pinafore dress and red Dunblane Primary School sweatshirt. Before putting on her socks, she asked if she could have a plaster to put on her ankle where Kit Kat, the grey cat, had scratched her the day before. It was very minor, but children seem to love decorating their wounds, and I stuck on a *Pocahontas* plaster.

The morning's news stories were fairly typical of the time: a threat of new loyalist terror in Northern Ireland; complaints from the Government about Brussels trying to enforce a 48-hour week on Britain; and opposition leader Tony Blair pledging to buy back the newly privatised Railtrack. The *Stirling Observer* led with news of a fatal road crash. Inside was a report on changes to the traffic system in Dunblane. Bridgend had become a one-way street, and the town's traffic was about to be disrupted for weeks while one carriageway of the main road was closed to allow maintenance to the bridges over the river and railway.

There were announcements about the Dunblane Pre-School Play Association Spring Fayre, the Cathedral Sunday School, the Local History Society and a dance in the Victoria Hall on Friday. The Dunblane crime desk's only report was of the theft of a two-wheeled generator/air compressor.

Breakfast went smoothly and Sophie ate up all her Coco Pops. Her only upset came when the post landed on the mat. There were two items, both for me. She complained that she never got any letters, which wasn't really true, and that 'it's not fair for me'. My mail wasn't of immediate interest and was left unopened. When, many days later, I looked inside one of the envelopes I found a magazine from the National Trust of Scotland. In it was an article on guns entitled 'Locks, stocks and barrels'. 'Look beyond the fact that firearms are designed to kill', it read.

We went out of the front door to find that the car was covered in ice. There was fresh snow on the ground and it was very slippery under foot. Together we scraped the car windows, delaying our departure by a few minutes, and I didn't get Sophie to Kids Club until 8.35 a.m. I went to the back entrance of the school, which was closer to the hut in which Kids Club met, as I wanted to avoid a long icy walk from the car. Even our short walk was treacherous and I was concerned that Sophie might fall. Inside the hut it was warm and welcoming, as always. Sophie took off her coat and went over to stand by Eddie. We said goodbye and for once she didn't give me a kiss. I still find myself wondering why not, but I left with the indelible image of a grown-up five-year-old girl standing quietly on the other side of the room.

From Kids Club she would have gone up to her classroom, where the twenty-eight children changed for their gym lesson, leaving no time for the register to be taken. Two children were absent. At nine o'clock the class went to the school hall for an assembly for all the younger children and when that had finished Sophie's class walked the short distance from the hall to the gymnasium. Sophie would have been wearing a T-shirt, shorts and a pair of pumps, all bought at Asda in Perth and all clearly labelled with her name. Waiting for the class were gym teacher Eileen Harrild and supervisory assistant Mary Blake. Mary was to relieve Gwen Mayor, who was due to go to a meeting. According to Eileen the children were excited and she had to restrain them from starting to use the equipment straight away. Until that moment they were a bunch of typical five- and six-year-olds. It was about 9.35 a.m.

★

Earlier that morning Thomas Hamilton had been scraping ice off a white van parked outside his house in Stirling. Neighbours say he was cheery. He then set off to drive to Dunblane. His movements, later analysed by the police, had been recorded in part by CCTV cameras. He was seen by witnesses, first at the back entrance, and then two minutes or so later at the front entrance of Dunblane Primary School. He parked the van in the school grounds at around 9.30 a.m. Using pliers he'd bought in January, he cut telephone wires, presumably intending to disconnect the school's phones. He had, in fact, severed the lines to neighbouring houses. He walked unchallenged into the school, went first to the hall and then into the gym.

★

I spent my first two hours at work in my office, going once or twice along the corridor to check on things in my laboratory, where a number of students were doing research projects. I had to catch up with some paperwork and was hardly disturbed. There was a brief phone call from one of the librarians letting me know about a problem over books for one of my courses. I walked to the MacRobert Arts Centre ticket office in time for its opening at eleven o'clock, to buy some tickets for the next Singing Kettle concert. Then I went back to my office. It was about ten past eleven. Within seconds my colleague Lewis was at the door, saying that he'd been phoned by one of our students who'd heard on the radio about a shooting incident at Dunblane High School. Lewis quickly corrected himself – no, it was Dunblane Primary School.

What do you do when you hear unbelievable news? Was it anything to worry about? Surely if it had been important, someone would have tried to contact me. The school had emergency contact numbers. Apart from Lisa's call from the library, the phone hadn't rung and no messages had

# DUNBLANE: NEVER FORGET   87

been left on my answering machine. I tried calling the Dunblane police office, but it was engaged all the time. Soon others with children at the school were at my office door. One of them said he was getting a lift up to the school – did I want to come?

I went to the lab to tell my research group where I was going and said that I'd see them later. What was I thinking, as Sylvia drove Mike and me through Bridge of Allan, up the hill and on to the Dunblane bypass? Possibly that these things only happen to other people. Sylvia turned off the bypass into the top end of Doune Road. Immediately we encountered a police roadblock. Mike and I got out of the car and were directed to the Westlands Hotel. We were given cloakroom tickets; presumably the plan was for us to give personal details when the number was called, but no one seemed to know what was happening. I saw Olwen sitting with another ex-Arnhall Nursery parent. Within ten minutes somebody came in and announced that the incident involved just one class, Mrs Mayor's. Parents with children in that class were to go to the house on the right-hand side of the school entrance.

There was no panic. Olwen offered to stay with me until I had news and we walked the short distance down Doune Road to 'Cairnbaan', the house beside the school. There were crowds of anxious parents milling around. From behind a barrier, set up opposite the school entrance, the media had a grandstand position to record the scene. I don't remember who was in the house when we arrived. Gradually I realised that others I knew were there: Hannah Scott's mum and dad, Karen and David; Emily Morton's parents, Kathryn and Les; and Megan Turner's mum and dad, Kareen and Willie. This was for real, these were people I knew whose children were in Sophie's class. We were offered cups of tea, but the police gave us nothing, no information at all. Occasionally a police officer would bellow out something, sometimes getting angry with an anxious parent. There was talk of twelve children dead. Earlier one father had challenged Supt Joseph Holden, the officer who'd been given responsibility for providing the victims' families with information, about the number of fatalities. Holden wouldn't confirm a thing.

Eventually, at some time after 12.30 p.m., arrangements were made for us to go into the school. We could have walked there in seconds if the police had cleared a path, but instead we were taken in ambulance service mini-buses. Social workers went on the first bus, one group of parents went next. The rest of us waited for at least another ten minutes. Our vehicle had problems negotiating the sharp turn from the house into the school and effectively parked next to the flashing press cameras. It couldn't have been set up better for them.

We'd been transferred from one hell to another, this time the school staffroom. Although some families were called out immediately – we weren't told why – the rest of us were made to wait and wait and wait. The officer in charge, Insp. Euan Ross, was unhelpful and rude. He kept promising that we would have information in a few minutes, but none came. We got sandwiches, but it was information we were desperately hungry for, and by starving us the police had heightened the tension in that room to a level that was unbearable. It is surprising how calm most people seemed to be. Insp. Ross was asked if we could speak to a senior officer and failed to find one, even though we now know that Supt Holden was close by. Holden had decided not to come and see us, concerned because he couldn't tell us anything, even though the world outside already had plenty of information. The police wouldn't even tell us whether or not the incident was over. One mother concluded that the lack of explanations meant that there must be a hostage situation.

Holden later admitted that he didn't have a clue what was going on in the staffroom. Lynne McMaster was heavily pregnant and in some distress, Isabel MacBeath had a baby desperately in need of nappies and Martyn and Barbara Dunn were trying to keep their young son Alex entertained. The 'help' we were given was members of the clergy, dressed in black, wandering among us, silently touching us on the shoulder. It was as if the angels of death had arrived. School staff and doctors from the health centre were also there, but they and the clergy were all under police instructions not to tell us anything. This was torture for everyone concerned. We were trapped, only allowed to go to the toilet if accompanied by a police officer – in Isabel MacBeath's case, an angry male one.

During our agonising wait I hardly spoke. For much of the time I sat or stood in a group with Olwen, Kareen, Willie, Karen and David. Les and Kathryn were at the other end of the room. Kathryn Morton told me later that she'd consoled herself with the thought that nothing awful could happen to me again. Sophie must be all right and so Emily would be all right too.

Every parent will on occasion experience those awful sensations in the pit of the stomach when you feel there is something wrong with your child. I used to have them in the late evening if Sophie cried out from her bedroom, disturbed by a dream. I'd go upstairs in a cold sweat only to find her settling back to sleep again. There are also those heart-rending times when your child is sobbing as if nothing in the world could ever make things better. Yet somehow something always does. And then there are those other moments of more concern, instances of real danger, often over before you have had time to react but which leave you shaking afterwards. I remember one when a waitress in a restaurant stumbled next to our table and nearly poured boiling water over Sophie.

None of those experiences had equipped me for dealing with the emotion of sitting and waiting for news that could mean my daughter was severely traumatised, permanently handicapped or dead. In the end, thinking through the awful possibilities had numbed all feeling, and the fact that my friends must have been working through those same possibilities was of no help, quite the opposite. We said supportive words to one another, but these weren't getting through to the places inside where they were needed. There was no comfort. Eventually, at least an hour and a half after we'd arrived, people came into the room at intervals and called out family names. Kareen and Willie and Karen and David went just before me. I suspect we mumbled something like 'I'm sure it will be all right' as we parted.

I know exactly at what time I was called. Olwen had stayed with me, having checked that her youngest daughter Lowri (then in Primary Four) was safe somewhere else in the school. I had just asked her what time school finished for the Primary One pupils. I had no idea because I'd only ever collected Sophie from Kids Club. 'It's probably about now', Olwen said, and when I looked at my watch I saw that it was about twenty to three, the time Sophie had been born. Then I heard the North family being called and we were led away by three people – Elspeth, a social worker, Derek, a plain-clothes police constable, and John, a uniformed constable, my family liaison team. They took us to one of the huts and we all sat down.

Derek began to speak. 'Mr and Mrs North …' I interrupted him. Didn't they know that I was a single parent, hadn't they been shown the school record card with Sophie's information? What had they been doing while we were waiting? I had to explain that Sophie's mother was dead and that Olwen was a friend who'd waited with me. Derek, speaking very formally, started to tell us that there had been a shooting incident and sixteen children and two adults were dead. That was it. As soon as he said 'sixteen' I knew that Sophie was one of them. That was roughly the number of family groups who'd been waiting in the staffroom. Sophie had been killed. So had her teacher, Derek told us. And for the first time there was confirmation that the incident was over, the perpetrator was dead. I was devastated and furious at the same time. In the next few minutes I made it abundantly clear how awful it had been to be left waiting for so long to be told this news. I got the feeling my family liaison team agreed. They too had been waiting for an hour or so with no information except the name of the family they were to tell.

Weeks later I learned that Sophie had been shot five times. She'd been fatally wounded by bullets through the head and chest, and had also been shot in the hand, the buttock and the leg. I was told that she would have died instantly. That would have been at around 9.37 a.m. I was informed of her death five hours later.

Derek tried to arrange for a car to take me home, but couldn't get one. I said I would walk. Elspeth accompanied me. When I got home the answer machine was full of messages from family and friends, each call more desperate than the last as more news of the massacre was broadcast. Some had contacted the help line, but couldn't be told anything without my permission. I tried to make some phone calls but couldn't because there were no lines available. Dunblane's telephone system was saturated.

The rest of my day was a blur. Phone calls, the identification of Sophie's body at the chapel of rest at Stirling Royal Infirmary and a restless sleepless night. Next day my doctor prescribed sleeping pills to help me get enough rest and gain some strength for what lay ahead. Helped by friends and my liaison team, I muddled through those next few days. I had to give a police statement and there was a funeral to arrange. Derek registered Sophie's death at the Registry Office. I couldn't face going back there, not to record another death.

In those two and a half years since Barbara had died there had been three main strands to my life: Sophie, work and me. I had only had the energy to concentrate on the first two and had neglected the third. Sophie was no longer there, and my ability to work was fractured again. I had to find the energy to take care of myself.

All sorts of feelings were churning inside me. The irrational one was of failure. I'd failed Sophie, God knows how, but I hadn't been there to protect her, I hadn't taken enough care. I'd failed Barbara. I said I would do everything possible to take care of her daughter and now she too was dead. Others around me were sharing the grief of Sophie's death, but they couldn't share the enormity of what I was feeling. I turned in on myself and personal relationships became strained. Above all I wanted some control over this new life. I would object strongly to other people sorting things out for me, speaking on my behalf, setting my agenda. I had to be true to myself from now on.

---

The Thirteenth of March 1996 was a day that affected millions of people around the world. Several years later I have tried, by watching the television news coverage and reading press reports, to get an idea of what happened and how others would have experienced that day. It was a time when many myths were born and I was interested in their origins. I wanted to understand what motivated some people to behave in the way they did, to understand how a community and its people respond to an event like the Dunblane massacre, whether there are lessons for others.

When Thomas Hamilton entered the school he was carrying four handguns and enough bullets to kill everyone there. In the assembly hall he used one of his two Browning 9 mm pistols to blast two shots into the stage. Then he walked into the gym. Within a three- to four-minute period he had fired another 103 times, changing pre-loaded magazines periodically. He shot mostly at the three teachers and twenty-eight children in the gym, but also fired once at a Primary Seven pupil who was walking outside, and for a brief time he went out of a back exit and fired four rounds at a group of Primary Four children and nine shots at a Primary Seven classroom. Grace Tweddle, a teacher with the Primary Four children, was wounded, but mercifully no children were hit. Olwen's daughter Lowri was one of the Primary Four class, though Olwen didn't know this until she walked home from the school with Lowri after she'd left me.

Hamilton returned to the gym and, at point-blank range, fired more shots at some of the children who lay injured on the floor. One of the survivors recalls being able to see the detail on Hamilton's boots before he fired another bullet into the child's back. Hamilton switched handguns and killed himself with a single shot from one of his two Smith and Wesson revolvers.

The world outside the Primary School was alerted when headteacher Ron Taylor phoned the police at 9.41 a.m. He had been on the phone when his deputy Senga Awlson came into his office on her knees to tell him there was a gunman in the gym. After making the emergency call, Taylor rushed to the gym, joined by trainee teacher David Scott, who had seen Hamilton shoot himself from the window of the art room. The scene was one of utter carnage. Gwen Mayor and fifteen children lay dead; a sixteenth was mortally wounded. The seventeen murder victims had received a total of fifty-eight gunshot wounds. Eileen Harrild and Mary Blake, both badly injured, were in a storeroom off the side of the gym where a number of the wounded children had gathered. All but two of the children in the class had been shot. Six of the surviving victims had very serious injuries, four were seriously hurt, three had minor wounds. Two victims had sustained non-gunshot injuries.

Ron Taylor went back to the office area and shouted for someone to call the ambulance service. With janitor John Currie he went back to the gym where others were already tending the injured children. The janitor kicked away the pistol lying at Hamilton's side and removed the revolver from his right hand. Two Dunblane policemen arrived at 9.50 a.m. and the first ambulance was at the school at 9.57 a.m. Medical staff from the local clinic arrived and the task began of assessing the victims' injuries.

Stirling Royal Infirmary had been notified of a major incident at 9.48 a.m. and staff from there arrived a little later. The injured were gradually taken to hospital. All were away from the school by 11.10 a.m. Nobody took the names of the injured children at the time, though consultant paediatrician Jack Beattie considered that even the most ill child was capable of giving his name. The police later said this was a deliberate decision on their part, that checking names would have caused vital delays. This omission contributed to problems with identification.

Senior police officers had arrived between 10 and 10.15 a.m. One of them was DCS John Ogg, who was given overall charge of the investigation. DCC Douglas McMurdo and Chief Constable William Wilson were also quickly on the scene. Members of staff, especially those from the school nursery, bore the brunt of the horrendous task of identifying the dead children and were sometimes harassed because they couldn't be certain of a child's name. There were difficulties and people couldn't cope, but that was inevitable. At around 12 noon the gym was evacuated on the advice of a scene-of-crime officer who thought that Hamilton's body and camera case might be booby-trapped. A bomb disposal officer, who didn't arrive until mid-afternoon, gave the all-clear at around 3.30 p.m.

Supt Holden, the officer responsible for informing the victims' families, had arrived at the school at 10.10 a.m. His first duty was to put a cordon around the school; his task with the families came second. The class involved was known immediately, yet Holden says he didn't have this information until 10.30 to 10.40 a.m., and it wasn't until 11 a.m. that he informed parents who'd already gathered in another house beside the school. The only information provided was the class involved. The families with children in Gwen Mayor's class were asked to go to 'Cairnbaan' and left in the hands of more junior officers. Many of us hadn't even arrived at the school by then and didn't see Holden at any time. He admitted that no use was made of the record cards to contact the families directly involved. At 3 p.m. Holden was given other duties and left the school, at least half an hour before the last parents he was charged to inform had been told of their children's deaths.

The police decided not to tell any of the victims' families anything until everyone could be told, so problems with identification were going to lead to an agonised wait for everyone. This was a huge error of judgement. If they were so concerned about families being informed at different times, this wasn't apparent when we were finally told. The last sets of parents were made to wait for more than an hour after the first parents had been told. The families were told that their children were dead by family liaison teams. Central Scotland Police say that we should be extremely grateful for this. I was certainly grateful for all the help my team gave me in the days and months afterwards; but did I need to wait for hours to allow the team to be assembled? Social workers had been called to the school in the morning and were also directed to 'Cairnbaan'. They too were given no details of what had happened. At around 12.30 p.m. they were transferred to a room in the school where police officers were waiting and they were briefed between 1.30 and 1.45 p.m.

Three years later I learned that others had been prepared to tell us the awful news several hours earlier. Anne Beaton is a district nursing sister and midwife in Dunblane. She'd once come to the house when Barbara was ill and I met her again in 1999 when we both addressed a meeting of the Emergency Planning Society. Very shortly after the shootings she was sent to the school by the health centre manager and was among the first in the gym. After all the injured had been taken to hospital and there was nothing more they could do, probably at around 11.30 a.m., the police took the Health Centre staff to the school library and told them that the families would be brought to them while the news of the children was broken. They were also told that they must not say anything without police permission. After waiting in the library for about an hour and a half, they were told they weren't needed. Some were sent to the staffroom to be with us, but still under instructions not to say anything. Others left the school.

The *Daily Record* was probably the first newspaper to hear about a shooting in Dunblane. Its office was contacted by someone from Falkirk, who'd picked up a message on a scanner and had heard a police officer screaming down the radio waves for doctors and an ambulance, 'We've got dead children'. Tim Bugler of the Central Scotland News Agency told me how he had gone to the Stirling Sheriff Court that morning and was waiting to cover the day's cases. After a sudden flurry of activity, the Procurator Fiscal announced that many of the cases had been cancelled for the day, because an emergency would prevent all police officers from attending the court. Back at his office, Tim learned from the ambulance service that the emergency involved a shooting at Dunblane Primary School. At 10.40 a.m. he sent out the first news story.

On BBC Radio 5 Live Diana Madill was having a discussion with correspondent Stephen Sackur, covering an international meeting on terrorism in Egypt. She had to break off the conversation to announce that news was coming through of a shooting at Dunblane Primary School. Before she had finished her sentence she had to add that the death toll had risen from one to a number of fatalities. The source of the information was the education authority. A later report from Reeval Alderson quotes the ambulance service as saying that as many as a dozen children were dead.

Soon there were hordes of reporters in Dunblane and television cameras recording images of people rushing to the school, mothers running down Doune Road with young children in buggies. Reporters described their own arrival as a circus:

> Large lorries parked in unfamiliar places, throbbing generators, cables slung across streets. Excited voices, lots more cars, cameras, crowded hotels. And strangers like me walking at a frantic pace round town, passing grieving faces and offering the same quick, weak acknowledgement while rarely meeting their eyes [Anton Antonowicz of the *Daily Mirror*].

Within three hours of the shootings, an estimated 500 members of the media were in the town.

A lot of details had been broadcast by one o'clock. If a television set had been switched on in the staffroom we'd have known what was happening. On the lunchtime news bulletins the massacre was already being described as one of Britain's worst mass murders. It was now said

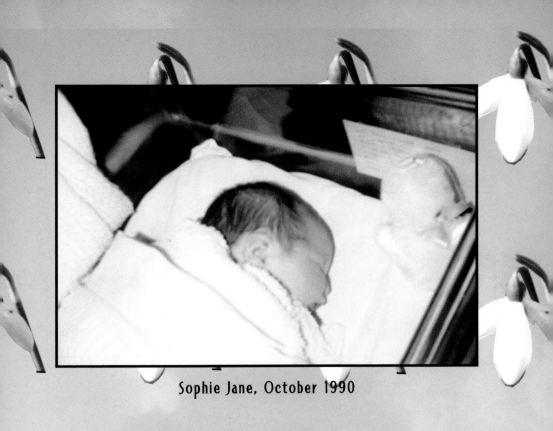

Sophie Jane, October 1990

Sophie (left) with Hannah Scott, December 1990

ABOVE: Mick, Sophie and Barbara, Oregon, August 1991

RIGHT: Sophie with Barbara on her first birthday, October 1991

Barbara and Sophie at nursery

RIGHT: Barbara and Sophie in the Blue Mountains, New South Wales, December 1992

BELOW: Mick and Sophie in Sydney, December 1992

LEFT: Sophie and Mick at Morag and Michael's wedding, August 1993

BELOW: Mick and Sophie at North Berwick, August 1993: this is one of the last photographs Barbara took

Sophie with Mount Shasta, California, in the background,
August 1994

ABOVE: Sophie's fourth birthday party, October 1994: (left to right) Mick, Rosie, Lowri, Sophie, Jamie T., Emily

LEFT: Sophie stands in front of that enormous hole, the Grand Canyon, March 1995

Sophie with Kit Kat in her bedroom at Dunblane, summer 1995

LEFT: Sophie in her new school uniform, July 1995

BELOW: Sophie's fifth birthday, at her granny's, October 1995

Sophie and Rosie at the play park in Dunblane, 3 March 1996

TOP: *Galanthus byzantinus* 'Sophie North': the Sophie snowdrop

ABOVE: The 'Gwen Mayor' rose

LEFT: The 'Innocence' rose

RIGHT: Willowbank House, Dunblane, in September 1994

BELOW: Mick at work on the book in his room in Balmain, Sydney, June 2000

that thirteen children and two adults were dead and that one of the adults was a teacher. The source of this information must have been Chief Constable Wilson. During the morning he'd spoken to reporters at the school gates:

> There's thirteen children dead at the moment, two adults and a number of children in hospital. We're obviously having a tremendous business sorting out who's who and what's what and please bear with us.

When asked, 'Where did it happen, sir?' he confirmed that it was in the gymnasium. Asked to confirm that a man was in custody, he said that it was 'different to that'. It wouldn't have taken much intelligence to guess from this that the gunman was also dead. He added that he could say no more until the parents had been informed. He'd already said plenty. Where had that inaccurate figure of thirteen children dead come from?

At the Cullen Inquiry the police seemed mystified about how news of the number of casualties had reached reporters. I don't have a problem with the fact that information was released by the education authority or the ambulance service. This was a major incident and the public had a right to know. Yet the police have behaved as if they weren't involved in any early release of information. In his submission to Lord Cullen, the Chief Constable wrote:

> Unfortunately, before an official police announcement could be made, there was a great deal of speculation in the media about the number of children who had died as a result of information being released by other sources. This caused problems to those officers dealing with the families of the dead and injured.

In a prepared statement at an October press conference, Wilson had the nerve to say:

> It would have been entirely unacceptable to us as professional police officers to proceed to release information if we were not

entirely certain of its accuracy. Again this is not meant as an attack on the parents . . .

In an attempt to wrest and maintain control over the release of information, Central Scotland Police called in Supt Louis Munn, the press officer from Strathclyde Police. He had experience from the Lockerbie disaster and now he came to Dunblane, as he put it, 'to feed the media beast'. This reflected police priorities: information for the press deserved an experienced officer from an outside force; information for relatives could be cobbled together by whoever was available from the local constabulary. Munn arrived in Dunblane at around 12.30 p.m. and made the official announcement of the number of casualties at 1.45 p.m. The announcement was immediately broadcast on BBC's *Reporting Scotland*. It was the first time anyone knew that as many as sixteen children had been murdered and you can hear the reporters' shocked gasps as Munn speaks. At that stage, however, none of the families whose children were dead had been told a thing. Chief Constable Wilson had already told reporters the incident had occurred in the gym, but Munn would only say that it had taken place in the school. He was obviously putting a lid on the release of information.

In an article entitled 'Handling the Media at Dunblane', which he later published, Munn blamed others for leaking information. Overlooking Wilson's conversation with the reporters, he wrote that 'information, over which we had no control, was released to the media. This could have resulted in relatives at the scene receiving the wrong facts from the media.'

By lunchtime politicians, union leaders and experts were being interviewed. School security was their initial focus: parallels were already being drawn with the murder of a pupil at Hall Garth School in Cleveland, two years earlier, and with the killing of headmaster Philip Lawrence outside an Inner London school in December 1995. Everyone said that their thoughts were with the victims' families. What would they have said if they'd been aware that we were sitting in ignorance, not knowing for certain whether we *were* 'victims' families'?

Scottish Secretary Michael Forsyth, Dunblane's MP, and George

Robertson, his opposition shadow and a Dunblane resident, were already on their way from London on the 12.15 p.m. shuttle flight, 'two rival politicians with politics totally forgotten'. Both were visibly shocked. Announcements had been made at Westminster, first by Scottish Office minister George Kynoch at a select committee meeting and then to a near-empty House of Commons by his ministerial colleague Lord James Douglas-Hamilton. By 3.30 p.m. many MPs had gathered to listen to a brief statement from the Leader of the House, Tony Newton, and to responses from his Labour shadow Ann Taylor, Archie Kirkwood of the Liberal Democrats and SNP leader Alex Salmond. Prime Minister John Major conveyed his thoughts from Egypt where he was attending the conference on terrorism. He emphasised that he was reacting not as a politician, but as a parent.

There had been a lunchtime news briefing at Stirling Royal Infirmary. The paediatrician in charge, Jack Beattie, made a brief statement about the number of casualties. Reporters said that the distress of the hospital staff had been all too apparent. As the day progressed, news was carried that three children had been airlifted to Yorkhill Hospital for Sick Children in Glasgow and that two boys and one adult were now at Falkirk Infirmary. Later reports brought better news on the conditions of the adults and most of the injured children.

At around 3.30 p.m. BBC Scotland reported that the murdered teacher was Gwen Mayor. At the same time, as I was taking the first agonising steps back to my empty house, reporters were occupied with another press briefing at the Victoria Hall in Dunblane. The Chief Constable announced the number of casualties, correctly this time. Seated with him were Michael Forsyth and George Robertson. Although Hamilton's name wasn't released for another two hours, all three would have known the identity of the killer and were no doubt reflecting on their past dealings with him. I imagine this had been preoccupying many others within the Chief Constable's force since ten o'clock. Many months later we learned how one of the first police officers on the scene had sent a message using a mobile phone. Inadvertently it was recorded on a domestic answering machine. His shocked, angry message indicated that he'd identified Hamilton immediately.

At the afternoon press briefing there was fulsome praise for the school's headteacher Ron Taylor. What about the other school staff – weren't they equally heroic? The emergency services, too, were applauded for their work. I have no wish to diminish what anybody did that day in awful circumstances, but a myth is created, almost as a reflex reaction to every tragedy, that all the emergency services are faultless. This uncritical praise might be good for public relations, but it made it harder to tease out the truth of how the police handled the situation. At 3.30 p.m., as the press briefing was being held, a police officer put his head round the school's staffroom door and asked, 'Is there anybody left?'. In fact there were two families left, four parents who'd yet to be told that their children were dead. The police had made them wait for six hours before giving them news. That certainly wasn't praiseworthy.

The media made comparisons with war zones; the reporters had never seen anything like it. Writing about their experiences and feelings, most reporters commented that it was like no other disaster story they'd covered. A number noted the lack of black humour shared after other horrific events. Many described how drained and emotionally exhausted they were once they got away from the town. Reporters said that on the first day they were received well by the people of Dunblane, who were open and talkative. Erlend Clouston of *The Guardian* described how:

> . . . not many hours after the shooting groups of young men and women were hanging around the Dunblane media centre, offering anecdotes about Hamilton and the way he ran his sports clubs. Nobody had forced them to come.

The press believed that, while there had been some invasion of privacy, they had generally showed considerable restraint. But by the second day the mood in the town had changed. There was far more hostility to the invading media circus.

Many reporters praised the way the police dealt with the press and the role of Louis Munn. It seems that they were well served. Munn later stated, 'If you feed the beast, the beast will be happy, otherwise the beast will go looking for food.' British Telecom engineers had been brought in by 2 p.m. to help set up a media centre. If the police could do this for the press then why not for the victims' families? Extra phones were not available at the school until 3 p.m. and when I got home I couldn't get a line out of Dunblane, even at 4 p.m.

By the early evening, television viewers were being told that the bereaved were being comforted and that we'd identified our children at a temporary morgue at the school. All the identifications were in fact carried out at Stirling Royal Infirmary and were not completed until late into the night. Were the media told this untruth to prevent us being harassed at the hospital later? The killer's name was broadcast, though the media seemed to have known it all day. At a 6.30 p.m. press briefing it was confirmed that Gwen Mayor had been killed. Those who knew Gwen Mayor would have recognised her earlier in a class photograph that Sky News had shown at five o'clock.

The class photographs were taken at the start of the autumn term by the Stirling firm of Whyler Photos. Two versions were obtained by the media. It's easy for me to distinguish the two. In the photograph shown on Sky, Sophie is almost out of her chair, so keen was she to smile for the camera. The BBC television programme *Decisive Moments*, which tells the stories behind some of the key photographic images of the year, described how one of the photographs had got into the public domain. During the day Whylers had given their complete collection of class photographs to the *Daily Record*. The money they were paid was donated to the Dunblane Fund. The photograph used by the *Daily Record* was not the same as Sky's. In *Decisive Moments* Louis Munn explains that he made the decision to give the class photograph to the media to save the families from being hounded for pictures. He said he didn't release it until 10 p.m. It appears Sky obtained their photograph from Newsflash, a Stirling news agency. I don't know their source, but it would be comforting to know that no one profited from the handover of that photograph.

At around 9.45 p.m. Louis Munn read out the names of the victims to the media corps assembled at the Victoria Halls. It was as if he were reading their names from the register that hadn't been taken earlier in the day.

Next morning there was saturation coverage in the media. BBC

Scotland and Scottish Television had become part of the story after they'd both received copies of Hamilton's letters to the Queen, Michael Forsyth and others – posted by him. I didn't watch television or read the papers, but had I done so I could have learnt a lot about Sophie's killer. Forensic psychiatrists were asked to speculate on Hamilton's character and the motives for his outrage. Reporters had already found out plenty. Some had known a lot beforehand. Within hours the press had put together a huge dossier that should have had the police revoking his firearms licence years before. Some of the stories were no doubt fictitious, but the majority painted the same picture of Hamilton as we gained later at the Cullen Inquiry. Alan Mackay, a BBC Scotland reporter who lived locally, had found a surprisingly large number of Dunblane people who were prepared to tell him about their dealings with Hamilton. When we later met Angus Macleod, the *Sunday Mail*'s political editor, he told us about a story he'd prepared on Hamilton in March 1994 prompted by rumours that had been sweeping Dunblane. It was never published because the paper's lawyers got cold feet.

At a morning briefing the Chief Constable revealed that he, too, was a resident of Dunblane and said how traumatic it had been for him, living in the town and knowing some of the parents. Reporters said that a thorough forensic and ballistic investigation was going on. Television viewers saw pictures of the damaged school: a classroom window with bullet holes amongst the pasted snowflakes and flowers.

As more details of the atrocity became known, the media turned its attention to gun control, reminding the public of the Hungerford massacre. Experts were already saying that there should be no rush to judgement, no knee-jerk reactions. I wonder if these were the same 'experts' who counselled caution in changing the law after Hungerford and had ensured that handguns remained legal. A significant number of politicians were, however, already trying to put gun control on the agenda.

At Prime Minister's Questions from the House of Commons, virtually all of the questions to John Major included a wish for him to convey sympathy to the people of Dunblane. Tony Blair said that Britain was 'a nation in mourning. This was no war, no catastrophe of nature. It was the slaughter of innocents. Politics is silent today.' For John Major, words seemed 'inadequate, it must not be forgotten'. There were a number of questions from backbenchers asking for media restraint and praising the courage of teachers. Conservative Robert Hughes asked that there should be a minute's silence on Sunday. At 9.30 a.m. on Sunday, 18 March activities all over the country came to a halt as the silence was duly observed. David Steel, ex-leader of the Liberal Democrats, said that he'd been married in Dunblane Cathedral. He and a number of others asked for a new look at firearms. John Major would not be drawn on this.

At 3.30 p.m., Michael Forsyth made a statement. He outlined what had happened and the heroic efforts there had been to save lives. He announced that there would be a Public Inquiry, to be chaired by Lord Cullen, and that the Queen and Princess Anne were to visit Dunblane. George Robertson responded with a speech full of emotion. He said that there were 'real children gone, real families affected'. Other Scottish MPs expressed support for Dunblane. In response to one, Michael Forsyth said that 'this is a tragedy which has struck a chord with parents everywhere'.

Some expressed the hope that the Inquiry would be held in the not-too-distant future. Although its scope was still to be discussed with Lord Cullen, there were immediate requests from MPs that gun control should be considered. Some politicians weren't going to let the prospect of an Inquiry postpone or diminish discussion. Plaid Cymru leader Dafydd Wigley led the way. After conveying sympathy from Wales he added that 'playing with guns means playing with lives, by people whose personal indulgence comes before assuming safety of communities'. There were further calls from Labour, Liberal Democrat and Scottish Nationalist MPs. The Conservative MPs largely toed the government line: this was a matter not to be discussed just now. But some didn't agree. Ex-minister David Mellor immediately published his view that handguns should be prohibited.

Ron Taylor spoke to the press for the first time in the afternoon, his words no doubt reflecting what many thought: 'Evil visited us yesterday and we don't know why, we don't understand it and I guess we never will.'

Listen to the news after nearly every disaster and, wherever it happens, you will almost certainly find that the media have focused on a community that is particularly affected. There is then a set pattern of reporting. The community is always described as close-knit, its clergy will be interviewed, local dignitaries will be asked how the community will respond and the reply will be that everyone will rally round, feeling for those who have been most affected, helping and supporting them as much as possible. But some of this will be a myth, a response to media attention. The events of 13 March had happened in what appeared to be a classic close-knit community, at a small-town school that most of the young children attended. It was certainly a small community, many of whose families were directly affected. Most people would have known at least one child at the school, many would have known some of the victims. Local residents – from BBC Scotland's Alan Mackay to George Robertson – all emphasised how close-knit Dunblane was. In fact it almost seemed compulsory to include 'close-knit' in any comment about Dunblane. Alan Mackay described the initial scenes he had witnessed, doors being opened to parents, cups of tea being offered, people hugging and comforting one another . . . The features of a caring community, yes, but close-knit? That implied everyone pulling together. The vast majority of the people interviewed were devastated and lost for appropriate words, but wouldn't they have been anyway? It wasn't just in Dunblane that people were feeling distraught.

Hundreds of people in Dunblane experienced trauma on the Thirteenth of March, parents waiting anxiously to be reunited with their children, relatives and friends hanging on for news. Every person would deal with this trauma in his or her way and, no matter how close-knit the community, there would be no uniform recovery process. The idea of Dunblane as a close-knit community took on a more worrying dimension when, for a few, it was the community itself that was going to be devastated, it was a terrible thing to have happened to the town. And in all of this, it became apparent that for some of the interviewees the community's grief would become greater and of more importance than that of the individuals directly affected. Supt Munn said that some of the interviews he set up were arranged 'to divert the media away from the parents, mainly by providing alternative storylines'. But some of those alternative storylines gave a rather distorted picture, laying the foundations of problems that were to affect the families for months to come.

Some of those interviewed claimed that councillors and counsellors would be visiting the bereaved, that the school governors would be talking to them. It was, of course, 'that kind of community'. These people never arrived at my door, at least not then. Without approaching the families, some in the community were already talking about memorials and funds. Their own tragedy already seemed distinct from ours.

The vast majority of people in Dunblane responded with love, care and generosity. Local shops joined in with offers of help to the families. Many townsfolk who were interviewed did provide a balanced perspective which emphasised what community spirit should really offer: support for the bereaved and the families of the injured for as long as necessary, a community working together and sharing our hurt. It would be a very long healing process. It perhaps goes without saying that much of the initial help came unpublicised from those not immediately concerned about a town's image. One of the first was from local people through the Dunblane Bereaved Families Fund, organised by the local Leprosy Mission. We were brought carrier bags of shopping. I found this a little strange at first – a food parcel for me – but it was a tangible and practical response, a generous gesture of support during those first terrible days.

Most of the town's shops closed on the Thursday. Parents took the day off work, preferring to stay at home with their children. I'm sure there were many in Britain who wanted to stay closer to their children. On the Thursday evening a special mass was held at Dunblane's Catholic Church, the Church of the Holy Family, at which Canon Basil O'Sullivan read a message from the Pope.

I'd always been sceptical about high-profile post-disaster visits by politicians, not least Margaret Thatcher's penchant for photo opportunities after other people's tragedies. I understand, however, that the visit by John Major and Tony Blair to Stirling Royal Infirmary and the school was very dignified, even though the press later reported that some squabbling had gone on behind the scenes. I think I was asked if I wanted to meet the Prime Minister, but declined.

Isabel MacBeath did request a fifteen-minute private meeting. Listening to this bereaved mother in the school's nursery, John Major would have been left in no doubt of the families' deep concerns about their treatment by the police. The meeting brought an instant but totally inappropriate response. Within minutes DCS Ogg had arrived at Isabel's house and proceeded to intimidate her. He ushered her houseguests from the room before telling her angrily that she 'didn't know police procedures'. Police procedures come first, care for distressed parents of murdered children is relegated to a secondary place.

This experience of how the police treat victims' families as an inconvenience was by no means unique. It has been revealing to learn how others involved in tragedies have fared. Police officers had used similar words about their procedures when dealing in a rude and insensitive manner with the families of the Hillsborough tragedy in 1989. And at the Emergency Planning Society meeting in 1999, John Mosey, whose daughter was killed on board Pam Am Flight 103, said of the various police forces with which he'd had contact:

> Too often these busy men, professional men, convey their attitude of 'I've got a major criminal investigation on my hands, don't mess my day up!' At times like these, grieving relatives must be expected to be a little demanding.

He might just as well have been talking about Central Scotland Police, for whom the Dunblane families were an inconvenience many years later.

On the evening of Friday, 15 March the people of Dunblane held a vigil at the Cathedral. The town's ministers, meeting on the evening of the Thirteenth, had planned it as an opportunity for the community to get together. They never expected as many as the estimated 5,000 who turned up, some staying until very late. Messages were left at the Cathedral on pieces of paper, the start of a Book of Commemoration. At the Sunday morning service, which replaced the anticipated Mothering

Sunday service, the Cathedral's minister, the Revd Colin McIntosh, said he believed that 'a whole nation, perhaps even the world, will remember us not for the tragedy that took place here, but because of the way we met it and with God's help overcame it'. Viewing the service many months later, however, I found its contents rather remote from the rawness of my feelings at the time. It was a service for the community.

It was Michael Forsyth or perhaps the members of the media themselves who encouraged the departure of 'the circus' from Dunblane that Sunday after the BBC had broadcast the service. Few of the reporters had any regrets about leaving, as they had been drained by their experience of Dunblane. The funerals of the victims were to take place away from the gaze of the media.

I had to make some decisions about Sophie's funeral and decided that she would be cremated at Falkirk, where we'd stood together just six short months ago looking at the Book of Remembrance. Eventually the Book would include an entry for Sophie, words that can be read by visitors every 13 March. It was so hard to draw this line under her life, yet there was no reprieve. Each of us who'd been told of our child's death emerged from the school a hundred steps ahead of anyone else in knowing what the news had meant. From the moment that Derek had told me, I knew precisely that Sophie would never be with me again; we would all have to make her live on through our individual and collective memories of her. I didn't want another impersonal service like Barbara's, when the crematorium minister had based what he'd said on a rushed conversation minutes before the service. I am not religious, but I wanted a religious service for those of Sophie's relatives and friends who have faith. It had to be something that would warm us with images of the real little girl we knew and loved. I needed a minister who had known her.

The Revd Ian Stirling's daughter Nicola had been a friend of Sophie's at Arnhall Nursery. Ian had been one of my nodding acquaintances, one with a dog collar. The family had moved away from the area a couple of years before, and from his parish in Ayr Ian knew how devastated the nursery would be. A number of children in the class had gone there, four of whom – Sophie, Emily, Hannah and John – had been killed. Ian drove to Dunblane to see if he could help. As well as comforting those at the nursery, he agreed to conduct Sophie's funeral service. He visited me twice over the weekend and we sat together while I told him stories of Sophie. He, too, had things he remembered about her. Those stories were translated into a most sensitive, moving and loving oratory at the service.

In the morning before the funeral I said goodbye to Sophie. She lay in a small white coffin in a flower-filled room at the funeral parlour. She looked beautiful, dressed in her *Lion King* sweatshirt and trousers. Many of us have recalled Disney associations from that time. For others it was *Pocahontas* socks or *Lion King* songs, but for me it was a *Pocahontas* plaster and a *Lion King* sweatshirt. I touched her gently, worried that I'd find evidence of the bullet wounds. I put her sooky beside her and left. When I saw the coffin later I didn't want to imagine her in it. This would be the moment of parting.

The funeral was held on the afternoon of Tuesday, 19 March and attended by scores of family, friends old and new, people from my work, present students, former students, people from Barbara's work and those who knew Sophie at nursery or at the health centre. I wanted it to be a private occasion, which it was and remains.

Afterwards, in Dunblane, I couldn't face being in the house where guests were chatting as they drank tea. It was too noisy. I went for a walk around the town with John, an old school friend who had travelled up from London. We walked along the path by the Allan Water and up to the Cathedral. Then, for the first time in a week, I went back to the school. The scene was overwhelming. A bank of flowers stretched along Doune Road, covering half the distance from the school to our house. Among the flowers were toys and messages from children. Cards asked the question in everyone's mind. 'Why?'

On his visit to Dunblane John Major had been asked whether the gym should be demolished. No doubt reflecting a widely held view, but perhaps without giving thought to all the consequences, he'd answered, 'Yes'. The Prime Minister sealed the fate of the building. Derek asked me what I thought about this, but I didn't have a clear view. However, if the building were to be demolished then I should go and see where Sophie had died. The day after Sophie's funeral I was taken there by Derek and Elspeth. I didn't know what I expected, I'd never been inside the gym and had only glanced through the windows on my way to Kids Club. It was smaller than I'd thought, darker too, as its windows had been covered over after the massacre. There were patches on the walls where bullet holes had been filled in. This place had once echoed to the sound of happy voices. Now there were no sounds. Its days had ended with children's screams and sobbing. I placed a bunch of flowers in the middle of the gym. Elspeth told me that I'd put them in the right spot. At the end Sophie had been at the centre of things. The gym was demolished on 10 April.

Since the massacre, most of my thoughts had been directed inwards, but prompted by other events I decided to give voice to how I was feeling about Sophie's death and how it had happened. On Friday, 15 March the Queen had visited Leeds to open the Royal Armouries Museum. She chose the occasion to speak in public for the first time about her grief for those at Dunblane. This was expressed, however, in a speech that included praise for the magnificent museum she was opening: 'The weapons of war, which can be as beautiful as they are terrible, are often products of the very finest design and craftsmanship.'

I don't find anything beautiful about machines designed to kill, and shudder at the very thought of guns being described this way. Others, including the veteran peace campaigner Lord Donald Soper, had already responded critically. I wanted my say. I wrote a handwritten letter, 'to whom it may concern':

> As a grieving parent I wish to express my anger at the insensitivity of the Queen's visit to open the new Royal Armouries Museum within two days of the events at my daughter Sophie's school. In whatever context it was meant, the juxtaposition of sympathy for myself and my fellow bereaved parents and a phrase linking beauty to any weapons was deeply hurtful. I feel it reflects an attitude to weaponry which could in some way have contributed to what happened here in Dunblane.

I didn't intend sending it directly to the Queen, I just wanted someone to know how I felt. I decided that the best route might be via George

Robertson. I'd never met him, but had a connection through Olwen, as his daughter Rachel and Olwen's eldest daughter Carys were school friends. Derek arranged to get the letter to him. A few weeks later I received a response from Sir Robert Fellowes, the Queen's Private Secretary. He told me that he had shown my letter to the Queen and expressed his and the Queen's sympathy. Reading between the lines I got the impression that there was some embarrassment at the timing and content of her Leeds speech. In view of subsequent comments from gun enthusiasts, including the Queen's husband, Prince Philip, I have no regrets about making my feelings about guns known so soon after the massacre. If others were going to be complacent and excuse weaponry because it was 'beautiful', I wasn't.

The Queen and Princess Anne were due to visit Dunblane on the Sunday. Invitations were about to be sent out to the families of the victims, but in view of how I felt, Derek ensured that I wasn't sent one. It was partly as a response to the Queen's words that I decided to make a media statement. Derek had asked me if I wanted to say something while the reporters were still in Dunblane. At first I didn't want to, couldn't see the point, but changed my mind over the weekend. I needed to say how devastated I was, I wanted to thank people and I wanted to put on record that I'd had enough of guns. As the media had now left Dunblane, I prepared a written statement. Rosie's dad Stuart helped me by consulting a colleague of his who regularly dealt with the press. I gave the statement to Derek:

> Seven days ago I lost the most precious gift I ever had. My daughter Sophie was such a very special little girl. Two and a half years ago at the age of three, her sparkle and love helped me through the pain of her mother Barbara's death. This time Sophie is not here to help, but the wonderful memories of her are so strong and vivid that in some way she is still here to make sure her dad is okay.
>
> My friends, family and the local community are an endless source of strength. I will need them all for a long time and thank them for being here not just for me, but also for the families of

Sophie's classmates and teacher, Gwen Mayor. I also thank all those in Scotland and the rest of the UK, indeed throughout the world, for all the love and sympathy they have showered on us over the past few horrendous days. I will never meet many of those who have written to me, and I wanted to use this opportunity to say that I shall be eternally grateful.

I wanted to say one other thing. For the sake of her fifteen dead friends, her teacher, all her other poor classmates, all the children at Dunblane Primary and Sophie herself, please no more guns and certainly no more worship of guns.

Incredibly, the statement was considered to be too political and its release was blocked by the police! Derek explained this on our drive to the gym the following Wednesday. I was as angry as my numbness allowed. Derek, too, was angry, and guessed that if the statement weren't released through the police I would not only arrange to release it myself but also tell the media that it had been blocked. That any attempt was made to stop a bereaved father commenting about guns tells us a lot about the reluctance of the establishment to have the boat rocked, even after something as horrific as the Dunblane massacre. Derek pulled strings for me and the statement was released the next day. Part of it was broadcast on the television news on Thursday, 21 March – 'No more guns and no more worship of guns'. The same day, Home Secretary Michael Howard announced a firearms amnesty.

During that week there had been better news of the surviving victims. One by one they were making progress and going home. For some the physical damage would repair relatively quickly; for others it would affect them for a lifetime. No one would know what mental scars they would carry with them into the future. On Friday, 22 March Dunblane Primary School reopened, though usual school hours would not be kept until after the Easter holidays. I'd not watched any television since the massacre and by chance the first thing I saw was headteacher Ron Taylor as he walked back into the school. 'This is a very important day for us because it marks the beginning of our recovery.' A line, albeit a thin one, was being drawn under the tragedy.

The community was ready to move on. A *Stirling Observer* headline in early April said 'normality' was 'slowly returning', no doubt reflecting how some of the community wanted to feel. The gym was still there, the cemetery was strewn with floral tributes and the victims' families were still coming to terms with what had happened. There was a forthcoming Public Inquiry and lots of issues to be addressed. Yet some in the town, so willing to talk at the beginning, had grown tired of it already. 'Weary' became a popular word. We'd find that a few people wanted to frogmarch the community into moving on. In fact, some had never stopped moving on, and we had a lot of catching up to do to make sure that we had some control over the aftermath of our tragedy.

# PART THREE

## MARCH 1996–APRIL 1998

The events of 13 March 1996 in Dunblane resulted in loss of unimaginable proportions. The impact was – and is – wide indeed, and it is no understatement to write of a world-wide expression of concern and sympathy which centres on the small city of Dunblane. Those affected by the tragic events have been offered help and support of family and friends, the Churches and all the helping agencies both statutory and voluntary

DUNBLANE SUPPORT CENTRE REPORT

# CHAPTER FIVE

# A Public Private Tragedy

## March 1996–August 1996

'On 21 March 1996 it was resolved by both Houses of Parliament that
it was "expedient that a Tribunal be established for inquiring into a
definite matter of urgent public importance, that is to say, the
incident at Dunblane Primary School on Wednesday, 13 March 1996,
which resulted in the deaths of 18 people"'

(*CULLEN REPORT*, FOREWORD)

During a recent interview I was asked when the scale of the tragedy had
first hit me. It was, I think, on Thursday, 21 March when I went to Gwen
Mayor's funeral in Dunblane Cathedral. Apart from brief words at
Sophie's funeral with Kathryn and Les Morton, and Ross Irvine's dad
Ian, I hadn't spoken to any of the other bereaved parents. I'd sent a
message to Karen and David Scott through mutual friends. Hannah's
funeral had coincided with Sophie's and I'd not had the strength to go to
any of the funerals of the other children. Now in the Cathedral I came
face to face with the evidence, if any were needed, that this was a tragedy
that had not just affected me.

The massacre sent waves of shock and horror around the world. Waves
of sympathy and love rolled back. Those of us who'd lost loved ones
would not grieve alone, but neither would we be able to. I felt as if a
burden of responsibility had been placed upon me to do something, to

ensure that lessons were learnt and changes made to reduce the risk of such an outrage ever happening again. Surely that is what every right-minded person would have wanted. It wasn't appropriate for me to hide away meekly, hoping that others might do things, because often they don't.

The Dunblane massacre was in many senses everybody's tragedy. Countless people, especially those with young children, would have felt as though something had been taken from them that day, hope and faith now damaged or lost. It was comforting that so many shared our sorrow, but this meant that part of our grief had been taken over, a portion of our children's memories had perhaps been hijacked. The victims were no longer our children: they were seen as angels, God's children, and they'd become Dunblane's children, more a part of the community than they had been when alive. Somehow each of us was going to have to find a way of achieving a balance between our own private grief and the reality of being part of a public tragedy. That would be all right if those promises of help for as long as we needed were kept, and as long as the community could deal with the public aspects of the tragedy as well as the private grief. In particular, the people of the town must avoid thinking that it was unbecoming for the victims' families to say things in public and remind others about what happened.

Local 'experts' had already been advising others in the community on how they should approach us. The families later heard that some people thought that we wouldn't want to talk about our children. Far from it. We learned that 'The Council' had told people to stay away from us, though no one I knew from Stirling Council had any knowledge of this instruction or its origin. It appeared to be an excuse to hold back information. However well-meaning this advice was, it set up unintended barriers.

There were a variety of responses from people around the world. Many had a feeling of helplessness, but also a wish to reach out to those of us who had been most affected. There were letters, poems, gifts and money, addressed directly to the families, or sent to the school or the town. Some were totally unconditional offers of help and care. Others were sent because of past personal experiences, now shared with one or more of us. Other messages came with 'baggage' attached – a religious belief, a personal problem, or a desire to become more involved. There were a few people, however, who responded to the tragedy by venting sick feelings on the victims' families and the mail had to be screened. But the vast majority of messages were sent with the best of motives.

At first the letters came in ones and twos. The first I received was from a family in Rutherglen near Glasgow. What started as a small trickle rapidly built up into a torrent, so much so that a couple of weeks later, after I'd gone for an early morning walk, I had difficulty opening the front door because of the number of letters piled behind it. I counted them, over 150 that day. The mail came addressed to the family of, or to the parents of Sophie North, or was one of a set of identical letters to be distributed among the families. When the post was screened many of my letters arrived with their envelopes sliced open. Dunblane was getting masses of mail. The staff at the sorting office did an amazing job and continued to help when the families needed to distribute mail within Dunblane. Volunteers were drafted in to deal with all the letters. I am sure most of them did the job with tact and care, recognising that they were playing their part in a community response. There were a few who reflected on this as a chore, an obligation to deal with a heavy burden placed on Dunblane.

It became easier to respond to some of the messages once the flood subsided, when a smaller number of letters could receive my full attention. But it was never possible to write to every one of the thousands who got in touch. I promised myself that one day I would try to write back to everyone. I haven't managed that, and this book, perhaps, is a means of letting everyone know what happened and thanking them for their kindness.

So much of me wanted to sort out my feelings about Sophie's death by myself. I understood how much friends and family would be suffering, but I wasn't in a state to have people lean too heavily on me for support, for explanations. But did I want to meet people who'd experienced the same loss as me? Would that be helpful? Central Regional Council had arranged a meeting for the bereaved families on the evening of Friday, 22 March: a room had been booked at Scottish Churches House, an ecumenical conference centre in the middle of Dunblane, opposite the Cathedral. I was nervous about going, even more so when I became agitated about my press statement from the day before. I was worried that one newspaper might have misrepresented what I'd said, making it appear that I was speaking on behalf of all the families. What would the others think of this person, whom many had never met, speaking for them? After sending an explanatory letter to them all, I decided to go to the meeting.

When I arrived at Churches House most people were already there, seated in a large circle. A Council official introduced himself and asked if we wanted him to stay. We made our first collective decision: we wanted to be on our own. He gave us a few contact phone numbers and left. It was to be the first of many, many meetings. There we were, different people from diverse backgrounds, a cross section of Dunblane. There were the electricians, the bank officer, the IT manager, the teachers, the ship's surveyor, the pathologist, the academic, the insurance salesman and many more. Some had left children at home that evening, others had left an empty house. Last week all of us had had young families. It was immediately apparent that whatever differences there were between us, these were nothing compared with what we had in common. The bereaved families, with Rod Mayor joining us on many occasions, found strength in one another's company and gave support to each other. The nature of the group and its size, over thirty of us, made sure of that. Those who were strong at one time would help those who weren't, roles that would be exchanged frequently as the grieving went on and the issues we had to deal with increased.

We introduced ourselves. Mothers said they were somebody's mum, fathers somebody's dad. Willie Turner slipped and introduced himself as Megan's mum. Karen Scott started the main conversation by asking if anybody was angry and we all agreed that we weren't. Numb, bereft, but not angry. Hamilton was mentioned, but apart from the August flier nobody knew much about him. We talked about the police and how things had been on the Thirteenth, but not for long. Isabel MacBeath described how she'd been visited by DCS Ogg. Duncan McLennan spoke about our need to get legal representation for the Public Inquiry. No one had told us what we had to do and not for the only time we had a sense of being marginalised. We didn't have much time, as the preliminary hearing had been fixed for 1 May, less than six weeks away. Duncan's brother had suggested that we contact Peter Watson of the Glasgow firm of Levy and McRae. The Law Society of Scotland did eventually place a press notice about legal representation, but if we'd waited until it appeared in late April there would have been little time left to prepare. Other groups involved in the Inquiry, the Crown Office, the Council, the Police and the gun enthusiasts were no doubt off their legal blocks within hours of the shooting.

We noted down each other's names, addresses and phone numbers. I agreed to type up a list for the next week, and in so doing became the group's secretary. We decided to switch days and meet the next Thursday, and that's how the Dunblane bereaved parents became the Thursday group. We met in the Churches House lounge, where we felt more comfortable and relaxed, but went back to the conference-room for joint meetings with the families of the injured children. Many of their immediate concerns differed from ours and they got together on a Wednesday evening. As the Public Inquiry got closer and the campaigning started, or when we needed more information, our two groups met together.

Most of us preferred meetings where we could sit and chat and not be overwhelmed by decision-making, although there was no way of avoiding that during those first months. When the meetings were more formal we could always relax together afterwards by adjourning to the Tappit Hen, the pub across the street. From our first conversations it was obvious that there were disparities in the amount of information the families were receiving. Not being kept in the dark was a key issue. I'd been blessed with a family liaison team who passed on every scrap of information. I extended my secretarial duties to produce a weekly newsletter, a summary of what we'd discussed at meetings and other information that ought to be shared. There was minimal formality — these newsletters weren't minutes — and agendas were put together spontaneously.

Some families found the meetings more helpful than others and not everyone came. That was perfectly understandable. Each person had their own way of dealing with grief and the newsletter allowed everyone to be kept up-to-date. Issues were dealt with confidentially, contact with anyone outside the group made privately. The victims' families were the last ones to seek publicity, except when it came to gun control, and that happened later. When there were problems, one of us would send off a letter or make a phone call. At that stage our appearances at public meetings were rare, though these seemed to induce discomfort in others. By the end of March and into April, others in the community were already commenting on money, gifts and many other matters on which they'd suddenly become 'experts'. Some were already writing articles about their role in the aftermath of the shootings.

The first of the Thursday group newsletters was distributed on 9 April. That week the topics included a change of time for the next meeting, holiday offers that the council had been receiving, the *Sunday Mail* petition against handguns, an invitation to Michael Forsyth to join us at one of our meetings and our legal representation at the Cullen Inquiry. I also mentioned that I had tapes of a concert sent from Texas that George Robertson had passed on to me. These were the first of many such musical gifts, including recordings of newly composed songs. By the time of the next newsletter the meetings with Peter Watson and Michael Forsyth had been arranged and the date for handing in the *Sunday Mail* petition was almost finalised. There was news that a grandparents' group had now started. It had seemed a lifetime, but it was only a month since the shootings and we seemed to have got ourselves organised.

I'd made my first visit to Dunblane Cemetery twelve days after the shootings. I saw the thousands upon thousands of flowers covering the open ground and stood and listened as the wind rustled eerily among the bouquets' polythene wrappings. The flowers had been moved from Doune Road on the night before the school reopened. In a triangular plot flanked by two roadways were two parallel curved rows of lairs, each lair marked with a small name plaque, the graves of Gwen Mayor and eleven of the children. I'd not known what to do with Sophie's ashes, but decided immediately on that visit. At lunchtime on Thursday, 29 March a few friends and I held a brief ceremony when I placed a small wooden casket containing Sophie's ashes in the ground. Her lair lay at the end of one of the rows. She was the last of the Dunblane victims to arrive at the Cemetery.

I'd gained some confidence from being with the other parents, and at the end of March felt strong enough to write to *Scotland on Sunday*. It was a personal response to a letter they'd published which had suggested that, in support of the case for gun control, all of the children's funerals should have been televised. The lack of news coverage of the funerals had surprised some, especially media representatives from abroad. It contrasted, they said, with the attitude towards televising funerals in Northern Ireland. My letter appeared on 7 April under the heading 'Private grief, public action':

> Your correspondent Tom Gill suggests that it may not have been wrong to have shown on television the funerals of the children killed at Dunblane. My daughter Sophie's funeral was a beautiful, moving and dignified ceremony which would, I am sure, have made 'emotional TV'. Nevertheless, Sophie's funeral was a celebration, a private occasion for those of us who had shared in the joy of her life. It was not an occasion for all those millions of people with whom we share the horror of its ending. I am glad the TV and the press respected our wishes to have that private time to remember her during a very public period.
>
> I know from the cards and letters I have received that there is already tremendous support for the tightening of legislation on the private holding of firearms, and it did not require the televising of funerals to achieve that. I do so agree with Mr Gill that one of the greatest commemorations to our children would be the total lawful ban of firearms from households throughout the UK.

Willowbank House was no longer a home warmed by a child's happy voice. It was safe, though, a place of refuge where I didn't have to see people. I could feel intimidated by the phone or the doorbell, though at other times I would sit for hours waiting for someone to call, not daring to phone and impose my misery on someone else. It was impossible to get it right; I was muddling along. There were social evenings with friends, the devastation temporarily relieved by talk and laughter. It didn't always work and I often switched off and sat staring at the ceiling or out of the window wondering what the hell had happened. Out in the town everything still seemed grey, the chiming of the cathedral clock a doleful sound as I walked home in the evenings. Inside the house I'd take my sleeping pills, go to bed and be safe for a few hours.

I cleared out the fridge and freezer; I couldn't keep the food I'd bought for Sophie forever. Lollies, cereals, spaghetti shapes, yoghurts went into the waste bin. In one room or another reminders of the past would leap from their hiding places: Barbara's bride's favour kept for Sophie, blank Father's Day cards, a card from friends wishing Sophie a life filled with happiness. Bit by bit, I moved Sophie's things up to her bedroom, but I was in no rush, and for months the kitchen remained a picture gallery and the lounge retained a semblance of the family room it once had been.

Gifts continued to arrive in the town. Some were displayed at a drop-in centre that had opened in the High Street. This was too public a place for me and I never went in. The families had little direct contact with community 'leaders', but we wanted to be kept informed, especially if things were being sent or offered in memory of our children or if there was any hint that our children's deaths were being exploited. Council officials maintained contact with us and asked for our opinions on various suggestions they'd received. One idea we vetoed was a proposal for a book called Dunblane Remembered. The author had apparently prepared books for previous tragedy towns. We saw copies of Hungerford Remembered, a glossy book full of advertisements for local firms and old black and white photos of the town. Although the mayor, Ron Tarry, had written a supportive message in their book, we found the idea distasteful. There was very little reference to the Hungerford massacre. Instead, the book seemed to convey the message, 'Let's pretend it didn't happen and get back to normal'. The inclusion of a photograph of a group of children called 'Cowboys and Indians, 1980', in which some boys were pointing guns, was in terrible taste.

Some gifts, intended for the community to share with the families or specifically sent to us, disappeared. Two examples illustrate why the victims' families sometimes felt left out. Hundreds of people from all over the world used the Internet to express their feelings about the tragedy, perhaps the first time this had happened. A Dunblane site was set up and the messages were collected into a standardised form that could be downloaded and printed. The Internet book was annotated with beautiful lettering and drawings. I didn't discover its existence until a long time afterwards, coming upon it by chance while checking other things online. I printed it out and arranged for it to be bound so that we could pass it among the families. I contacted Jim McNulty and Rik Bean, the people involved, to thank them. Jim wrote back to tell me that he'd taken bound copies to Dunblane in 1996. 'You would have to see the original book to appreciate the beauty of the paper, graphics, binding etc. It really is a beautiful tribute to the children, and to how they touched all our lives.' According to a story printed in *Reader's Digest*, one copy went to the school, one copy was for the Cathedral and one for the town. Nobody in the town thought to pass on one of the beautiful tributes to the families so they could see it.

Mystery also surrounds *The Andrew Poems*, a book of poems by Shelly Wagner from Virginia. Shelly's five-year-old son Andrew had accidentally drowned. Some time after his death she began to write poems about him and the tragedy that had befallen her family, and the collection was published in 1994. Immediately after the Dunblane massacre, parents and teachers of a kindergarten in her hometown sent copies of the book to us. Shelly included a letter with each one. Each book was inscribed for an individual family. I was very touched when I received my copy, but most of the other families never got theirs. There was an intensive search for them but they never turned up. Shelly generously replaced the missing books. She visited us in 1998 and read us some of her inspirational poems.

There was often confusion about where the gifts should go and the first public signs of resentment surfaced. Some members of the School Board and PTA appeared to be more concerned about benefits the school might derive from the massacre. In letters and comments made at the end of April, they castigated Stirling Council for withholding offers from them. Teddy bears sent from all over the world, including Oklahoma, a city that had suffered its own tragedy in 1995, were given to local people, including the victims' families. It was a lovely gesture, but some didn't like this. I couldn't believe it when I read that Gerry McDermott, a spokesman for the School Board, had branded the give-away 'offensive'. He claimed the school had not been consulted, although soft toys are mentioned in the minutes of the School Board meeting held a few days earlier. Meanwhile rumour-mongers had already begun drip feeding poison into the community, disturbed by the money and who was going to get it. We got the impression, substantiated by what some reporters told us, that some prominent locals were overly concerned about individuals becoming 'personally enriched' and that 'these people wouldn't know how to deal with money', wasting it on 'fitted kitchens, cars and drink'.

*These people*, the victims' families, were more concerned with having to deal with a major aspect of the massacre's aftermath, one that many other townsfolk could avoid. We were preparing for the Public Inquiry. The remit appeared broad. Lord Cullen was asked to look into the circumstances surrounding the events at the school. He chose three in particular: control of the possession and use of firearms and ammunition; school security; and vetting and supervision of adults working with children.

Some of us had already met Scottish Secretary Michael Forsyth when we took the *Sunday Mail* anti-handgun petition to London. In early May he came to one of the Thursday meetings in Dunblane and listened carefully to our views on gun ownership. He was obviously surprised and shocked at the size of the arsenal that Hamilton had been allowed to keep at home. He assured us that parliamentary time would be made available later in the year for changes in legislation. The nature of the legislation would depend on what Lord Cullen recommended, and until it had received his report the Government wouldn't commit itself to a particular position.

When Peter Watson came to talk to us in April we were generally impressed with what he had to say. Like many lawyers, he had quite a lot to say. Peter had represented victims of previous disasters, including Piper Alpha and Lockerbie. He reiterated what we seemed to know already, that following a disaster the establishment tends to come in quickly to occupy the centre ground. Those most directly affected get pushed aside. Without further delay we agreed to ask him to represent the families of all the children in the class as well as Eileen Harrild and Mary Blake. It made sense for all of us to have the same lawyer and it was almost certain that Lord Cullen would insist on it. Peter and his assistant Sandra Biggart met with us in Dunblane on a number of occasions in the run up to the Inquiry. Our counsel, who would be cross-examining witnesses on our behalf and making our final submission, were Colin Campbell QC and Laura Dunlop.

Peter Watson warned us that we should not try to ask for too much from the Inquiry. We should focus on one or two key issues. Gun control was uppermost in our minds and we wanted as much attention as possible drawn to this. In retrospect we should have asked more questions about other matters, about the way the police and the Procurators Fiscal dealt with Thomas Hamilton, but how could we ask questions when we didn't yet have the evidence and were in no condition to think clearly? We were being rapidly bounced into the Inquiry. The haste was justified to be in our interests – it would help with our grief – yet in the long term the conduct of the Inquiry has left a legacy that, by failing to provide answers to vital questions, extended the grief and despair.

The preliminary hearing was held on Wednesday, 1 May 1996, just seven weeks after the massacre. All the proceedings took place in the Albert Hall in Stirling. Lord Cullen sat facing the legal representatives at the front of the hall, with seats for members of the public provided behind the legal teams. The victims' families observed the proceedings from the upstairs circle, out of the view of the media. We had also been provided with space in the Lesser Albert Hall where we could sit and discuss what was happening, away from the public arena. A crèche was available so that parents with young children were able to attend. A disadvantage with this arrangement was that the Lesser Albert Hall was also the waiting area for the witnesses, some of whom we had no desire to set eyes on, except when they were on the stand. Through an appalling lack of tact and thought, Insp. Euan Ross, the officer we last saw in the school staffroom informing us brusquely that we would get information in a few minutes, had been detailed to take care of us at the Inquiry. We asked for him to be replaced. He was.

The preliminary hearing was held four weeks before the main hearings began and lasted one morning. Legal teams had to apply to Lord Cullen for authorisation to represent those persons who appeared to him to be 'interested in the circumstances leading up to and surrounding the incident'. Scotland's senior law officer, the Lord Advocate Lord Mackay of Drumadoon, and the counsel appointed by him to act on his behalf, Iain Bonomy QC, had the responsibility of presenting evidence to the Inquiry in the public interest. The preliminary investigation was being carried out under his authority largely by Central Scotland Police under the direction of the local Procurator Fiscal, John Miller. In addition to ourselves, the parties represented were the family of Gwen Mayor and twenty-nine members of the teaching staff at Dunblane Primary School, Stirling Council (and the pre-reorganisation local authorities), Central Scotland Police, Ron Taylor (the headteacher of Dunblane Primary School), Lothian and Borders Police and the Scottish Police Federation. Three representatives of shooting organisations were allowed to participate in the closing session. The Dunblane Primary School Board sought representation, but was turned down. Lord Cullen told its lawyer that its interests were already served by other parties.

During May the Dunblane Support Centre opened in Portakabins at the Braeport Centre near Dunblane Cathedral. It later transferred to purpose-built accommodation on the same site. This was part of the response of Stirling Council, which, following local government reorganisation at the beginning of April, had taken over responsibility for social services from Central Region. The Support Centre was established as a specialist resource to 'support and service the community and those involved with, and affected by, events in Dunblane'. It was staffed by a co-ordinator, an administrator and seven full-time and part-time support workers with backgrounds in counselling, therapeutic work, crisis intervention, group work, stress management, welfare benefits and addictions. It was to be available for all who wished to use it, in and outwith the community.

It would be inappropriate for me to comment on the effectiveness of services I didn't use myself, but I know that many in Dunblane found the Support Centre extremely helpful, often essential. It provided somewhere for them to go and chat, to find somebody to ask about problems that were making it difficult for them to get on with their lives. Each month during the first year between 325 and 459 people contacted the centre. Its three-year report reveals that there were between 170 and 187 visitors to the centre every month up until the end of 1998. It provided a central location for disseminating information and was used by others to get messages to the victims' families. For a short while I had regular meetings with the co-ordinator Colin Findlay, to ensure a flow of information was maintained. Support workers provided help for the injured families group and the grandparents' groups and also facilitated meetings of other parents who had children at the Primary School. News updates were provided.

The need for a Support Centre within the community had been highlighted by evidence produced by The Disasters Working Party, set up by the Government to learn lessons from previous disasters. In the aftermath of disasters a range of individual, family and community difficulties may be anticipated: stress is experienced by 40–70 per cent in the first month, and by 20–40 per cent after the first year; and 15–20 per cent experience chronic levels of anxiety which remain high for longer than two years. Some people, including a prominent local councillor, considered the Support Centre to be a waste of money. Perhaps it was too obvious a reminder of what had happened in the town. Apparently we should just move on. Counselling and care weren't what was needed. They hadn't taken on board what Susie Orbach had written in *The Guardian* immediately after the shootings.

Dunblane will never be in the past if there is any sense of a pressure to be over it. The tragedy marks everyone in the community, particularly those children and parents who were touched with a direct loss, for the rest of their lives.

Paradoxically, the only possibility of coming to terms with the trauma, which is to say, finding a way for it eventually to have a place, as opposed to the whole place, in one's life, is by ensuring that there is no sense of a hurry, no tension, for people to put this behind them.

As the Inquiry got closer, the families began to receive reams of paper from our lawyers. Every day the postman delivered witness statements and submissions and, once the hearings had begun, lists of witnesses and summaries of evidence. It was difficult not to begin to feel swamped by it all. My concentration was poor and the things I was reading were mind-boggling. Not having read the press reports, only now was I piecing together Hamilton's history. Could it really have been over twenty years ago since he had been in trouble with the Scouts? Could there have been so many complaints about him and had the authorities been so impotent when it came to stopping him? Could so many people in Dunblane have known him? And was he really licensed to hold so many guns and so much ammunition, even though his activities were frequently under investigation by the police?

A week before the main hearing we had a meeting with Lord Cullen and the Crown Office team. They told us that everything possible would be done to spare us having to listen to sensitive material about the victims and to prevent these details getting into the public domain. It would be inevitable that matters relating to Thomas Hamilton would dominate the proceedings, we were told, but we must never think that those who had been injured or had lost their lives would be forgotten. The meeting was amicable and I think most of the families went home that evening relatively optimistic that the Inquiry would be fair and open.

I went away to England for a long weekend. May had been a difficult month. Not only had there been all the things relating to the massacre, but I'd had to spend a number of days trapped in bed with sciatica. I disliked being totally reliant on other people. The time away was a welcome release from many pressures that had built up. There were some difficult things to do. I was visiting my mum and Barbara's family to explain what had been happening, what I had found out from the pathologist, whom I'd seen a few days earlier, and what I thought would be taking place at the Inquiry. I wanted to show them some of the gifts I'd received. In London I had my first meeting with Gill Marshall-Andrews to discuss the formation of a new gun-control group.

I was reluctant to go back to Dunblane and its Public Inquiry after the weekend. I didn't know what to expect. The reporters and cameras were all right, the families were filmed as we went in and out of the building but our privacy was largely respected. Within the Albert Hall, however, things were far worse than I'd imagined. Each day there were over five hours of evidence and cross-examination. Witnesses had sworn on oath to tell the truth. During those first few days, however, not only did I have to experience the pain of hearing evidence relating to Sophie's death, but it became apparent that we weren't going to hear the whole truth.

The Inquiry began on the morning of Wednesday, 29 May. In his opening address to Lord Cullen, the Lord Advocate read out the names of the victims. One of the first people to give evidence was Eileen Harrild, the gym teacher shot by Hamilton. Her account of what happened was harrowing enough, even though the Inquiry was spared the worst of the details. From Eileen's testimony there could be no doubt about Hamilton's murderous intent. When he entered the gym he was already pointing the gun in front of him as if he were at the firing range. He immediately shot at her and the other adults.

Other evidence on Day One included the briefest of summaries of the victims' injuries from two pathologists: the full reports were available to Lord Cullen. We heard that Hamilton's autopsy had revealed that he was perfectly healthy and not taking drugs of any description. Evidence was provided that Hamilton had persistently asked one of his boys' club members, a pupil from Dunblane Primary School, about the layout of the school and the time of the assembly. He had been given the wrong time, 9.30 a.m. From his time of arrival at the school it was surmised that Hamilton had intended to cause mayhem in the assembly hall where two or three hundred young pupils had been gathered earlier.

There was a lot of forensic and ballistics evidence. We heard about Hamilton's guns, details of their serial numbers and the bullets he had fired, eighty-nine Swedish and sixteen American bullets. It was horrifying to learn that the latter were soft-nosed, designed to stay in a target and inflict the maximum amount of damage. Now why should a sports shooter want those? Similar bullets such as the dum-dum are banned from use by armies by the Geneva Convention, but we heard that it was perfectly legal for target shooters to use them.

The horror in the gym was described by the first policeman and the first ambulance technician on the scene and by consultant paediatrician Jack Beattie. All these witnesses gave evidence that was hard to listen to, but none was saying anything with which we could disagree. Things were to change with the arrival on the stand of the last witness that day, DCS John Ogg. It was going to be extremely important for us to know that the whole truth would emerge at the Inquiry. There was more to it than that. As a group who felt badly let down, the families had to know that we could trust the Inquiry and that required an honest and open approach by everyone. On that first afternoon, our hopes were dashed by John Ogg, and I cannot overemphasise the irreparable damage that did.

Ogg spoke in an abrupt tone, presumably honed during numerous appearances at criminal trials. He was asked about the events of 13 March and how his force had dealt with them. We had to take on trust what he said about the events in the gym, but it was a different matter when he came to talk about how the police had dealt with us. We were flabbergasted and angry when Ogg, the senior investigating officer, told Lord Cullen that we had all been told of our children's deaths at least an hour earlier than had been the case. The journalists assembled below were unable to see us, but many reported the audible groan that had come from our gallery during Ogg's evidence. There seemed little doubt to us, given the certainty of his answer, that we had just heard the official police version of events.

Next day he was still on the stand, this time being cross-examined by our counsel and others. He continued to defend his story, though he began to fudge it a bit: he was only going by other people's reports, it was Holden's responsibility. The counsel for Central Scotland Police asked when he had first become aware of complaints about the police handling of the conveying of information to parents. He lied. He said he had only heard in the last two or three days. His visit to Isabel MacBeath on 15 March had been conveniently forgotten.

The first afternoon at the Albert Hall left a bitter taste in my mouth. We'd had to listen to Ogg's testimony and in a piece of gratuitous insensitivity the Crown had chosen to show a photograph of Hamilton's body lying in the gymnasium. Elspeth, my social worker, gave me a lift home, but I couldn't face seeing anyone else. I got in the car and drove, ending up at the Backwater Reservoir in Angus where on 14 March 1993, Sophie, Barbara and I had picnicked together for the last time. I stayed out until it got dark, crept back into Dunblane and went to bed.

Day Two began with Ogg and then there was more harrowing evidence, this time from headteacher Ron Taylor and his assistant, Senga Awlson. Thomas Hamilton's mother was called to give evidence. Following her divorce, her son had been adopted by her parents and had been brought up thinking that she was his sister and that his maternal grandparents were his parents. Much of the evidence on Day Two involved Supt Holden, the man who on 13 March had been responsible for informing relatives. Like Ogg, he had no doubts about when the families had been told – the early incorrect times. He wouldn't be budged and his rigidity left no room for doubt. There seemed no possibility that the police might have got it wrong.

On Day Two I learned some other disturbing information. Much of Hamilton's typing had been done at the university and there was a possibility that he had been there two days before the shootings. I was puzzled how an outsider could have arranged this typing service on campus. I'd seen no statements from anyone at the university and there was no indication that the person concerned would be called to give evidence. The next day brought further evidence of Hamilton's link with the university and over lunch I expressed my anxiety to some of the other parents. One knew the identity of the typist, a secretary in the department adjacent to mine, just along the corridor from my laboratory. I was horrified and heard later that her role was common knowledge on campus. Going back to work would be difficult, but worse now I knew that only days before Sophie was shot dead, her killer had probably been along the corridor from me.

The evidence continued to be painful on Day Three. Various witnesses related how they had met or spoken to Hamilton on the phone or in and around Stirling in the days before the shooting. There was more information about Hamilton's weapons and ammunition. The gun that killed Gwen Mayor and the children had been purchased from a gun dealer in York in September 1995 by mail order using a credit card – a routine transaction, apparently, except that Hamilton had returned the gun and negotiated a reduction before accepting his Browning 9 mm pistol. His ammunition, the bullets he used in the gym, had been bought from shops in Glasgow or Stirling. With increasing incredulity we listened as a member of the gun club where Hamilton had last shot enthused about shooting, telling Lord Cullen that it was a very social activity and that there were competitions in which shooters fired at humanoid targets – one called 'police pistol 1'. Referring all the time to Tommy, he spoke as if he had no grasp of the enormity of what his fellow shooter had done with his guns. The activities he described were so alien to us. After all that talk of the murderer and his murder weapons, the weekend came as a welcome break.

The final-year students, the ones whose courses I'd had to abandon in March, were getting their results that Friday and had invited me to a party. I wanted the opportunity to congratulate them and celebrate their success. The evening was enjoyable, but it wasn't easy to find any comfort, even in relaxed surroundings. Many things have been done in Sophie's memory, but one of the more touching was by that Class of '96. They'd met Sophie at a party I'd given at home in November and again when one of them got married in December. She'd charmed them all. During the year they'd been preparing a yearbook with entries about themselves and the members of staff. I was very flattered by what they wrote: 'Wherever we go we will be pushed to meet a man who matches Dr North – we will miss you.' But I was even more touched by the page that read: 'The yearbook is dedicated to Sophie North.' At the bottom of the page was a picture of a snowdrop. To mark their leaving, Lewis gave each one of them a slice of polished wood on which he'd painted a snowdrop. He had one for me as well, another treasured gift, made even more special because Lewis's wife Evelyn had just named a new variety of snowdrop after Sophie, *Galanthus byzantinus* 'Sophie North' (syn. *G. plicatus* ssp. *byzantinus* cv. 'Sophie North'). Evelyn had originally found the plant in the garden of their house in Doune Road, a stone's throw from the Primary School.

At the weekend I escaped briefly from Dunblane, driving north on the A9 and back to some of the places where we'd been on Barbara's last weekend away. I picked some heather at Findhorn and took a pebble from the beach at Lossiemouth. It was but a brief respite and on Monday I was back in the Albert Hall at the Cullen Inquiry.

After the distorted evidence of Ogg and Holden I was already disenchanted with the Inquiry. During that second week some of the liaison team police officers suggested to their families that the time they'd been told of their child's death was probably earlier than they'd thought. This had every appearance of a concerted attempt to bully families into changing information they'd recorded honestly in their statements. The Inquiry relied heavily on evidence provided by Central Scotland Police and now its officers were trying to get the families to change their statements. How could we ever trust the police again? I'm pleased to say that my police officer was not among those involved. Derek very pointedly told me that he and I agreed on the time I'd learnt of Sophie's death, even though 2.45 p.m. was later than the Ogg/Holden times.

Martyn and Barbara Dunn were among the last parents to be told. Their social worker Margaret Aland volunteered to take the stand so that the truth could be heard. She had to endure some of the most hostile cross-examination of the whole Inquiry. It was quite clear from her evidence that the police times were wrong, but no officer was called back to the stand to account for the discrepancy. The attempted arm-twisting of some families was never revealed. Because the discrepancies were obvious, we no doubt thought that Lord Cullen would be aware of what was happening and would be suitably damning of the force in his Report. At the very least it was now obvious that the claim by Central Scotland Police that on 13 March they had acted in a way to protect our feelings was a sham. The truth was, we didn't matter. We had been a low priority then and were continuing to be one at the Inquiry. And it didn't matter whether or not we were upset that they couldn't give the correct times. Until then I might have been prepared to overlook the additional trauma that police procedures had caused on the day of the massacre. Now I knew they were trying to cover it up and I resolved not to let them be able to get away with this.

During that second week at the Inquiry we learned a lot more about the Scouts and Hamilton's boys' clubs and camps. On Day Six another female witness was also subjected to very hostile examination. Doreen Hagger had attempted to draw her Regional Council's attention to Hamilton's activities at the boys' camps by throwing gunge over him in Linlithgow in 1989. After the massacre, stories had appeared in the press that Hamilton had once threatened her with a gun. Had this alleged incident been reported to the police in 1989 it would, one assumes, have led to immediate revocation of Hamilton's firearm certificate. There were some doubts about the validity of this story and it was right that the truth should be established. However, Doreen Hagger was treated as if she were on trial and, because of the nature of the Inquiry, she had no counsel to defend her. She stuck to her story. Next morning it seemed as if every officer who'd been stationed at Linlithgow had been brought in to prove that the gun incident couldn't have taken place or that it was never reported. Lord Cullen didn't believe Doreen Hagger's story. It may not have been true, but when it came to getting at the truth different standards were being applied. The doubts about the gun incident should not take attention away from the fact that Doreen Hagger's perception of Hamilton as a danger was more astute than that of Central Scotland Police.

By Day Seven, Thursday, 6 June, I'd had enough. I missed the opportunity to hear Paul Hughes's damning evidence about the memo he'd written in September 1991 (after his visit to Hamilton's camp at Mullarochy Bay) and about his recommendation to his superiors that Hamilton's firearm certificate should be revoked. I was already on my way south along the M74, running away.

That evening at the Forton Services motel the receptionist asked me how things were in Dunblane. I couldn't tell her how the town was feeling: I didn't know. I learned how difficult it was going to be revealing this part of my life. It was hard to tell people, especially strangers, what had happened. It still can be. In my motel room, surrounded by the papers from the Inquiry, I began to plan what I would do in the next few days. I needed to be in London on the Saturday and in the West Midlands on the Sunday afternoon. I forced myself to get on the phone and contact friends.

I arranged to stay with John in London. Before going back to John's house on the Friday evening, I visited my younger sister Janice. The weather was hot and oppressive and by the evening the northern sky was constantly lit by flashes of lightning. As I drove to John's in this apocalyptic atmosphere, I found myself approaching a police roadblock, just like the one in Doune Road, Dunblane, three months earlier. Memories flooded back. I was told to divert down a side street and got lost for a while. In bed that night, with thunder crashing outside, I wondered whether there would be any peace anywhere.

By the next day some purpose was restored when I went to Gun Control Network's first meeting. On the Sunday I drove to the West Midlands to join some of the other Dunblane parents at a memorial service for Charlotte Dunn. Charlotte had briefly attended primary school in Cradley before her family had moved to Dunblane a few months before the massacre. The Dunns were due to move back to the West Midlands at the end of March and within days of Charlotte's funeral, Martyn, Barbara and their young son Alex had to leave Dunblane. We kept in touch through the newsletters and phone calls. Martyn and Barbara travelled back to Scotland for important meetings. Charlotte's service set the tone for many later occasions – an event to celebrate a special life, with songs from *The Lion King* and children from her old school singing and dancing. (Martyn and Barbara eventually moved back to Dunblane.)

I spent Sunday night with other friends, and then took all day and half of Monday evening to haul myself back to Scotland. Against my better judgement, I went back to the Albert Hall and the evidence on Tuesday, Day Ten. At the start of the Inquiry a large number of the families had attended, but the numbers had now dwindled. People would call in, rarely staying long as they tried to return to work or catch up on other aspects of their lives. It took considerable stamina to sit in the Albert Hall, day after day, enduring the weight of evidence that suggested that Hamilton could and should have been stopped.

During the two days I'd missed, the Inquiry had been given details of the criminal intelligence system operated by Central Scotland Police. Now there was evidence about Hamilton's firearms applications. For two days, almost every witness was a serving or ex-police officer, describing his or her part in the process that permitted Hamilton to own guns. This evidence preceded the appearance on the stand of the man responsible for signing the firearm certificates, DCC Douglas McMurdo, who in April had been appointed as Assistant to Her Majesty's Inspector of Constabulary.

McMurdo gave evidence for the whole of Day Thirteen and part of Day Fourteen. Peter Watson had told us at our first meeting that the establishment would find a scapegoat, a single head to serve up on a platter by the end of the Inquiry. We were now listening to him. During tough examination, McMurdo's answers were often evasive and there was a lack of basic common sense to some of them. Underlying them all was an attitude, expressed not only by McMurdo but also by other senior officers, that Hamilton's troubles were with boys' clubs, his continual complaining, his smokescreens and his deviousness, but not with guns.

In spite of all the problems he'd experienced with Hamilton – McMurdo had even considered suing him – the Deputy Chief Constable believed that this catalogue of troubles had nothing whatsoever to do with Hamilton's fitness to own guns. As for revoking Hamilton's licence, McMurdo had been concerned about the consequences of an appeal to the Sheriff – unnecessarily so, as in all the time he'd had responsibility for firearm certification, he'd only had one experience of an appeal against a revocation, which the appellant lost. On the subject of the Hughes memo, McMurdo's attitude was bizarre. He never asked Hughes himself why the licence should be revoked and appeared to put little trust in what his junior officer had reported or implied. Hughes has since been promoted to the rank of chief inspector, which makes it all the more surprising that his views on Hamilton were summarily dismissed.

McMurdo's attitude seemed to minimise the possibility that some gun owners commit criminal acts. He couldn't have taken account of the fact that mass murderers around the world are often lone men holding a deep-seated grudge. In answer to Colin Campbell, Douglas McMurdo conceded that the only way to avoid handguns falling into the wrong hands was to ban them. But he stubbornly maintained that, given the same circumstances, he would still have approved Hamilton's licence. His evidence highlighted faults in the law and faults with those like him who were entrusted to administer it.

That third week of evidence ended with further revelations about Hamilton's involvement with firearms and with his GP confirming that he had not been seen at the clinic for two decades. The GP cast doubt on the ability of doctors to vouch that anyone would be a fit person to own a gun, a message that was coming loud and clear from many in the medical profession.

After that I began to lose the plot. There no longer appeared to be an obvious structure to the Inquiry proceedings. Lord Cullen and the Crown Office team presumably knew what was happening, but to a concerned onlooker like myself things were not at all clear. Naïvely I'd expected that a Public Inquiry would be conducted in a way that would help the public to understand. When Shadow Scottish Secretary George Robertson and Scottish Secretary Michael Forsyth appeared as witnesses, answering questions about their dealings with Hamilton, their evidence was preceded by some explanation from Iain Bonomy. It would have been helpful if this had been the norm with other groups of witnesses.

The influence of the gun lobby on the thinking of some in the police service became apparent when evidence was given on a draft report from Her Majesty's Inspectorate of Constabulary, produced after a thematic inspection of the procedures used by Scottish forces to administer firearms administration. From the sections of the report that were read out at the Inquiry, it appeared that the inspection was prompted by the shooting community who wanted to see the police improve their service to them. As our counsel was to describe it, the document read much like a promotional feature produced by a company like Marks and Spencer or British Airways, designed to please its customers. The gun owners were being treated as if they were customers of a police service. Yet the 'customers' of the police should be the general public, not the shooters. Some of the suggestions in the report would have relegated public safety below the convenience of the shooting community. The renewal period had already been extended from three to five years and there were moves to introduce postal applications.

Towards the end of the Inquiry a crucial issue arose. It wasn't possible to question Scotland's prosecutors, the Procurators Fiscal, about their reasons for not taking Hamilton to court. The police claimed that one of the reasons they couldn't do anything about Hamilton's firearm certificate was that he'd not been charged with any offence. During my now less frequent visits to the Albert Hall, I heard some of this discussion. Much of it was almost impossible to follow, the arguments couched in legal language with examples drawn from cases no lay person would know. The outcome was disappointing for those of us who wanted to believe that all relevant evidence would be heard. Examining the prosecution service in depth was not possible; this was one boundary that the Scottish judicial system would not or could not cross.

The Inquiry concluded with a series of expert witnesses who gave evidence on firearms, the sport of shooting, school security and Hamilton's psychiatric state. After a week's adjournment, the final three days were mostly taken up by the final submissions of those represented at the Inquiry. And then it was over. The events surrounding the deaths of our children had been sifted through and examined in detail. But would it be enough? We would be able to judge once the Report was published, probably in late September.

---

As the Inquiry neared its end I'd attempted to turn my mind to work. I was on sick leave, but had to stay in touch. I went into my laboratory, to help get a summer student started on her project, and visited my colleagues in Glasgow to see how well I could focus on research. It was tough. I wasn't ready for work. I tried to relax by watching some of the Euro 96 soccer matches. I also went to meet the Singing Kettle after their concert at the MacRobert Arts Centre when Sophie and I should have been in the audience.

All through that difficult period, gifts and kindness continued to pour into Dunblane. Singer Chris de Burgh had arranged to give a concert at Stirling Castle. For months he'd been asking whether he could do something for the families. He wanted to sing to us. On a balmy summer's evening on the Castle Esplanade he fulfilled his promise and sang his poignant songs for us and to an audience of 5,000. We met up with Chris before and after the concert at a local hotel. The evening was magical and just for a few moments it was possible to forget why we were there and why an international singing star had wanted to meet us.

That evening with Chris de Burgh was the first time the families had been out together. A group of us decided to use some money we'd been given to go out together again to hear the Eagles play at Murrayfield. Later in August we were back there, at the national rugby stadium in Edinburgh, with thousands of rugby fans for the Dunblane International – a match between Scotland and the Barbarians in aid of the Dunblane Fund. It was a grand occasion and the Scottish Rugby Union were generous hosts to all the families, including the surviving children from the class. There were memorable moments, including a fly-past and the singing of 'Flower of Scotland' before the kick-off. But I struggled when I saw Sophie's ex-classmates happily playing in the hospitality suite. I was so glad for them and their families, but it brought home to me too starkly that Sophie wasn't there.

There were special gifts. Laurie, a mother from California, made contact with me asking if she could send the families a book of pictures and words prepared by children at her daughters' school. When the book arrived it was quite unique. Dozens of children had made drawings and added messages, conveying their feelings about what had happened to our children. Some messages reflected a maturity we'd not always found among adults. These Californian kids were not frightened to acknowledge what had happened. It was made more touching because Sophie and I had driven through their hometown on two of our American trips and had stayed in the neighbouring city.

There were beautiful quilts from Alaska and Nebraska, a grandfather clock made by prison inmates, which is now kept in the Churches House lounge beside an embroidered picture, 'Remembering Our Children', which we'd also received. A pewter plate arrived from Malaysia and is now on display in Dunblane Public Library. One of the more unusual gifts was the Crystal Tree, a seven-foot wrought-iron structure decorated with seventeen angel crystals, commissioned on behalf of the people of Liverpool who had known their own tragedy. The school didn't know what to do with it and locked it away in a storeroom with various other gifts. I first saw it through the window of the storeroom, light glistening from the crystals in an otherwise gloomy space. It deserved to be on display somewhere better than a school storeroom. The families asked for it to be placed in the Cathedral, where it was allowed to stand for the Memorial Service. It now sits in one family's dining-room, waiting for a permanent home.

The generosity of those who donated gifts in response to the tragedy ought to be marked in a more permanent way. It would be good to think that many of the gifts sent to Dunblane could be collected together and put on permanent display in the town. This was suggested to me by the curator of a local museum in Stirling.

Some of the flowers donated to Dunblane were planted in a new garden created next to the Four Ways Roundabout. They surround a sculpture of a fox and bear, 'Friends Forever', donated by the Towsontowne Rotary Club of Maryland, USA. Flowers were very important in the aftermath, from the bank of massed bouquets that stretched along Doune road to the Sophie North snowdrop and two new roses. Rod Mayor had contacted Cockers Roses in Aberdeen to arrange for a rose to be named after Gwen and encouraged the bereaved parents to choose a rose for the children. With funding from the Dunblane Fund, 'Gwen Mayor' – a peach and apricot Hybrid Tea rose – and 'Innocence' – a salmon apricot bushy patio rose – were named. Both are sold as charity roses. The sales of 'Gwen Mayor' contribute to the Gwen Mayor Trust set up by the Educational Institute of Scotland (EIS) to support educational activities in Scotland; those of 'Innocence' help the Children's Hospice Association of Scotland (CHAS).

So much kindness, and from people who didn't know much about us, except that our children and their teachers had been killed or injured. That would change. What had happened to our loved ones had become more public as a result of the Inquiry. Now, for the sake of publicising our gun-control campaign, many of us were about to allow parts of our lives to become more public too. For eighteen weeks we had supported the gun-control campaign by proxy, but with the Inquiry over we wanted to play a more active role. We were still hurting: we wanted to tell everyone why, and what we thought of the menace that had devastated our lives. We were going to talk to the media, because we wanted the public to know what we thought about guns.

# CHAPTER SIX

# 'No More Guns and No More Worship of Guns'

## April 1996–October 1996

'I had something that took skill and dedication, that I found gave me immeasurable pleasure – that was bringing up my daughter'

(MICK NORTH, *NEWSNIGHT*)

I'd never liked guns. I could feel sick watching movies that included gratuitous gun violence. I never saw the funny side of people being shot in comedy programmes or cartoons. It is too easy to use guns to intimidate, to shock, to harm and the intimidation, shock and harm can be mediated at a distance – you don't even have to get close to the person targeted. Those who possess guns gain a power, and guns appear to attract some men for that reason. It is inevitable that their possession creates circumstances in which they are used in a disproportionate response, sometimes with lethal consequences.

Sophie knew my dislike of guns and we turned off the television whenever there was shooting. Her nursery had a clear and firm policy about guns. There were to be no toy guns and the children were actively discouraged from turning other objects into pretend guns. I have heard the argument that children, especially boys, will always pretend they have guns, and so what is the harm in giving them toy ones? This is said as if shooting at somebody else is an acceptable part of human behaviour, something to be fostered in our young. Is it? If so, it is a depressing thought. Shouldn't every effort be made to discourage this?

It is disturbing how easily people slip references to shooting into everyday conversations. 'I'll shoot you if you don't behave'. 'He should be taken out and shot'. Do they really mean these things? They don't say 'I'll stab you' or 'He should be strangled', so why these glib references to shooting? Is it because of the immense degree of threat they imply? Ex-boxing champion Jim Watt couldn't understand why some of us were extremely offended when he told a 'joke' about a firing squad at a fund-raising sportsmen's dinner for the Dunblane Fund less than a year after the massacre. It was no longer a joking matter, it never should have been. Another example: John Major in March 1991, laughing with Gulf War soldiers as he wields a military rifle he's been given, says, 'This will give me Cabinet authority of a sort.' A joke, perhaps, but too many take this kind of imagery seriously. Get a gun, they think, and acquire power, respect and authority. This may not be in the minds of the majority of shooters, but so long as it enters the minds of a few then we must worry about anyone having easy access to guns.

Before I knew anything about Sophie's killer, I was concerned about the way in which those who own guns talked about them. Shooting made them feel important and their obsession was disturbing. There was indeed a worship of guns. Even some of those at the heart of the tragedy seemed to excuse target shooting too easily, as if it had no bearing on Hamilton's shooting spree. Here is Provost Pat Greenhill, talking to Sky TV on 14 March:

> Always in a tragedy like this every single question is considered and asked and people will look at that. But it [shooting] was a legitimate hobby of the man. He never hid it. It wasn't unknown, I have to say. But never for a moment did we think anything like this could result from the activities.

In Great Britain target shooting was, with just a very few exceptions, the only legitimate reason for the ownership of handguns. Yet handguns are particularly dangerous because they are easily concealed and the majority of them are semi-automatics, capable of being fired many times in rapid succession. Their acceptance by some as sports equipment should not have made them appropriate as everyday objects that could be kept in the home. Guns are instruments of death, designed for one purpose – to kill. Is it healthy for a sport to use the tools of assassins, terrorists and mercenaries? A so-called sport should never be an excuse to continue exposing the general public to danger.

The Dunblane families were not alone in believing that our children would still be alive if previous governments had acted more in the public interest. In 1970 Her Majesty's Chief Inspector of Constabulary was asked by the Home Office to undertake a review of firearms controls. A report, the McKay report, was prepared in 1972 but never published. In 1973 the Government prepared a related green paper, said by the gun lobby to be highly restrictive in tone. Eleven broad-based categories of restrictions were proposed, but later in the year Edward Heath's Conservative government abandoned plans to tighten the gun laws, bowing to what *The Guardian* described as 'a model of parliamentary lobbying', a campaign by the Long Room Committee, a group representing Britain's gun users.

Another opportunity to tighten gun laws arose after the Hungerford massacre. Michael Ryan had been another loner with no previous criminal record and no known history of medical or mental problems. On the day in 1987 when he killed sixteen people and injured fifteen others, he was legally entitled to possess eight guns, three shotguns and five firearms, as all the necessary criteria were apparently satisfied. He was a member of two Home Office-approved shooting clubs. Unlike Hamilton, this man was known to the police only as being 'well dressed, of good behaviour, courteous and quiet'. Questions have been raised about the licensing procedures used by Thames Valley Police, but until evidence to the contrary is published it can only be concluded that the police had no option but to approve his firearm certificate. The law favoured the shooters. A person almost had to prove himself to be a criminal or personally unfit – i.e. have intemperate habits (drinking) or be of unsound mind – before being prevented from owning a gun.

The jury at the coroner's inquest held in Hungerford in September 1987 made only one recommendation:

> The Jury felt that semi-automatic weapons should not be generally available and that an individual should not be allowed to own an unlimited quantity of arms and ammunition. However, knowing that this subject is under review by the Government, the Jury makes no detailed recommendations.

The members of that jury had put their faith in the legislators, but many of the ministers and backbenchers of the Tory government were in favour of gun ownership. Home Secretary Douglas Hurd announced a review of firearms legislation, but the changes brought in by the Firearms (Amendment) Act of 1988 were very limited. The Act took some high-powered weapons out of circulation and there were a few changes to the procedures involved in the issue of firearms and to security requirements of firearms storage. Limits were placed on ammunition kept at home, semi-automatic rifles were banned. But the gun owners were able to keep their handguns. A Michael Ryan would still have been able to own one. Thomas Hamilton certainly was, and by 1992 he also had authority to keep as many as 7,500 rounds of ammunition at home.

One consequence of the 1988 Act was the setting up of the Firearms Consultative Committee (FCC), an advisory body to the Home Secretary. It was to consist of persons appearing to the Home Secretary to have knowledge and experience of one or more of the following matters: the possession, use or keeping of, or transactions in, firearms; weapon technology; the administration or enforcement of the provisions of the principal Act, the Firearms Act 1982, and the Firearms (Amendment) Act just passed. The group that dominated FCC proceedings were those described as 'other individuals with specific knowledge of aspects of firearms or aspects of shooting sports'. The committee became a conduit between the shooting community and the Home Office, pushing for changes in the regulations that over the next few years made gun ownership progressively easier. The FCC afforded little opportunity for those promoting gun control to have an influence on government policy.

The FCC was just one means available to the UK gun lobby to sway the Government. Gun enthusiasts always promote their own expertise as a reason for them to advise the Government, pooh-poohing the right of non-shooters to hold views on guns. In their eyes, if you don't shoot you have no legitimacy to talk about firearms. They would rather gun legislation were dictated by those with their finger on the trigger than by those who only see the pointing barrel. Shooters consider not only that they have an inalienable right to own their lethal weapons, but also that they have some special status when it comes to being heard by politicians. Too often, many of our legislators have accepted what this minority self-interest group have had to say.

If their spokesmen are to be believed, the shooters' view of themselves is a rather disturbing one. Gun owners are, they repeatedly say, the most law-abiding citizens, as if the mere fact of owning a gun grants one this status. Yet as soon as one of this 'law-abiding fraternity' commits an atrocity, they manoeuvre their arguments to make sure that the perpetrator was never actually one of them. He must have obtained his guns illegally; it was the fault of the licensing authorities, who should have spotted him and prevented him from becoming 'one of us'. This is a more worrying knee-jerk reaction to gun atrocities than the pleas for tighter gun control. To the gun owners, the easy availability of firearms is never a factor.

When it comes to remedies the gun lobby always expresses its earnest desire to do anything that would help – but never anything that would actually affect their activities. 'Every one of us would give up anything to bring the children back, but it [handing in guns] won't.' Easy words, because the children can't come back. The weapons should have been given up before a massacre was allowed to occur. The shooters argue that no matter how awful and obvious the devastation caused by guns, there should never be any emotional response. To be objective and detached, however, is to deny the reality of what happened. This is an issue which calls for an emotionally informed response. Any sane person would respond emotionally and would want their gun policy to continue being informed by the horror and despair occasioned by shooting. One must suspect the state of mind of the gun lobby who consistently turn a mask of disinterest towards the suffering brought about by these weapons.

Victims and their families are plunged into situations that give them a unique opportunity to publicise the case for change, to break the inertia. This is often the only way. For many who have had to deal with the damage inflicted by bullets, this is an immense burden and one they would rather avoid. It was so for the families of the Dunblane victims, but slowly and surely most of them became involved in a campaign that had a profound effect on firearms legislation in Britain.

None of us who sat through the evidence at the Cullen Inquiry could be accused of being ignorant about guns. We had been given a crash course on the 'sports equipment' that had ripped through our children's bodies. We had heard about the way in which 'sportsmen' use them, heard how powerful and dangerous they are, each piece of evidence making us more determined to campaign for tighter gun laws. We had noted the contrast between the stringent regulations that controlled the use of firearms by police officers and the ease with which private citizens could get guns. A clear message was necessary that guns were dangerous and their use by civilians had to be restricted. Legislative change would send out that message loud and clear.

Initially the Dunblane families didn't have the emotional strength to organise and lead a gun-control campaign. We were strong supporters of what others were doing. Later, when the time was right, we became actively involved. For me it started relatively early when I received a message from Ann Pearston whom I'd known when she lived in Dunblane. Her children had been at Arnhall Nursery and Sophie had been to their birthday parties. In a letter to the *Sunday Times*, published on 24 March, she had written:

> Next March when the snowdrops appear, let us remember Dunblane. But let us also be able to say, 'We made our feelings clearly known to those who govern us and seek to shape laws to protect us.'

Ann told me how she and some friends had begun an anti-handgun petition, the Dunblane Snowdrop Campaign, named after the only flower blooming in Dunblane on 13 March. The organisers, Ann, Rosemary Hunter, Jackie Walsh and Jackie's husband David, were local parents who wanted to do something positive, horrified at what had happened. They were not, as the gun lobby and others later claimed, professional campaigners out to exploit our grief. Ann asked me if I would come to their high-profile launch on Monday, 22 April, taking place in Inverness when the Scottish Grand Committee met there. The Committee consisted of all the Scottish MPs and had only recently started meeting in Scotland. Its previous meeting, due to be held in Glasgow on 15 March, had been cancelled as a mark of respect for the Dunblane victims.

I didn't know whether gun control would be a sensitive issue among the Thursday parents' group. We were still getting to know one another and I didn't want to impose issues that might be upsetting. At that stage we had hardly talked about guns. Others were becoming involved, too. Not long after I'd spoken to Ann Pearston I received a call from Peter Samson, a reporter from the *Sunday Mail*. I avoided direct contact at first. I asked Stuart, Rosie's dad, to check what Peter Samson wanted. The paper was running a petition calling for a review of firearm laws and a ban on the private ownership of handguns. There'd been an overwhelming response and the paper wanted some of the victims' families to be involved when the petition was handed to the Government. Megan Turner had once won a *Sunday Mail* Happy Smile contest and on the Sunday after the massacre Kareen and Willie had been shocked to find that the paper had used their daughter's photograph to launch its campaign. Although angry at first that no one had told them, they soon decided to give the petition their support. Once we knew that other families had been contacted, gun control became a major topic of conversation on Thursday evenings. I told the others about the Snowdrop petition and promised to keep them informed. Soon many of the others were offering their support to the Snowdrop campaigners.

I travelled alone to Inverness for the Snowdrop launch, catching an early morning train from Dunblane. It was going to be a tough day, but as I was to find out, campaigning for gun control would never be easy. I would have to draw deep on my emotional reserves. I was supposed to be anonymous, just an unnamed Dunblane parent who was at the launch to show support. Some of the reporters had guessed my identity. I refused to talk to them, but my presence ensured the press reported that the petition had the support of the Dunblane families.

When I arrived the Scottish MPs were in the chamber for a session of questions to Scottish Office ministers. Although the Conservatives were in power, they were represented by a mere handful of MPs in Scotland, vastly outnumbered by the three opposition parties – Labour, Liberal Democrats and Scottish Nationalists. Members were questioning ministers on a variety of topics, but especially on the latest crisis to hit the Government, BSE and its effect on the beef industry. Snowdrop's presence was acknowledged in a question from the Maryhill MP Maria Fyfe.

Afterwards, in the foyer, MPs were invited to sign the Snowdrop petition:

> Wherefore your Petitioners pray that your honourable House introduce or amend the law relating to the ownership and usage of firearms such that:
> 1. All firearms held for recreational purposes for use in authorised shooting clubs be held securely at such clubs with the firing mechanisms removed;
> 2. The private ownership of handguns be made illegal;
> 3. Certification of all firearms be subject to stricter control.

Political differences quickly became apparent. The response from opposition MPs was tremendous. All three leaders signed. Jim Wallace, leader of the Scottish Liberal Democrats and now Scotland's Justice Minister, held back, arguing that he never signed parliamentary petitions on principle. After a lengthy discussion with the campaigners he was persuaded to sign. The papers next day carried photos of Jim Wallace, Labour's George Robertson and the SNP's Alex Salmond in a unified public stance against handguns. Not one of the handful of Scottish Tory MPs was prepared to support the petition. Some had shooting interests, others said they would be waiting for Lord Cullen's report before making up their minds. Scottish Secretary Michael Forsyth argued that he couldn't set up a Public Inquiry, which was to report to him, and then prejudge the issue. The *Daily Record* unfairly slated him for this, but he was one of the few who did have a legitimate reason for not signing. I travelled back to Dunblane on my own, exhausted from my first brief experience of campaigning, but heartened by the enthusiasm of the other campaigners and the support and publicity they had gained that day.

Three days later a group of us, bereaved parents and grandparents, Gwen Mayor's daughter Esther and her partner Mark, were off to London. Accompanying us were the *Sunday Mail*'s Peter Samson, Melanie Reid, Angus Macleod and cameraman Ronnie Anderson. The editor Jim Cassidy joined us in London. There were mixed emotions and some excitement – first flights for Jimmy and Betty Ross, whose granddaughter Joanna had been one of the victims – but a lot of apprehension about the people we'd be meeting. Overshadowing it all was a feeling of great sadness. We were leaving Dunblane at the crack of dawn because our loved ones had been killed with a legally held handgun, and thousands of people had signed a petition to say that they'd had enough of them.

At Westminster we met Shadow Scottish Secretary George Robertson. I'd come to know George over the past weeks. He'd called at the house a few times to explain what had happened to my letter about the Queen, to give me a copy of Cullen's report on the Piper Alpha disaster and to talk about the Snowdrop Campaign. He gave us a brief tour of the Houses of Parliament before taking us to the Shadow Cabinet room. Here we had our first meeting with Tony Blair, then Leader of Her Majesty's Opposition, and Shadow Home Secretary Jack Straw. On the whole it was a comfortable and useful meeting. At that stage the Labour Party wouldn't commit itself to a precise position on gun control, but I came away with the clear impression of being listened to, our concerns about guns being understood. The same was true when we met Menzies Campbell, a senior member of the Liberal Democrats.

After lunch we loaded boxes containing the signed petition on to a minibus and accompanied them to the South Bank of the Thames where Ronnie Anderson took photographs for next Sunday's edition. We held up the boxes. Six of them were numbered 4–2–8–2–7–9: '428,279 SAY BAN THE GUN.' This amazing number of signatures had been collected in an unprecedented four and a half weeks. For a newspaper whose circulation is almost entirely within Scotland, a country with a population of only 5.1 million, this represented incredible support for the view that something had to be done about handguns, something drastic. Ronnie's camera caught us with strained smiles on our faces — not a reflection of happiness, for there was none to be had, though we later heard that gossips in Dunblane were accusing us of enjoying being in the limelight.

We met our MP Michael Forsyth at the Scottish Office in Dover House, Whitehall. A few days earlier Willie, Kareen and I had written a letter to John Major. We'd been told that we couldn't hand the petition to the Prime Minister, but had asked him if we could meet him when we came to London. There had been no reply, but Michael Forsyth now informed us that the Prime Minister should be able to see us. A few minutes later we were on our way to 10 Downing Street where John Major invited us into the Cabinet Room. We were joined by the Scottish Secretary and the Prime Minister's wife, Norma.

Sitting on the opposite side of the Cabinet table from John Major, I realised that I was feeling very weary and I began to have difficulty concentrating. Though my judgement was probably impaired, it was difficult to be anything but disappointed with that meeting. In contrast to our earlier get-together with the Shadow Cabinet members, this was not a relaxed occasion. John Major may have reacted to the tragedy as a parent, but that day he was a politician. What John Major had to say warned us that the gun lobby's arguments were still treated seriously at the top of the Tory party. One of these is that those who perpetrate atrocities with firearms can easily find alternative ways of committing them. The fact that a gun was used is considered irrelevant. It is an argument that overlooks both how much more likely these events are to occur when a gun is close at hand and also the extent of the damage that can be done with guns. That morning the Provisional IRA had attempted to blow up London's Hammersmith Bridge using Semtex. John Major told us in all sincerity that if Hamilton had not had his guns he could have tried to blow up the school with Semtex.

This was the first of a number of occasions when we were fed this ridiculous red herring. With a perplexing ability to put themselves into Hamilton's mind, politicians imagined a number of ways in which he could have carried out mass murder without his guns. Where are the clubs where men can practise the making and planting of bombs, and where are the 'sports shops' for the purchase of explosives and detonators over the counter? What we did know was that there were plenty of places to practise shooting and to buy guns and bullets.

The Prime Minister tried to reassure us 'guns aren't really the problem'. Why, in his Huntingdon constituency, one of the largest rural constituencies in England, they'd never had any problems – it wasn't anything his constituents wrote to him about. He wasn't listening to us and I began to feel patronised. Kareen Turner, getting equally annoyed, interrupted one of his deflective discourses by reminding him why we were there. It had been a gun that had been used to kill the children and their teacher and we had come to see him because we believed it was necessary to ban handguns. Those who had signed the petition agreed with us.

I had another worry about that meeting. Our small group hadn't always spoken with one voice, and that could be exploited by politicians and others. We would have to make sure that we didn't give them that opportunity, by working hard at promoting a united and consistent front.

Back at the Scottish Office Home, Secretary Michael Howard and Michael Forsyth formally accepted the petition and seemed to be attentive to what we had to say as we sat and drank tea. Neither of them would make a commitment, but they now knew that we wouldn't let the matter rest. Mere tinkering with the gun laws would not be acceptable this time. We departed telling Michael Forsyth that if they didn't do something about the gun laws we would be back again.

The day had been handled with great sensitivity by the *Sunday Mail*, something that did not go unnoticed. When Jim Cassidy left the paper in

September 1999, Roy Greenslade of *The Guardian* wrote that the editor's 'post-Dunblane ban-the-guns campaign was handled tastefully enough to be appreciated by the bereaved parents'. I also appreciate what Melanie Reid wrote the following Sunday. At the bottom of her weekly column appeared the following PS:

> I was privileged to travel to Westminster last week with some bereaved families from Dunblane. I cannot pretend to understand what they are going through, because their terrible experiences have taken them over a threshold the rest of us cannot pass.
>
> But I hope they will allow me to express unfailing admiration for their resilience, their warmth and their dignity. After being savaged by great depravity, they have risen to the heights of great humanity.

The *Sunday Mail* had given us a certain level of assurance about trusting the media. We were going to need that trust if we were to campaign successfully. With so little experience and without the benefit of any media training, we would have to learn fast how to interact with the press and television so that our message could be heard as widely as possible.

All across the country various groups of people, some known to the Dunblane families, others not, were also doing things to make sure that our law-makers were aware of the public mood – a mood largely in favour of tighter gun control. In what was probably the first move of its kind, Stirling Council agreed to support the principal aims and objectives of the Dunblane Snowdrop petition. A copy of the petition had been placed in the reception at Old Viewforth and Cllr Ann-Marie Strang expressed the hope that as many councillors, employees and visitors be encouraged to sign it.

Three days after we'd been persuading the British Prime Minister to tighten gun laws in Britain, another lone gunman with lawfully held guns wreaked havoc on the other side of the world. Martin Bryant killed thirty-five people at the Port Arthur heritage site in Tasmania. The response of John Howard's newly elected Australian federal government was swift. New firearms regulations were drawn up in a first-ever agreement between all the states. Australian gun laws had differed from state to state and were generally more lax than those in Britain, especially in Tasmania. To the defiant protests of the Australian gun lobby, but with the support of the majority of the Australian public, many weapons became prohibited. A buy-back programme and firearms compensation scheme were rapidly introduced and hundreds of thousands of weapons were surrendered by September 1997.

If the Australian government could act swiftly and decisively why not the British government? Why couldn't they also show an immediate response to overwhelming public demands? Some answers lay in the strength of the gun lobby within the Tory party and John Major's weak position at its head. His parliamentary party had been split and for a while the government's tiny majority had been put in jeopardy by a group of its own MPs, the Euro-sceptics. He and his ministers seemed reluctant to do anything that might upset the backbenchers.

A first opportunity to hear some of the gun lobby's arguments came at the beginning of May on *Words with Wark*, a weekly current affairs programme. The panel that discussed gun ownership consisted of *Sunday Times* columnist Joan McAlpine, the *Sunday Mail*'s Jim Cassidy, Guy Savage of the Shooters' Rights Association and Sean Gabb, the libertarian editor of *Free Life*. Joan McAlpine and Jim Cassidy unequivocally supported tough gun laws and a handgun ban. Most viewers would have been repelled by the views of the other two panellists. Savage, a gun dealer, appeared frequently for the gun lobby during the next few months, extolling the virtues of gun ownership and the right to bear arms. In a later interview he told a reporter that if a handgun ban were enforced he stood to lose more than the Dunblane victims' families. He was heard from less after that. Gabb wanted everyone to own a gun for protection and appeared to gloat at the thought of being able to use a gun to shoot an intruder. Ian Stirling, the minister who'd conducted Sophie's funeral service, participated in the programme and had also been contacted by the *Daily Record*. In an article, 'Don't betray Sophie', Ian advocated a change in the law: 'Scotland doesn't want guns.' The article was supported by a short editorial. Like all the tabloid newspapers and most of the broadsheets, the *Record* was taking a tough stance in favour of greater gun control.

Petitions provided an effective and immediate way of putting pressure on Parliament to change gun legislation and especially to introduce a handgun ban. A ban would not, however, address all the problems associated with gun ownership. Whatever the success of the anti-handgun campaign, it was imperative that the other dangers weren't overlooked as memories faded. The gun lobby's arguments had largely gone unchallenged because there'd been no organisation lobbying for tighter gun control. If shooters' views remained unopposed then the scene would be set for progressive weakening of any legislation introduced in the wake of Dunblane. This had occurred following the Hungerford massacre and the gun lobby was already at work when the parliamentary Home Affairs Committee began to look at handgun ownership in May 1996.

Gill Marshall-Andrews made the first moves after the massacre to set up a gun-control organisation. Gill had been concerned for some time about the influence of the gun lobby and the rise of a gun culture in Britain. Two years earlier she'd tried to set up an organisation, but failed through lack of interest and support. She contacted me and a number of other people with interests in gun control including Prof. Ian Taylor, a criminologist at the University of Salford, and Tony and Judith Hill, whose daughter Sandra had been killed at Hungerford. Tony's had often seemed a lone voice for tighter gun legislation and he'd been devastated by the events of 13 March, concerned that he hadn't done enough since 1987. But it wasn't Tony who hadn't done enough: there'd been too little activity in Whitehall and at Westminster.

During meetings at Gill's house during May and June, Gun Control Network (GCN) was born and its aims defined:

- The private ownership of handguns to be made illegal;
- Rifles and related ammunition to be kept only in approved gun clubs and weapons over .22 calibre to be prohibited;
- Multi-shot rifles and shotguns to be banned;
- Certification procedures for shotguns and rifles to be tightened,

more rigorously applied by police and the courts, and
extended to cover air guns;
- The minimum age to be raised to 18;
- A firearms control board to be established;
- De-activated and replica weapons to be banned;
- Sale of gun and ammunition to be more restricted;
- Regulation and monitoring of approved gun clubs to be tightened.

The major theme running through our objectives was that public safety should always come first, never again placed behind the 'rights' or convenience of the gun users. Society should work towards an overall reduction in gun ownership; if guns had no essential use then they should be removed from society. As at the start of the Snowdrop Campaign, I kept the other families informed about GCN's proposals.

But guns just wouldn't go away. One afternoon in late April, as I stood by the children's graves at Dunblane Cemetery, I was horrified to hear the sound of rapid gunfire from the local Whiteston rifle range, one of the ranges where Thomas Hamilton had practised. How could anyone think it appropriate to be using the range again less than two months after the shootings at the school? The next day, a Sunday morning, they were still shooting. I couldn't stand it and returned home in distress. We discussed the matter at a Thursday meeting. I spoke to the Support Centre co-ordinator Colin Findlay and he contacted the Army, the owners of the range. He got little reassurance. An Army timetable indicated heavy use of the range. During an eight-day period in June, for example, it would be used from 9 a.m. to 5 p.m. for seven of those days. Michael Forsyth had told us to contact him if anything was bothering us and so I wrote to the Scottish Office. The matter was passed on to the Ministry of Defence. We dealt with all of this as quietly as possible. The press only became aware of the situation when it was raised at a Stirling Council meeting in late May.

The Army agreed to suspend the use of the range until the Cullen Inquiry was over, but in July I received a letter from Defence Secretary Michael Portillo that didn't hold out any long-term hope. Whiteston was regarded as a valuable facility. I replied on 5 August setting out how we felt about the impossible choice we were being given – either to visit the cemetery only at times when the guns weren't firing, times determined by the Army, or to visit the graves when we needed to, with the constant risk of hearing gunfire. Fortunately no other correspondence was necessary. On the day the Cullen Report was published, Michael Forsyth informed us that the Defence Secretary had agreed that the range would be closed, the only appropriate outcome.

The families agonised over ways to express a strong collective view on guns for inclusion in our final submission to the Public Inquiry. Consensus was proving difficult to achieve. There were those, like myself, who thought that it would be impossible to argue against the vocational use of rifles and shotguns, and that it would be pragmatic to focus on a ban on handguns. This was a clear message and one that was being echoed throughout the country. Others argued that, as all guns are dangerous, it is not logical to restrict the prohibition to handguns: all guns should be banned and if there were ever an opportunity to articulate this, it was at the Cullen Inquiry, an opportunity to be seized.

On occasions our meetings became heated. We were tired, emotional people trying to get to grips with a subject about which we'd known little three months earlier. The victims' families numbered over sixty people, and it was no surprise that consensus was difficult to achieve. We formed small working parties to try to resolve the impasse. Eventually, because of the underlying togetherness within the group and after a passionate speech from one parent, the difficulty was circumvented. Our primary submission would be that all guns should be banned, but that if this were rejected, we would seek as an urgent and minimum step the immediate banning of the civilian use of handguns. Our counsel Colin Campbell would make the case supporting a total ban in his final submission to Cullen. He would highlight the dangerousness of handguns and the fact that the vast majority of these were used only for a pastime, target shooting.

The families were about to take a more active role in the gun-control campaign. The Dunblane Snowdrop campaigners came to our meetings to give us progress reports and to explain what would be happening when the petition was handed in to Parliament. This was arranged for Wednesday, 3 July, during a week's adjournment in the Cullen Inquiry. The campaign had been given assistance from a number of people and organisations. These included Ann Pearston's MP, Martin O'Neill, and others in the Labour Party; Alex Salmond and the Scottish National Party; the Scottish Office; and the *Sunday Times*.

An unexpected late addition to the itinerary was a morning meeting with Diana, Princess of Wales, at Kensington Palace. Diana had wanted to visit Dunblane after the massacre and apparently had been stopped by the Queen. Some of us were concerned that the meeting might not be in our best interests and that the gun-control message could get diluted by potential stories of the Princess of Wales comforting the Dunblane families. The publicity war between Diana and the Prince of Wales made this a strong possibility. Indeed, even as we waited at Edinburgh Airport for the early morning shuttle to London, we saw copies of the *Daily Record* reporting our forthcoming meeting with Diana; someone had leaked the news. A group of us decided not to meet her and stepped off the coach on its way from Heathrow Airport to Kensington Palace. We waited for the others in The Red Lion pub in Whitehall. Those who saw Diana told us how genuinely caring she was and I'll admit that as time went on I began to think I may have misjudged the situation.

Our itinerary at Westminster was similar to the one we'd followed with the *Sunday Mail* petition. We met with senior politicians inside the Palace of Westminster and over lunch at the Scottish Office. There was a photo call outside St Stephen's Gate, a large group of victims' families and campaigners standing behind a wall of about thirty boxes containing more than 705,000 signatures. The petition was handed over to Parliament and there were formal photographs with Home Secretary Michael Howard. In the House of Commons, however, the petition was upstaged by John Major's announcement that the Stone of Destiny was going to be returned to Scotland.

The gun lobby claimed, with no justification, that the petition overestimated the number of those in favour of a handgun ban. They said, for example, that children had been coerced into signing it. In fact the petition probably gave an underestimate of the support. Not everyone had been able to get petition forms in time and signatures were still received long after the official hand-in to Parliament.

It had been a long and arduous day, but more than worthwhile for the publicity it had generated. None of the families had yet spoken to the press, a policy maintained throughout the Inquiry. Peter Watson spoke on our behalf on matters relating to the Inquiry; the Snowdrop Campaigners spoke about the petition. But we didn't want the British public to think that there was nothing more to do now that the petition had been handed in. To keep up the momentum we wanted to tell the public exactly how the dangers of gun ownership relate to real people, real victims and real survivors. A lot of us were getting prepared to do the talking.

A week before the Inquiry finished I had to consult Peter Watson at his Glasgow office. At the meeting he encouraged me to consider talking to the media. GCN's launch was imminent and it would make sense to publicise this in interviews. Even so, I wasn't sure. Next day I heard that BBC2's *Newsnight* wanted me to appear on a programme to be screened on the evening the Inquiry finished. I didn't need any reassurance about *Newsnight*, a serious news programme with an excellent reputation. What I needed to think through was how much of myself I was prepared to give away in an interview. Not only would I need to articulate the case against handgun ownership, but I would also have to talk about the personal damage inflicted by the gunman's actions. I scribbled down everything and anything I could think of, trying to gauge how much of my soul I could bare. By the time I talked things over with the *Newsnight* team I'd convinced myself I was ready to reveal something of my personal life with Sophie. I agreed to the interview.

On the Sunday evening I found myself sitting in my living-room talking to Krishnan Guru-Murthy about what life had been like when Sophie was alive. I described the skill it had taken and the pleasure it had given me to bring her up. My contempt for the shooters' claims that they should be allowed to keep their guns because of the skill and pleasure involved in shooting would have been crystal clear from my comments. My interview was juxtaposed with re-enactments of parts of the Cullen Inquiry. These concentrated on the evidence of Paul Hughes and Anne Anderson and on Douglas McMurdo's lack of action.

The *Newsnight* interview was the first of many for television and newspapers during a very busy fortnight. On the penultimate day of the Inquiry, I spoke to BBC's *Reporting Scotland* and STV's *Scotland Today* in the car park of the Albert Hall. John Crozier, whose daughter Emma had been killed, gave a powerful interview to ITN. Some of the other parents gave an impromptu press conference that was shown on all news bulletins. As well as questions about Dunblane, we were asked our thoughts on an incident in the West Midlands in which a number of nursery children and their teacher, Lisa Potts, had been attacked by a man with a machete. It was a terrible incident and our sympathy went out to all those affected. Thankfully no one had been killed, and we all thought the same: if the attacker had been carrying a gun instead of a machete, lives would almost certainly have been lost. Many of the following Sunday's papers carried interviews with victims' parents. Britain could now read about the effect of Hamilton's outrage on the people most directly affected.

My interviews had a lot of impact. As an appendix to a list of top 100 TV moments that it published in 1999, *The Observer* added some other key moments from the history of television. Included was this comment from a viewer: 'A *Newsnight* interview with a grieving father. It was extremely poignant and overwhelming evidence against guns.' Many people at home and abroad saw that interview. It was screened in America and Canada and was shown in Australia during a time when their new gun-control measures were coming up against stiff opposition. Two members of the Australian gun-control movement, Fran and Michael, saw it at their home in Sydney. As a result they decided to try to meet me, at that time a complete stranger, when they visited Britain the following month. From that first meeting a very special friendship has developed.

Two weeks after the visit to Westminster with the Snowdrop Campaign, I had to go back for GCN's launch on 16 July. GCN was set up with a committee of seven, and four of us – Gill Marshall-Andrews, Tony Hill, Ian Taylor and myself – spoke to a packed committee-room. We explained why we'd set up the organisation, what its aims would be and why individually we'd become involved in a campaign for tighter gun control. I'd decided what to say while travelling down on the train the day before. I explained how Sophie had been killed with a lawfully held pistol by a man who practised with his deadly weapons over and over again at Home Office-approved gun clubs. I complained about lax attitudes and poor legislation: 'For all our sakes, no more guns and no more worship of guns. Please support the Gun Control Network.'

Ann Pearston was invited to speak to show that there would be close links between Snowdrop's petition campaign and GCN's longer-term objectives. Charles Coull, a close friend of the Ross family, and a man with experience of using firearms from his days in the Army, had joined the Snowdrop Campaign and had become an eloquent spokesman. He agreed to join GCN, strengthening the ties between the two groups.

Parliamentarians from all the major parties attended the launch. Tory backbencher Robert Hughes had to put up with some tough questioning from a Hungerford relative who blamed the Conservatives for the continuing gun culture. Bob Hughes became a good ally, one of the few Tories prepared to support a total handgun ban. After the launch I gave interviews on College Green and had my first experience of giving a live interview, on ITN's lunchtime news. I was later told that Julia Somerville of ITN had said that interviewing a Dunblane parent was one of her most memorable experiences. It had been a very effective launch and the next day's headlines emphasised that it had involved both Dunblane and Hungerford families. In the following weeks I received masses of letters in support of GCN.

The gun lobby realised that the situation was different from the one they'd encountered post-Hungerford. This time the public and politicians were getting to hear the arguments in favour of gun control and the shooters' case for maintaining the status quo would be scrutinised as never before. No longer would the perceived importance of their pastime be sufficient reason to avoid changes.

However, the shooters had been presented with an ideal opportunity to promote their cause in the Home Affairs Committee Fifth Report. The Committee consists of eleven backbench MPs: in 1996 there were six Tory and five Labour members, appointed to examine, among other things, expenditure, administration and policy of the Home Office and associated public bodies. In April 1996, in spite of the forthcoming Cullen Inquiry, it had decided to consider the possession of handguns. It must have been clear to its members that Lord Cullen would also be considering this, but they ploughed on regardless. One of the five minority Labour MPs, Chris Mullen, attempted to have the work suspended, but to no avail. The Conservative majority, including chair Sir Ivan Lawrence, seemed determined to pre-empt Lord Cullen's report.

The Committee called for oral evidence, taken as early as 8 May, only from the police, four members of the gun lobby (including two shooting MPs) under the umbrella of the British Shooting Sports Council (BSSC) and Home Office minister David Maclean. Although there was written evidence from a variety of sources, most references in the Report are to evidence from gun enthusiasts. In most cases these were dealt with and accepted uncritically. Much of the Report reads like a wish list for shooters – hardly surprising, as the Committee's special adviser was Colin Greenwood, a prominent and often outspoken gun expert who vigorously defends gun ownership. The Committee saw the BSSC's claims about the expansion of the sport, worryingly described as a 'vast explosion' in legal gun use, to be a good reason not to place any further restrictions. Research work from more independent academics was rubbished because others – gun enthusiasts whose subjectivity on the matter should have prompted extreme caution – had said so.

The Report threw out all suggestions for tighter controls over shooting. In particular it ruled out a total ban, or indeed any type of ban, on handguns. Select committee reports are usually agreed unanimously, demonstrating a cross-party consensus. This report, however, had the support of only six committee members, the Conservatives. The five Labour members voted against it and in favour of one prepared by Chris Mullen recommending a handgun ban and an extension of regulations over shotguns and air weapons.

There was a ferocious outcry in the media, the story making the headlines twice – once in late July, when the split in the Committee was first leaked, and then again on 1 August when the Report was finally published. The tabloids were particularly vociferous in their attacks on the Tory MPs. One of these MPs, Walter Sweeney, was quoted as saying that they had 'not been unduly influenced by the gun lobby'. An unbiased reader of the Report would have found this difficult to believe.

We had been told repeatedly that the political parties would not decide their positions until they'd had an opportunity to read Lord Cullen's report. To the acute embarrassment of the Government, its own backbenchers on the Home Affairs Select Committee had effectively produced a blueprint for no change. Gun legislation could no longer be claimed to command cross-party consensus. Although disgusted at the attitude of Sir Ivan Lawrence and his cronies, we recognised that the publication of the Report had actually worked in favour of the gun-control campaign, and allowed us to seize on the political dimensions of the debate. Home Secretary Michael Howard maintained that it was dreadful that the massacre should have become a political football, but those like ourselves who were pushing for change wanted nothing less than an open debate, and if this made the issue of gun control political then so be it.

The media always wanted to hear the views of the parents, not only on heavyweight matters such as the Home Affairs Committee Report, but on any incident that involved guns. Sometimes this was simply to give a personal touch to their stories, which didn't add much to the key arguments. Weariness soon overcame many of us and we couldn't respond to all the requests for interviews. When I got back from the GCN launch I couldn't do any more, even though I'd talked to the media for less than a fortnight. After that initial burst of activity I tried to be more selective. There would be no point in repeating the same comments in one programme or newspaper article after another. Apart from agreeing to participate in BBC TV's *Panorama*, I spoke mostly to overseas television companies. People abroad wanted to know why and how we'd been able to challenge the gun laws in Britain, and as the campaign gained success we were often approached and asked what advice we might give to other countries where gun control had become an issue.

Of all the interviews I gave that summer, the one that gave me particular satisfaction was with Ed Vulliamy. I'd read many of Ed's *Guardian* reports from the former Yugoslavia and before we met he'd sent me copies of these and his book, *Seasons in Hell*, about his experiences of the war in Bosnia. Ed was intrigued that I'd been in Slovenia on the day that Yugoslavia began to fall apart. We also shared a love of the great American outdoors. I told him of my travels with Sophie, our trip to the Grand Canyon and of another journey through the Painted Desert to Monument Valley in Arizona. He said he'd always looked forward to being able to drive his young daughter, then two, through the Arizona desert. I'd taken my opportunity in March 1995.

After he visited Dunblane Cemetery with me, Ed described it as the saddest place on earth, a sobering observation from a journalist who had seen so much atrocity. Ed gave me a lift to Glasgow on the day we met, and we talked throughout the journey. Remembering so much of what I'd said, he crafted our conversation into a memorable article, a powerful piece supporting the call for gun control. I still read his acutely observed stories from America in *The Observer*. Since we met in 1996 he's had to report from the USA on too many other gun outrages as the epidemic of school massacres has spread. He once wrote telling me that when he visited the site of one of these in Jonesboro, Arkansas, I had been on his shoulder all the time. 'Dunblane was everywhere.'

In September 1996 I was invited to contribute to the *Times Higher Educational Supplement* and wrote my first gun-control article. I set out my arguments in favour of a handgun ban and dismissed the handgun owners' claimed 'right' to shoot with their guns. The shooting lobby couldn't pass the buck for the macho images that appeared in gun magazines and for the shooting disciplines that involved targets in a human form. I wrote that 'there are alternative pastimes which can provide the pleasure that they seek. There are no alternative lives for our children.'

We knew where we were with the gun lobby, but there were hidden dangers among our 'sympathisers'. In late April 1996 a man calling himself Tobias Elias Bernstein approached the Charity Commissioners and registered an organisation called SAGE (Stop All Guns in Europe) Community and Charitable Services. He had two organisations, one for campaigning and one for educational purposes. Almost immediately press advertisements appeared, bearing a registered charity number and appealing for credit card subscriptions from putative members. Some people who'd met him were suspicious of his motives, but these were gut feelings. One parent, anxious to enrol anyone supportive to our campaign, contacted Bernstein and invited him to meet the families. Those who met him in Dunblane had differing opinions. Some were impressed by his sincerity as he described how his family had been killed in a road accident in the USA and that he wanted to use a family trust to support a worthy cause. Others appeared to have the same gut feeling I'd heard about already.

In August Bernstein prepared press advertisements that included, with the permission of the parents concerned, photographs of some of the Dunblane children. I wish I'd voiced my suspicions more, because on 21 August the Glasgow *Evening Times* revealed Bernstein as a convicted fraudster (real name William Bernson) who had been in gaol on 13 March. There'd been no car accident in the USA: he'd made that up. Within days of his exposure he'd left the country. I have no idea how sincerely he held anti-gun views – that no longer mattered – but there is little doubt that he was quite prepared to string along as many people as possible in his scheme, including parents whose children had been murdered. When the press caught up with Bernson in the Netherlands, he said 'I don't know what these people of Dunblane are upset about. I'm out £15,500.' He was last reported to be in a Mexican gaol in May 1997. This was an embarrassment for the Charity Commission, who have assured me that they did learn lessons from the incident. SAGE is still listed on their register, however. At our next parents' meeting we talked about what had happened and agreed we would be stronger from the experience. We must be sure of the people with whom we worked, especially now that the publication of the Cullen Report was only a few weeks away.

Around this time, August 1996, I had another occasion to wonder about the ability of some police officers to behave sympathetically towards the public. I'd offered to help Breakthrough Breast Cancer with a street collection in Stirling. The organiser, Gordon, gave me a certificate that indicated I was collecting on behalf of Breakthrough. For two hours I stood outside the Thistle Centre, feeling somewhat vulnerable, but knowing I was doing this in a good cause. I was then approached by two police officers who demanded to see my certificate, which I showed them. One of them informed me, with a rudeness that suggested he'd prejudged the situation, that it wasn't the right certificate. I told him that I was only one of a number of collectors and that Gordon would presumably have the certificate they wished to see. I was marched along the street to find Gordon.

Unlike me, Gordon was an experienced collector who, on no previous occasion or in any other location, had been asked to produce his council permit, the certificate the police wanted to see. Not thinking he'd need it in Stirling, he'd left it at home. Instead of checking a list of permitted collections that they undoubtedly had in their patrol car, the police officers started to threaten us with arrest. It seemed more satisfying for them to act tough and bully a couple of widowers than make a simple check. Had I not been in such a fragile state I would have been better able to stand up for myself. Gordon was forced to go to the Council offices and get another permit, during which time the collection was suspended and valuable contributions from the public lost. Immediately afterwards I wrote a letter of complaint to police headquarters. No doubt my personal situation helped speed the response and prompted a sort of apology. But the episode reinforced my view that some police officers behave as if they have no capacity to understand the public they're dealing with.

After the criticism of the Home Affairs Committee Report, the shooters began to complain that they were being scapegoated and vilified, made to take the blame for something they hadn't done. They missed the point: no one was saying they were guilty of murder or advocating that they should be convicted for wanting to own guns. They were being asked to stand back and look again at their 'sport' in the wider context of public safety and civil society. The danger that they, not necessarily individually but certainly collectively, posed by allowing these weapons to be easily available couldn't be ignored. New laws prohibiting handguns wouldn't make them criminals, though stubborn non-compliance of any new act of Parliament would.

During September the gun enthusiasts adopted more aggressive and offensive tactics. As if wanting to show that it could flex its muscles, The

British Association for Shooting and Conservation advised its members in one of its magazines not to co-operate with the police if stricter spot checks were introduced. Members were said to be 'under tremendous and unwarranted pressure'. The National Pistol Association (NPA) attacked John Crozier, accusing him of a hidden agenda. It is difficult to conceive what hidden agenda the father of a murdered child might have, save trying to ensure that a massacre doesn't happen again, and that was hardly a hidden agenda. The attack led to the resignation of the organisation's President, Conservative MP and former athlete Sebastian Coe.

The episode prompted some local reaction including an ill-advised editorial in the *Stirling Observer* from Alan Rennie, who described John Crozier as 'stirrer-in-chief'. In response Ann Pearston quoted Thumper, a character from the Disney film, *Bambi*: 'If you can't say anything nice, don't say anything at all.' In the next issue Alan Rennie tried to backtrack, but there was no doubt that he'd used his editorial to reflect a view, held by some in the Dunblane community, that it was unseemly for the families to be campaigning.

The publication of the Home Affairs Committee Report had pulled the debate firmly into the political arena. Stirling Council reacted by unanimously passing a motion, moved by Dunblane West's councillor Arthur Ironside and seconded by his Labour colleague Gillie Thomson:

> This Council notes that the large majority of the law-abiding public are opposed to the possession, ownership or carrying of handguns.
>
> We as a Council see no reason why Parliament should accept the recommendation of the Select Committee and believe that the Prime Minister should reject it out of hand. Council calls on the Government to bring forward legislation to outlaw the ownership, possession or carrying of handguns and to introduce salutary prison sentences for any breach.
>
> The Council reserves its position on the ownership, possession or carrying of any other firearm until after the Cullen Inquiry publishes its findings.

It was carried unanimously on 19 September and was later supported by COSLA, the organisation that represents all of Scotland's local authorities.

Differences between the political parties became more apparent. The Scottish National Party had been strong in their support of a handgun ban. Indeed their leader Alex Salmond had been one of the first politicians to speak in its favour earlier in the year. Labour appeared to be toughening its stance on gun control and there seemed a strong possibility that they would eventually agree with their backbenchers on the Home Affairs Committee and favour a total handgun ban. The Liberal Democrats seemed to be edging in that direction, too.

The Party Conference season began in late September. At the Liberal Democrat Conference the delegates narrowly voted against a total ban after a heated debate. The most significant event, however, was at the Labour Party Conference, following an invitation to the Snowdrop campaigners to contribute to their debate on gun control. I would like to have gone to Blackpool, where other GCN members were lobbying, but I couldn't leave Dunblane, not at the beginning of October. It should have been Sophie's sixth birthday on the Second. The debate took place the following day and I watched it live on television.

The stated aim of the debate's motion (composite 31) was 'putting the needs of victims before gun users'. Dr Richard Simpson, one of our Bridge of Allan GPs, was the first to speak in favour of tighter gun controls, his arguments strengthened by his experience as both a GP and a psychiatrist. He was followed by Michael McMahon, from the Hamilton North and Bellshill Constituency Labour Party, who moved an emergency resolution calling for a ban on handguns. He described how his fellow CLP member Thomas McIntyre had been murdered in 1990 by a gun club member using a legally held handgun. Waiting on the platform were the Snowdrop Campaign's Ann Pearston and Rosemary Hunter. Ann was called to speak by the Chair, Diana Judah, and greeted by sustained applause. The speech that followed was incredible. Into thirteen minutes of calm, controlled delivery, Ann spelled out all the facts of what happened in the gym – the carnage, the number of bullets fired, the number of children dead and injured, the number of adults dead and injured – and combined this with a powerful argument against the continued private use of handguns. An emotional speech, of course, and it certainly moved the delegates, but it never lost sight of the argument, that without Hamilton's legal ownership of handguns the massacre would never have happened. Ann concluded, as she'd told me she would, by referring to Sophie's birthday:

> Yesterday was a little girl's birthday. There were flowers and there were candles but there was no one to blow them out. That little girl was Sophie North. Compromise cost her her life.

When Ann finished the delegates rose to give her and Rosemary a standing ovation, as heartfelt and deserved as for any of their Party's leaders. Gerald Kaufmann, a veteran of over forty years of Labour Conferences, said of Ann's speech that there had 'never been anything like it'.

Shadow Scottish Secretary George Robertson followed Ann to the podium. He added his personal thoughts and his recollections of the massacre. Ann's message 'will not be forgotten', he promised. Shadow Home Secretary Jack Straw had already signalled movement in Labour's position. They were about to support a total handgun ban. The Conservatives criticised Labour for having politicised the debate. Their party chairman Brian Mawhinney claimed that Labour had broken ranks by inviting Ann Pearston to address its conference. Some accused Labour of making political capital out of the deaths of the children. However, as Joan McAlpine wrote in one of her sensitive and well-judged commentaries in the *Sunday Times*, 'Personal tragedy is political too'.

Ann Pearston had the agreement of the families to speak and was expressing views that were widely held throughout the country. Any party that ignored this fact was badly out of touch. Ann would happily have spoken at the Conservative Party Conference the following week, but she was not invited. Indeed the Tories avoided any formal debate on the issue. John Major was asked about gun control at one of his informal question-and-answer sessions, but apart from that the governing party steered clear of the debate. In a timely observation on the Tories'

Bournemouth conference, *The Guardian* revealed that at least seven members of the current Conservative Cabinet were shooters.

Everyone was now anxiously awaiting the publication of Lord Cullen's Report, although some in Dunblane already feared the return of the media to the town. The families viewed the media differently. To maintain pressure on the Government, a group of us met at the Croziers' house the weekend before the Cullen Report was released and gave interviews to the major television companies. Sitting in the conservatory, we talked passionately about our fears for public safety if the Government didn't take this opportunity to clamp down on gun ownership. Although our comments would not alter the contents of the Report, there was a possibility that we might be able to influence the discussions that were about to go on around the Cabinet table.

In another weekend interview Ann Pearston had hinted that, if the Government failed to introduce a complete handgun ban, one of the campaigners might be prepared to stand against Michael Forsyth in the next general election, no more than six months away. If unresolved, gun control could be an important issue. Ann's suggestion was, I believe, only made in passing, and she withdrew it shortly afterwards. Scottish Conservative MP Phil Gallie described it as 'blackmail'. However, everyone has a democratic right to stand for election. It is surely up to the electorate to determine whether a person and their policies are acceptable or not. 'Threatening' to stand in an election was certainly more acceptable than the blackmail of threatening to keep weapons illegally, which at the time is what some of the gun owners were proposing, should the law change.

I agreed to write another article. Entitled 'Don't put sport before safety', the piece in the *Sunday Times* of 13 October included the following comments:

> To have been allowed to have guns Hamilton and Ryan had both been deemed to be fit persons. Are there other such 'fit persons' with access to handguns? The answer is surely 'Yes'. It is impossible for doctors and psychologists to predict whether someone seeking permission to use guns will be safe for a short

period let alone for the full five years now allowed by the licensing procedure. Given the incidence of mental illness and behavioural disorders among the general public we have to assume that a significant number of handgun users will at some stage have problems which would make them unfit for gun ownership and thus put the general public at risk.

If we can't guarantee the behaviour of handgun users there is only one course of action and that is to ban their weapons, and to ban them completely.

It is too late for Sophie and the other victims of Dunblane, but it is not too late for everyone else.

As if to remind us how complacent things could get, that same week a class at Dunblane Primary School, which included children who had survived in the gym, were given worksheets depicting familiar objects and asked to fill in the missing letter in the names. One of the pictures was of a gun, the children asked to complete the word 'G_N'. Veronica Hutchison, whose daughter Amy had been badly injured by bullets from Hamilton's gun, told the newspapers how Amy had refused to colour in the picture. The workbooks were withdrawn from local primary schools. Guns should never be treated as if they are everyday objects.

In the following days there was plenty of press speculation about the contents of the Cullen Report and the Government's likely response. The gun lobby claimed they'd been told, off the record, that there would be no handgun ban. However, if all the press reports are to be believed, Michael Forsyth was working hard within the Cabinet to push for as tough a policy as possible. After months of waiting, we were about to learn the outcome of the Public Inquiry and find out whether all the pain had been worth while.

CHAPTER SEVEN

# Lord Cullen Reports: A Shortfall in Justice

## October 1996–February 1998

'What we have before us is exactly that, a compromise – a compromise that is not acceptable to the people of this country'

(LES MORTON)

For commentators like *The Observer*'s Euan Ferguson, Michael Forsyth's immediate announcement of a public inquiry into the shootings at Dunblane Primary School meant an 'early retreat behind the sanctity of a forthcoming inquiry'. Public inquiries are official responses to controversial cases, usually conducted by a senior judge. The judge takes written and oral evidence, which can be supported by investigations by a police inquiry team. In *Hillsborough: The Truth*, Phil Scraton describes how public inquiries are 'surrounded by allegations and counter-allegations, raising serious matters of responsibility and liability'. Although 'interested parties' hire legal teams 'to safeguard their interests and where possible, deflect liability', public inquiries are not part of criminal or civil proceedings. The term 'public inquiry' suggests a process that is open and provides the public, not least the victims and their families, with the opportunity to see that lessons are going to be learnt. 'Seen as "independent" and commissioned by the government', writes Phil Scraton, 'the presumption is that their recommendations will be treated with respect and implemented.' Yet the priorities of a public inquiry are not established by the public, since these decisions lie with the government minister involved in setting up its terms of reference. The outcome may therefore reflect more on the needs of an establishment, fearful perhaps of too many changes, rather than on those of a public in search of truth and justice.

Lord Cullen's Report on the shootings at Dunblane Primary School was published later than expected, on Wednesday, 16 October. It had been completed in late September and there has been speculation that its release was delayed by a fractured government's uncertainty about its response. The Government denied this, saying that it had not received the Report until the party conferences were over, just two days before its publication.

Cullen made a total of twenty-eight recommendations, twenty-three on 'the certification system relating to section 1 firearms [handguns and rifles]', one on 'the availability of section 1 firearms' and two each on 'school security' and 'the vetting and supervision of adults working with children and young people'. Of the twenty-three on firearm certification, seven related to the police, eight to the matter of good reason for ownership of guns, seven to the applicant's suitability and one to decisions and appeals. The Government accepted all of these in full except number twenty-four, the one on the availability of section 1 firearms. Cullen had recommended that a restriction, rather than a ban, be placed on the availability of self-loading pistols and revolvers of any calibre held by individuals for target shooting. The preferred restriction would be by disablement for which two possible methods were suggested. Lord Cullen added that if such a system were not adopted then the guns should be restricted by banning their possession by individual owners.

The Government adopted a different position, proposing a ban on the possession of all high-calibre handguns (above .22). The .22s would remain legal, though they would have to be kept at gun clubs under the most stringent secure conditions. This went further than Cullen's recommendation, but it was a compromise that would satisfy no one, a fudge somewhat typical of the last days of the Major government. The gun lobby was opposed to any ban on handguns, and those of us favouring tighter gun control saw no reason to distinguish between the dangerousness of handguns on the basis of calibre. It had been a compromise between cabinet ministers. Dunblane's MP Michael Forsyth was widely reported to have pushed his colleagues into accepting some kind of handgun ban, almost certainly against the wishes of Home Secretary Michael Howard.

In line with Cullen's recommendations, the Government would also introduce measures for stricter school security and checks on adults working with children.

The Dunblane families had access to Cullen's report some hours before it became available to the general public, an arrangement made possible with special permission from the Speaker of the House of Commons. We met in a room at the Dunblane Hydro hotel where each family was given an envelope containing a copy of the Report and a letter from Michael Forsyth outlining the Government's response. Needless to say, the reaction among the families was that both the Report and the Government's response fell short of our wishes. Some gave up reading the Report in disgust. I thought it was important to try to get to grips with Cullen's arguments as quickly as possible. To justify our position, we would not only need to say that we disagreed with his conclusions, but also explain our reasons. My initial impression was that Cullen had failed to look at the broad picture of firearms use. The Report had little to say about firearms in general. Although there was considerable detail about the measures that might make it more difficult to misuse those handguns used in target shooting, Cullen had not looked in detail at the wider question of whether target shooting of any kind was an acceptable pastime. His recommendations were based on the assumption that it was.

If we'd had the time, as we rapidly read through the Report, we could have gauged the reaction of politicians. A television set had been set up in the room so that we could watch the live broadcast from Westminster where Michael Forsyth and Michael Howard were presenting Cullen's findings and the Government's proposals to the House of Commons.

Cullen was praised for his meticulous analysis of events. Michael Forsyth had allowed DCC Douglas McMurdo sight of relevant paragraphs of the Report in advance. McMurdo subsequently announced that he couldn't continue as Assistant Inspector of Constabulary and was also leaving Central Scotland Police.

The families had agreed to give a press conference. We prepared a statement that Les Morton was going to read on our behalf. Les had spoken on the gun issue for the first time at a dinner that followed the Dunblane Rugby International at Murrayfield in August. His would be a strong voice for gun control over the next few months. We transferred to a room packed with cameras, microphones and reporters and sat or stood behind a long table, backed by a banner that read 'Dunblane Against Guns'. Les read our statement, the gist of which was that what the British public was being offered was an unacceptable compromise. It was powerful stuff and nobody could doubt the strength of the families' views, nor our sense of frustration.

The journalists were also keen to hear from Ann Pearston who had joined us at the press conference. She and the other Snowdrop campaigners had been putting in a massive amount of work on the anti-handgun campaign and the strain was beginning to tell. As she laid down the gauntlet to the Government, Ann showed some raw emotion, reflecting how we all felt. Saying the Government had not gone far enough, she added, 'We voted you in and, if you don't ban them all, we can vote you back out.' This, most probably, was what pro-gun MP John Carlisle was referring to when he accused the Dunblane parents of being 'hysterical'. Like some others who supported continued gun ownership he believed he could dismiss forceful criticism as hysteria.

The press conference began an exhausting evening for me. Immediately afterwards I gave live interviews on radio for BBC Scotland's *News Drive* and on TV for BBC 1's *Six o'Clock News*, BBC News 24 and BBC Scotland's *Reporting Scotland*. I rushed back to the Hydro for another live interview, this time with Jon Snow for *Channel Four News*. Most of the interviewers were asking me why the families weren't satisfied with the Government's response. They pointed out that there was at least to be a partial ban. Our response over the coming months would be consistent: if the politicians were able to recognise how dangerous handguns are, and can go this far, then why can't they take that one additional step and ban all handguns? On two occasions I was followed by interviews with Home Secretary Michael Howard. Asked to comment on what I'd said, he oozed sympathy, but went on to defend his government's compromise position as a fair one. Among his arguments for retaining .22s was their use in Olympic competition and the fact that a total ban would drive handguns underground. So much for his faith in the 'law-abiding' shooters.

In his report Lord Cullen had many critical words about the police, though he made no recommendations on accountability. At the time most people, including the families, were concentrating their thoughts on firearms. The families needed time to reflect on what had been said about the police. I'd been asked to say something about them in an interview I'd done the day before for BBC 2's *Newsnight* and with hindsight I know I wasn't critical enough. I still hoped that the police would accept responsibility for some of the things that had happened.

The interview formed part of a programme to be broadcast after the Report had been released. Like other programmes, *Newsnight* focused mostly on the gun debate. The programme centred around a live studio discussion chaired by Jeremy Paxman. Les Morton and David Scott represented the parents, with Ann Pearston adding another gun-control voice. The rest of the panel was made up of representatives of the shooters, the police and those with interests in school security and youth organisations. It was an unsatisfactory debate, as the television debates often were. The interests of balance and the limited time never allowed enough scope for arguments to be developed. David, assuming he'd been invited to discuss the handgun ban, was surprised to find himself probed about his views on school security. The issues of school security and child supervision were not nearly so contentious and might have been left for another occasion.

The programme makers had asked me to go through to the BBC's Glasgow studios to record some additional comments after reading Cullen's report. Before the live discussion started I met David and Les in the hospitality room. We were soon joined by other contributors, including the gun enthusiasts. I was exhausted and when I overheard one of these men begin to complain about how much he would lose if the Government's proposals went ahead. I couldn't take any more. I walked out of the room, I couldn't face having to listen to the bleeding hearts of the shooters who had no perspective on loss. When the programme was over, Les, David and I left immediately. Some may have thought that getting the promise of even a partial ban on handguns would satisfy us and make us feel better. I hadn't become involved in campaigning to make me feel better: I did it because fate had determined that I had a role in the debate, and for better or worse I would continue to campaign for more gun control.

The next day's papers viewed the Government's response to Cullen as fair, but many also saw it as a missed opportunity. Some papers, including the *Daily Mirror*, *The Sun* and the *Sunday Mail*, launched new campaigns for a total ban on handguns. *Scotland on Sunday* had asked me to write a piece for the following weekend and over the next two days I tried to gather my thoughts. Even though it was written hastily, I am proud of what I was able to put into words during that difficult week. Here are parts of 'A father's story':

> It is still difficult for me to take in that this report, by one of Scotland's foremost judges, concerns a massacre in which my daughter Sophie was murdered. Reading it was very hard, often traumatic. Anyone would have felt the same as it describes an event of unbelievable horror. Too often I had to attempt the impossible and forget my personal involvement so that I could continue working my way through its 174 pages. Was the report worth waiting for? Did it in any way justify the agony that I and the other families had put ourselves through when we sat and listened to the evidence in the Albert Halls in Stirling? Did it compensate in any little way for having the deaths of our loved ones so much in the public eye?
>
> Much of the report is an account of what happened on 13th March and details of Hamilton's dealings with various organisations, including the police and local authorities. I had

heard it all as evidence at the Inquiry. Nevertheless it is appropriate that these things have been recorded and analysed and, of course, that criticisms have been made and blame attached. Without a doubt a considerable amount of criticism is necessary.

I welcome the acknowledgement by Lord Cullen that it was entirely unacceptable that we were left waiting in the school for so long before being given any significant information about the fate of our children. Lessons must be learnt. The lesson here is that you do not treat anyone, and especially someone who is going to hear the worst possible news about their child or wife, as an inconvenience. That's how we were made to feel on 13th March and the police have been rightly criticised for this. I await my apology from them.

The sections dealing with Hamilton document a seemingly endless series of complaints, concerns and gut feelings about the man and his activities. My constant thought when reading this was, 'This man could have been stopped, this man should have been stopped, I need never have had to know who he was, Sophie should still be here.' Systems, and individuals within those systems, failed too often.

. . . One of the most telling passages in the report is within paragraph 6.69. Lord Cullen concludes that what Hamilton did was planned in advance but that it was planned in the context of the continuing availability of his own firearms and ammunition. In other words without his legally held guns and bullets he wouldn't have perpetrated a mass shooting.

It was the combination of a man and his legally held guns that resulted in my daughter's death and the 16 other unnecessary deaths, and so I feel very let down by what Lord Cullen has to say about firearms availability. He details how the existing practices can be changed but fails to address the bigger question of whether the so-called sport of shooting has any place in our society. Many of the 23 recommendations for changes in the certification system would not be needed if the guns they relate to are banned. The bottom line of our submission to Lord Cullen was that handguns should become prohibited weapons. The contents of the report more than justify that position.

The Government has amended Lord Cullen's recommendation 24, which concerns the availability of firearms. It concedes that some handguns, those over .22 calibre, must be banned. Access to other handguns would still be allowed but restricted to secure premises. A distinction is being made between handguns of different calibre, but those which would still be allowed are also deadly weapons. Many homicides in the USA are caused by them: Bobby Kennedy was killed and Ronald Reagan injured by them. Last year the Israeli Prime Minister Yitzhak Rabin was assassinated with a .22. Dunblane's gym teacher Eileen Harrild has testified that the calibre of the gun Hamilton was pointing at her was the last thought in her mind.

The justification for not banning .22 handguns is that they are used in the Olympic Games. This does not sanitise them, they can still be used to kill. Indeed it is time to ask why the Olympic Games, a Celebration of Life, should include a sport which involves instruments of death.

In their response to Lord Cullen the Government set out stringent security standards for gun clubs which will be necessary to protect the public. The standards set are a clear acknowledgement of the dangerousness of .22 handguns. By allowing their continued use the Government is compromising public safety. Lord Cullen's report sets out the reasons why handguns are dangerous, and since public safety comes way ahead of the privilege of anyone to shoot, there is only one logical conclusion – they should all be banned.

Over the next few days the other parents and I will be urging the Government to think again and go that one step further and agree to ban all handguns. If they do not we shall be asking MPs to think very carefully about what this issue involves; it is about the right of every member of the public to be safe versus the privilege of a minority who wish to pursue a pastime. If the

Government do not change their minds, yet believe, as I do, that this really is an issue which transcends party politics then they should allow a free vote.

Since 13th March we have had to deal with the glare of publicity, gun lobby hostility, general insensitivity including the recent accusation of hysteria from John Carlisle MP and, more surprisingly, criticism of our involvement in campaigning from my own local councillor, Ann Dickson. However, the families of the victims of the Dunblane massacre have drawn strength from one another and from the knowledge that we are pursuing something with which millions of our fellow citizens agree. We believe that the majority of the people in Great Britain have been with us in our campaign for tighter gun control and the banning of handguns. We will continue to make our reasoned arguments with dignity. If we are not qualified to speak on gun control and describe the effects on our lives of the misuse of guns, then who is . . . ?

In providing a mechanism for collecting together many of the facts relating to Hamilton – his activities with boys' clubs and his ownership of guns – details of firearms legislation and use, and, albeit to a less satisfactory extent, what had happened on the day of the massacre, the Public Inquiry could be seen as worthwhile. But was this the only way in which the Government and others could get to grips with the problems involved? My overall experience of the Dunblane Inquiry suggests that the public's expectations were not met. The limitations of Cullen's recommendations had made it necessary for the campaign against handguns to continue. There were other issues as well, to which I shall return after I've described the culmination of that campaign.

A number of people questioned whether a judge should have been asked to make recommendations on the Government's firearms policy. David Mellor was one who had argued that, in this respect, the Inquiry was unnecessary. He suggested that cross-party talks could have provided a mechanism for introducing tighter gun laws. Although he hadn't recommended the banning of any category of firearm, Lord

Cullen had recognised, in the precise, measured language that characterises the Report, that this was a political area:

> At the same time I am very conscious that proposals such as a ban on the possession of a certain type of firearm raise questions which are peculiarly within the province of the Government and Parliament to decide.

The Government's response had advanced the gun-control debate. Prohibiting guns was now politically acceptable. The Firearms (Amendment) Bill was published within two weeks, on 1 November. The Government faced problems with parts of the Bill from two quarters. The opposition were anxious to assist the Government with most of its proposals, but as these parties and some government backbenchers supported a total ban on handguns, there was a good possibility that a successful amendment could be tabled to achieve this. On the other hand, there was a core, almost entirely made up of die-hard Conservative MPs, who were opposed to any significant changes to the gun laws. In order to keep its own supporters in line, especially those in the House of Lords, the Government announced that there would be no free vote on the Bill: all members of their party were supposed to vote for the partial ban. The opposition parties were prepared to make this a matter for the conscience of individual members and would not whip their MPs through the lobby.

At first the gun lobby reacted as if the Cullen Report had vindicated their position, but only because Cullen hadn't recommended a ban. Had the Government stuck with Cullen's recommendations, however, I suspect that the shooters would have protested about every single safety measure that was introduced. As our counsel at the Inquiry had put it, the shooters 'do themselves few favours by their apparent reluctance to countenance material change'. They no doubt felt they'd been caught on the back foot and had misjudged the strength of feeling at Westminster and throughout the country. The Government was accused of 'using the tragedy for political gain'.

The shooters began to mobilise and lobby in the hope that they could scupper the legislation. Many joined a new organisation, the Sportsman's Association of Great Britain, which distributed leaflets. Their circulation included Dunblane. A bereaved father found one lying on the bar of a local pub and was offended to see those of us who were campaigning described as 'a noisy hysterical group of social terrorists currently leading all the political parties by their noses'. Unable to comprehend how so many of Britain's population could be against their 'sport', the leaflet claimed:

> While the anti campaign relied largely upon children signing something they may not have understood, we are comprised of paid members and have far greater credibility in the eyes of prospective members of parliament.

The Sportsman's Association began to organise rallies, which received little sympathy from the media. Newspapers published photographs of largely male crowds, belligerently protesting about a loss of 'rights'. One line they continued to push was that if an applicant for a firearm certificate were properly checked by the police (they claimed that this had not happened in the case of Thomas Hamilton), the 'good' would be distinguished from the 'bad'. The 'good' could then be trusted with any number of lethal weapons. They didn't consider, or wish to consider the possibility that one of the 'good' could at some point in his gun-owning life become 'bad'.

In the pursuit of their case against banning handguns the gun lobby began to overstep the mark and their spokesmen dealt out misinformation. An example of this, frequently repeated by the Sportsman's Association's Michael Yardley, was that Hamilton had possessed illegal weapons. There was never a single shred of evidence for this. Hamilton had held all his weapons legally. But to further its argument that there wasn't a problem with legal weapons, the gun lobby invented a scenario in which Hamilton also had access to illegal guns, placing him outside their 'law-abiding' fraternity. Some shooters tried to gain sympathy by fabricating and promoting a story that Hamilton had committed his atrocity in part to destroy the sport of shooting. At the launch of the Sportsman's Association, Michael Yardley claimed 'Thomas Hamilton wanted to inflict this pain on the community of Dunblane and he wanted to destroy the sport of shooting', while another spokesman, Albie Fox, said: 'That man was out to get two lots of people – the parents of Dunblane and revenge on the shooting community that had rejected him.'

It's been claimed that Callander Rifle and Pistol Club prevented Hamilton from joining in March 1996. This is not true. His membership application didn't proceed because Hamilton had failed to provide a supporting reference. This was hardly rejection. Indeed it seems that, rather than ostracise him, his fellow shooters remained tolerant of his idiosyncratic shooting style.

The Shooters' Rights Association literature went way over the top, claiming that 'the spectre of the most pernicious and evil legislation to stalk Europe since the reign of the Third Reich is about to be forced upon the British nation'.

Another tactic sometimes used by groups who lack public support is to attempt to blacken the names of those with opposing views. The gun lobby was quite happy to invent stories about gun-control campaigners, inviting its supporters to provide information that might help. Following on from the attack on Dunblane parent John Crozier, shooters increasingly targeted the Snowdrop Campaign's Ann Pearston, branding her as a 'a non-poll-tax-paying IRA sympathiser' – a person whom none of us who knew her would have recognised. The accusations were completely false. Ann had received at least two death threats and was subject to abuse on the Internet. There were nasty phone calls to other campaigners. One man, angered that a friend was no longer able to shoot, was gaoled in 1998 for malicious calls made to Snowdrop's Rosemary Hunter. In 1997 a gun club member began to send hoax bombs and other obnoxious mail to both the Labour Party and Gun Control Network as a display of his displeasure. He, too, was gaoled for his activities. All of this was from the group who call themselves the most 'decent and law-abiding' in the country and ask us to trust them with lethal weapons.

In another bid to gain the public's support, gun enthusiasts talked about standing at the next general election, then a few months away.

Elizabeth Law, wife of the secretary of the Shooters' Rights Association, announced that she would stand in Michael Forsyth's Stirling constituency. The press vilified her for suggesting that the electorate in Dunblane would wish to see a gun lobby candidate on the ballot paper. She backed down.

We gun-control advocates embarked on a vigorous lobbying campaign of our own. Our aims were well known, motivated by a wish that no one else should have to suffer through a gun massacre. We wanted to ensure not only that the Government's proposed ban on high calibre pistols and revolvers became law, but that it was extended to include all smaller-calibre handguns. We knew that at least four Conservative MPs were prepared to defy their party whip and vote for a total ban. If just a handful more of their Tory colleagues could be persuaded, there was every chance that an appropriate amendment could be passed. At the end of October Les Morton and I went to Westminster on the first of a number of visits by Dunblane family members. Our first day involved various meetings with sympathetic MPs to assess the situation and make sure they were aware of what we were trying to achieve. We spoke to the Liberal Democrat leadership, the Scottish and Welsh Nationalist MPs and Shadow Cabinet members George Robertson and Jack Straw. Robert Hughes, one of the Conservatives who wanted a total ban, sent out an invitation to all his fellow Tory backbenchers to meet us. Only two others attended, Hugh Dykes and Terry Dicks, both of whom were already supportive. We had spoken on the phone to the fourth Tory MP who wanted a total ban, David Mellor, and he gave us his full support. It was frustrating that so few Conservatives were prepared to come and listen to our case. The media continued to play an important role and Les and I agreed to do a few interviews for television and radio, emphasising our view that the Government should be prepared to take that one step more and ban all handguns.

Next day we learned from an article in *The Scotsman* that two Scottish Conservative MPs, Phil Gallie and Bill Walker, had been offended that we hadn't spoken with them. Gallie said, 'I'm amazed that they did not seek a meeting with us'. Walker added, arrogantly:

It was an unfortunate error not to see us. In a democracy, it is a big mistake not to see as many people as possible and an even bigger mistake when they belong to the Government party.

They would have been welcome to come to Robert Hughes's meeting. Realising that this provided an opportunity to meet another constituency within the Tory ranks, Les and I flew back to London the next week to meet them. It was not a good meeting. Neither one of them showed any willingness to deviate from his party's position. Bill Walker in particular took an obstinate and superior line, assuming that the argument that 'we are legislators who have to see the broader picture' justified everything he said. He told us how Hamilton could have killed the children with an articulated lorry! Of the two of us, Les is considered to be the one more prepared to argue, the more easily riled by inappropriate comment. He thought that having me alongside him would be a calming influence. That day we reversed roles, I was more than a little irritated by the patronising attitude that greeted us. It became apparent that this meeting was more about the two men being seen to have listened to us rather than their actually listening to us. The next day we read about our meeting in the papers. Neither Les nor I discussed the meeting with the press, but the MPs wanted to let everyone know that they had taken the trouble to see us.

In the event of any ban, gun owners were to receive compensation for the weapons that were handed in. The amount the Government needed to pay out was inflated by the gun lobby, as was the risk of job losses, with claims that thousands of people would be thrown out of work. The public were supposed to sympathise with the shooters, but few did. Compensation was also an issue among MPs and in order to minimise the opposition to the Bill, particularly among its own backbenchers, the Government upped the amount of money available. By mid-November £100 million had been allowed (some gun lobbyists had set the amount required as high as £1.5 billion). Nevertheless this wasn't enough for some. The second reading of the Bill was opposed in the House of Commons by thirty-one Conservatives and three Labour MPs. They either wanted more concessions or were intransigently opposed to a handgun ban. The Government did, however, get the Bill through this stage. The crucial vote was to come.

The Bill had reached the stage at which amendments could be proposed. Robert Hughes, one of the Tories in favour of a total handgun ban, put forward an amendment whose effect would be to include all lower-calibre handguns among the prohibited weapons. The vote on this amendment was expected to be close. All the opposition parties were in favour, as were the four Tory rebels, and it appeared that everything hinged on the votes of the Northern Ireland MPs, especially those from the Unionist parties.

A large group of Dunblane family members and Snowdrop campaigners visited Westminster during the week before the vote, talking to as many politicians as possible. Those who were there found it difficult to gauge how the Unionist MPs would vote. What was their attitude to a Bill that did not apply to Northern Ireland where the gun laws were different, a place that had seen so much carnage over the past decades? Would they vote for a Bill that would signal a safer environment, or would everything be dictated by party politics and the need for the Unionists to remain supportive of the Government, perhaps in return for favours during the Peace Process? The division on Bob Hughes's amendment took place on the evening of Monday, 18 November. It was defeated by twenty-five votes, a much larger majority than expected, boosted by the surprise absence of a number of Labour and Liberal Democrat MPs. None of the Ulster Unionists supported the amendment, but it would have lost anyway. The opportunity to get a total handgun ban in this parliamentary session had gone.

Two weeks after the vote on 29 November the full details of Gwen Mayor's murder were heard at a fatal accident inquiry at Stirling Sheriff Court. She was shot six times. One bullet literally 'blew out' her brains. Sheriff Principal John Maguire recorded that the cause of death was gunshot wounds as a result of being 'repeatedly and unlawfully shot' by Thomas Hamilton. He rejected a plea made on behalf of Rod Mayor to find that her death might have been prevented by a complete ban on handguns.

Having succeeded with its Bill in the Commons, the Government now faced the hurdle of that establishment bastion, the House of Lords. Here opposition to any changes to the gun laws was even fiercer than in the Commons and certainly more entrenched. There were various attempts by pro-gun peers to block the bill. The Government had failed in its promise to have legislation in place by Christmas.

The speeches from the Lords debates on the Firearms (Amendment) Bill, like all parliamentary business, can be read in Hansard. They provide an informative insight into the extent to which some peers were prepared to go to couch their self-interest in the pseudo-logic of the gun lobby. Lord Gisborough, for example, on 16 December delivered the familiar 'sympathy but' line: 'My Lords, we all sympathise with the parents of Dunblane. But, however distraught people may be, emotion makes bad law.' Impartial observers had, however, commented that much of the emotion was coming from the gun owners who appeared distraught because the public had woken up to the fact that their hobby compromised public safety.

Lord Gisborough also used another familiar argument, that the shooters were being made scapegoats: 'Thus British shooters have all been found guilty for another man's crime on the premise that if one goes berserk, the others must follow.' No one was saying they were guilty of a crime, nor that all others would follow. Having just one of their number 'go berserk' was enough. Why, when their sport served no other purpose but to provide these men with entertainment, should the public be exposed to any more risk? Arguments that society was safer without guns were met with anachronistic references to the nobility of the sport of shooting and the assertion, yet again, that the guns' owners were the most law-abiding group.

There were many establishment figures who supported this position. Douglas Hurd, the Home Secretary who oversaw the inadequate Government response to the Hungerford massacre, was a typical example, saying that the proposed legislation wouldn't work and that the 1988 legislation had, in contrast, been measured. Short-measured would be a more apt description, its shortcomings allowing another lone gunman to carry out mass slaughter using legal weapons. Just before Christmas 1996, Prince Philip, a keen shooter himself, blundered into the debate. During an interview on BBC Radio 5 Live, he dismissed calls for bans on guns. With a crassness that has characterised some of his other public pronouncements, he asked whether, if someone had gone into the gym and attacked the children with a cricket bat, we would now be asking for a ban on cricket bats? Of course we wouldn't, he suggested, so why a ban on guns? His argument was preposterous, denying the reality of what had happened, trivialising the fact that it would have been impossible to create carnage on the scale at Dunblane with anything other than a gun. It denied the fact that Hamilton wanted to kill himself and could only do so with a gun. It denied the fact that, in contrast to a cricket bat or a golf club (another piece of sports equipment the gun lobby have claimed to be more dangerous than a gun), a firearm is designed to kill, its sporting use a secondary one.

The gun lobby spokesmen rushed to use Prince Philip's 'common-sense' support as evidence that the anti-handgun campaign was misguided. Hurriedly organised opinion polls seemed to indicate public support for his views until the polls were shown to be rigged. The families agreed that only one of us would comment and David Scott provided a balanced and calm response – no hysteria, no publicity seeking and no points scoring.

The campaigning continued throughout the winter. Both Snowdrop and GCN were receiving *pro bono* help from advertising agencies prepared to put their resources behind the campaign. On 18 November the Sportsman's Association had placed a full-page advertisement in *The Scotsman*. In the interests of balance, and aware that the Snowdrop Campaign had few resources, the newspaper printed without charge a Snowdrop advertisement prepared by Edinburgh agency 1576. In January GCN launched two posters, produced by Saatchi and Saatchi. One depicted a grave with the caption, 'A .22 handgun makes the same size hole as a magnum'; the other carried a photograph of Senator Robert Kennedy, assassinated with a bullet from a .22 handgun in 1968, with the words, 'If a .22 handgun is less deadly why can't he be less dead?' The posters had the 'distinction' of prompting ninety-four complaints to the Advertising Standards Agency, the largest number received for any advertisement in 1997. Gun owners had been urged to write and complain, but the regulator rejected the complaints. GCN was also receiving help in setting up its own web site. The organisation had limited resources and little opportunity to communicate with its supporters except through media events such as the poster launch and web site.

The most controversial piece of campaign publicity was a forty-second long cinema advertisement produced for the Snowdrop Campaign in March 1997 by Delaney Fletcher Bozell. It depicted a .22 handgun being fired at a target in a shooting range. Sean Connery provided the voice over:

> It is said that a total ban on handguns, including .22s, would take away innocent pleasure from thousands of people. Is that more – or less – pleasure than watching your child grow up?

The advertisement closed with the words 'REMEMBER DUNBLANE, BAN ALL HANDGUNS' on the screen. There were worries, even among the gun-control campaigners, that using the 'voice of James Bond' to promote gun control was sending out an ambiguous message and might even be hypocritical. The gun lobby had a knee-jerk reaction, sending in complaints even before the advertisement had been screened. Fifty-six objections were received in total. The Advertising Standards Agency again rejected the complaints. The gun lobby was never interested in having the dangers posed by its sport out in the open: it was too used to cosy relationships with some sympathetic politicians away from the public gaze.

The shooters continued their rallies. The numbers who attended increased from a few hundred at first to several thousand by January, but never demonstrated the mass support claimed by their spokesmen. The placards they carried frequently reflected their blinkered perspectives. At one rally held in London on 11 January a man is seen holding the sign '16 pensioners die in Scotland from E. coli. Will MPs ban butchers shops?' They were increasingly portraying themselves as a persecuted minority, having failed to convince anyone outside their ranks that theirs really was a sport that millions enjoyed. The press remained largely unsympathetic and reported on worrying aspects of the gun culture such as gun club members getting into trouble with the law or a flourishing children's gun club in North Devon where children, some as young as eight, could learn how to handle and shoot a range of handguns and rifles. A *Guardian* article concluded with evidence that ten-year-olds had already learnt the gun lobby mantra, 'It's not guns that are the problem, it's people'.

During late January and early February, the Government suffered two defeats on the Firearms (Amendment) Bill in the House of Lords, largely at the hands of unelected hereditary peers. One of these defeats was on proposals for compensation, the other on the ban on holding .22 pistols at home. There was a danger that, with parliamentary time running out as the General Election approached, the Bill would be destroyed. Then on 11 February the peers agreed to give the Bill a 'free run'. 'GUN BAN IN THREE WEEKS' proclaimed the *Daily Record*.

In a Commons vote on 18 February the Government reversed the Lords amendment on keeping pistols at home, though not without massive opposition from its own supporters. Ninety Tory backbenchers, including six former ministers, voted against the Government. The double standards of the 'law-abiding' shooters were reflected in this comment from Jill Knight MP, one of the Tory members of the Home Affairs Select Committee: 'Whatever happens some people are going to break the law'. She said it as if this blackmail were a good reason for not passing the law. By 20 February the Bill had passed through the Lords, and on 27 February it received the Royal Assent and became law. Andrew Billen of *The Observer* described the outcome as 'perhaps the most effective petitioning by the British of their Parliament in history'. Large-calibre handguns like the one that had killed Sophie were banned. On 5 March it was confirmed that Hamilton's guns had been destroyed.

To us this success was a partial one. The campaigning continued. With a general election in the offing, eventually announced for 1 May, it was important that gun control remained on the political agenda. GCN wrote to all prospective parliamentary candidates asking whether they would support stricter gun control, including a total ban on handguns. The vast majority of the respondents indicated their support. While the opposition candidates were willing to participate, only a meagre twenty-seven of the nearly four hundred replies came from prospective Tory candidates – the majority of whom thought that enough, or even too much, had been done already. GCN announced the results at a Westminster press conference on 24 April to which politicians from all the parties had been invited. Alun Michael, then shadow Home Affairs minister, gave an assurance that if elected Labour would keep its promise and introduce legislation to remove .22s from private ownership. This was supported by Kay Ulrich for the SNP and Diana Maddox for the Liberal Democrats. No Conservative politician turned up. GCN's message was that anyone concerned about gun safety should not vote Conservative.

The press conference marked the formal end of the Snowdrop Campaign. The campaign had extended well beyond the initial achievement of presenting its petition to parliament, and had been an essential part of the lobbying process ever since. There had, however, been some disagreement among the campaigners about when to wind things up. Ann Pearston, the best-known face of the anti-handgun campaign, wanted to see things through until the election, but the others wanted to bow out earlier. Some of their differences spilled over into unfortunate articles in the press. With GCN able to take over the administrative work of the Snowdrop Campaign and the prospect of a new government more sympathetic to tough gun control, it was now appropriate for Snowdrop to wind up. Ann announced this at the press conference. Their achievement had been magnificent.

On 1 May 1997 the country voted to go in a New direction, Tony Blair's Labour government being elected with a huge majority. Nowhere was the outgoing Government's demise more complete than in Scotland where, on a 7.75 per cent swing, its party lost every seat. In the Stirling constituency, Michael Forsyth was defeated by Labour's Anne McGuire by 6,411 votes. Like her party, Anne McGuire considered gun control to be a key issue in the election. In a personal pre-election message to the electors of Stirling, she'd written:

> Finally, on a personal note, I regard a total ban on handguns as unfinished business. Labour is committed to legislating for a ban.

I will work tirelessly until these weapons are removed from our communities.

Michael Forsyth was a gracious loser. He had done a lot for us since the massacre and had fought hard in Cabinet to give the Conservatives' firearms bill the strength it had. We wanted it to be stronger, but he undoubtedly did as much as he could to persuade his colleagues of the case for gun control. He was later knighted and more recently given a peerage, to become Lord Forsyth of Drumlean. Shadow Scottish Secretary George Robertson was re-elected and appointed to Tony Blair's cabinet as Defence Secretary. After two years he left the cabinet to become Secretary General of NATO and was also elevated to a peerage, becoming Lord Robertson of Port Ellen. The post of Scottish Secretary was given to Donald Dewar who, after devolution in 1999, became Scotland's First Minister.

It is impossible for me to judge whether policies on gun control influenced voting preferences. It is likely that what had happened in the campaign since March 1996 had, at the very least, contributed to a general impression that the Tories were out of touch with the wishes of the electorate, dithering between placating their gun-loving supporters and satisfying the wishes of the majority of the British public. Michael Yardley, standing as a 'Sportsman's Alliance – Anyone but Mellor' candidate, opposed David Mellor in Putney. Only ninety voters put their X against his name. That was thirty-one more than the tally gained by Raymond Saint of 'Country Field and Shooting Sports' in Michael Howard's Folkestone and Hythe constituency. The gun enthusiasts had certainly lost. The Labour Party manifesto had stated that 'in the wake of Dunblane and Hungerford, it is clear that only the strictest firearms laws can provide maximum safety' and, with a Labour government in power, a total handgun ban was on its way.

On 6 May the press confirmed that the new government would introduce a bill banning all remaining handguns and there would be a free vote. Next day I received a phone message from George Robertson to say that Tony Blair wanted to contact me. The Prime Minister wished to invite the Dunblane families to 10 Downing Street so that he could tell us himself about the new Firearms (Amendment) Bill. On 12 May we met Tony Blair, Donald Dewar and Anne McGuire in the Cabinet Room. In relaxed surroundings we were given a tour of 10 Downing Street in the company of Cherie Blair, who was seeing some of the rooms herself for the first time. The atmosphere was so different from that tense day in April 1996 when a smaller group of us had first met John Major. Our meetings with the then Labour Opposition had always been more constructive and now they were in power they proved that they had listened. Tony Blair later said that his Government had 'paid its debt to the people of Dunblane'. What the Government did was to put in place a measure that would make the whole population safer. It was an issue beyond Dunblane.

The new Bill was first debated in early June. Although Parliament's gun enthusiasts (especially those in the House of Lords) tried to water it down again with amendments and bluster, voting in favour of exemptions for the disabled and for international competition, the Bill eventually became law on 27 November. The final step in the legislative process drew little attention from the press, who'd assumed it had been a foregone conclusion since Labour came to power. As the Bill passed through Parliament, the hand-in of higher-calibre handguns was completed between 1 July and 30 September 1997. The .22 handguns became prohibited weapons on 1 February 1998 and their hand-in was completed by the end of that month. The guns were destroyed and the gun owners compensated, though not entirely to their satisfaction. The compensation process and the shooters' dissatisfaction rumble on.

Looking back on the anti-handgun campaign, it is now possible to appreciate that it was achieved in a remarkably short time. When he was asked about the six most remarkable events he had witnessed in his lifetime, veteran Labour MP Tony Benn included Dunblane. He did so because of the public response it had provoked and what that response had led to. I can't assess precisely how much of that success was due to the campaigning and how much to other circumstances, including a volatile political situation and the Dunblane connections of both the Scottish Secretary and his Shadow; but it seems doubtful whether so much would have been achieved without our willingness to take a public stance against guns.

The handgun ban was achieved in spite of, not because of, what Lord Cullen had recommended. The whole process of the Inquiry fell short of what I, as a victim's father, might have expected. Above all, it should be an opportunity for truth and justice. In this context, truth means the accurate presentation of all the facts that are relevant to the events; justice equates with accountability.

It is too easy for those who become entangled in the aftermath of a tragedy to find themselves marginalised. This becomes amplified when an inquiry, purportedly set up in the public interest, goes ahead without adequate explanation. At first we were told nothing about the Cullen Inquiry or legal representation, and had to take our own steps to remedy this. Had we not started meeting together and been able to resolve the matter as a group, it is doubtful whether we would have had time to prepare. We had to appoint our lawyer before we knew whether our legal costs would be covered, a risk we had to take. Although our costs were paid out of the public purse, we weren't to know that at the time. We were given certain assurances about the Inquiry – the meeting with Lord Cullen and the Crown Office lawyers was useful in this respect – yet it provided an expectation of openness that wasn't fulfilled. We received lists of witnesses and other documentation from our lawyers, but had no clear overview of the strategy being adopted by the Crown who were, it has to be said, there to represent the public interest. The key participants in the Inquiry were lawyers and its procedures and language, so familiar to them, were an alien world to many of the families. Our own lawyers could help up to a point, but lack of familiarity doesn't aid full participation in a supposedly public process. At the very least, shouldn't it be possible for a government agency to produce a booklet on public inquiries that explains in lay terms what is going on?

The Public Inquiry began within weeks of the massacre, giving many of the parties little time to prepare. The victims' families were still in a distressed state, and it has only been possible to appreciate some of its shortcomings retrospectively. This raises a general question. Public inquiries are set up as 'one-offs', a single opportunity to establish and resolve all the problems. They have a 'once-and-for-all' quality and when they're over it is convenient for some parties to conclude that everything is done and dusted. Is this not expecting far too much from the process and those involved? It diminishes the possibility of considering evidence that may come to light later. Should there not be a process that allows a review, if necessary, after a set period? An area of concern from the Dunblane Inquiry is the many rumours about Hamilton's links with police that have surfaced since the Inquiry. There are suspicions about the motives of those who have circulated them, yet there are very serious implications if any of these rumours are true. Can they be investigated appropriately once an inquiry is over? Lord Ewing suggested to me that it should have been possible for Cullen to present a detailed but interim report. After a suitable period of time, which would have allowed a little healing, then the Inquiry could have been re-opened and other issues raised, especially ones on which new information had become available.

The collection of evidence for the Dunblane Inquiry and the selection of witnesses were undertaken by the Crown Office and the local Procurator Fiscal. Through these processes they provided the parameters of the Inquiry, which meant that they determined its course, no doubt in consultation with Lord Cullen. It would be impossible to consider calling every possible witness – no one would benefit from such an open-ended Inquiry – and some limits have to be placed on the evidence that can be heard. The question then arises as to how the limits are determined and to what extent the selection process pushes the Inquiry in prescribed directions. Certainly not all the available evidence needs to be presented, and with some of it, such as details of the victims' injuries, I can see why it was unnecessary and also inappropriate to present it in public. Nevertheless I remain puzzled, at the very least, about some omissions, which no doubt reflect differences in the details wanted by Cullen and the details that I thought I needed to know.

First of all, there is the link between Dunblane and Thomas Hamilton. Hamilton's actions were well planned, and we can assume that he deliberately targeted Dunblane. He seemed particularly drawn to the town and had involvement with a number of its residents. Yet the evidence on this was selective. An inquiry aimed at getting to the heart of a problem should have explored all the links. We know, for example, from what Lord Ewing told the House of Lords, that Hamilton's problems with Dunblane went as far back as 1971. Lord Ewing regarded this old Dunblane connection to be important and concluded his speech by saying:

> My reason for explaining all this is that in my humble opinion, honestly and sincerely expressed – I am in a minority of one – the Dunblane situation has been completely misread. Hamilton's perceived problems were all based in Dunblane. They were not firearms problems at all. They were perceived as related to the town; everything that happened to Hamilton had the Dunblane background to it.

The events he described never came to light at the Inquiry. Lord Ewing has told me that he didn't volunteer to give evidence because he didn't want to distress the families further, but nothing he revealed would have caused us any greater upset. He was also concerned that it all happened a long time ago and, given the close proximity of the Inquiry to the massacre, might be seen as a diversion. But this wasn't thought to be the case with Hamilton's dealings with the Scouts in 1974. Was it the town of Dunblane itself that didn't want to be distressed? A number of townsfolk, including its councillors, had known Thomas Hamilton more recently – they'd told the media as much – but none of them was called to give evidence to shed more light on Hamilton's relationship with the town. Was this omission simply an example of over-sensitivity towards the feelings of a community or individuals within it? I'd like to know more.

There are other gaps. Neither of the chief constables who were in charge of Central Scotland Police during the period of Hamilton's gun licensing was called to the stand. Wilson's absence was even more surprising, given the criticism of his force's operations on the day of the shootings. I've also been puzzled why there was no evidence from the university secretary who'd typed Hamilton's letters. She knew what he was writing and might have provided valuable insights into his state of mind; others who'd seen him less often were questioned on this. While not suggesting there are sinister reasons behind this, I'm questioning whether, with such omissions, an Inquiry can be considered thorough. Another question mark hangs over Cullen's willingness to state in his Report that he was 'satisfied that he [Hamilton] was not a member of the masons', when very little evidence was presented on this. Discrepancies and deficiencies in the gun registration process were not fully explored, giving the gun lobby an opportunity to criticise the conduct of the Inquiry.

If establishing the truth is one of the prime aims of a public inquiry then no avenues should be closed off. At the Dunblane Inquiry constraints were in place that prevented a complete exploration of the role of the Scottish prosecution service, the Procurators Fiscal. They had failed to proceed with charges against Hamilton on a number of occasions and although they are independent of the police service, the Procurators' actions did affect how Central Scotland Police behaved. The lack of charges was cited by DCC McMurdo as one of the reasons why he felt unable to revoke Hamilton's firearms licence. At the Inquiry the Crown argued that the Procurators Fiscal should not be subjected to in-depth questioning, an argument which was accepted by Lord Cullen. Regardless of whether anything new would have been revealed, the barriers placed by the legal system on the questioning of 'their own' suggest that public inquiries can never be entirely open. The establishment boat can never be rocked too much.

This was also exemplified by the Inquiry's attitude towards the discrepancies between the police and the parents in the times we were told of our children's deaths. Had there been a ruthless determination to establish the truth and to demonstrate that only the whole truth was acceptable, then those police officers who'd distorted the times ought to have been recalled to the stand to explain the discrepancy.

And what about that expectation of justice, the matter of accountability? Cullen's report sets out a number of recommendations, none of which deal with accountability for the events surrounding the massacre. It has been too easy for those criticised in the Report to duck their responsibilities by saying that the matter has already been dealt with by Cullen. Lord Cullen did not and could not implement his own recommendations, and neither was he responsible for following up any of the criticisms he made. The response required those parties criticised, whether individuals or the management of organisations, to act honourably and consider their positions. As I'll detail in the following chapter, no one from Central Scotland Police accepted responsibility. Both 'watchdogs', Her Majesty's Inspectorate of Constabulary and the local Joint Police Board, were content to say afterwards that matters had been dealt with by Lord Cullen. They hadn't been. In this respect the outcome of the Public Inquiry was far from satisfactory.

Is there a way of remedying this? One way would be to give the responsibility of following up a public inquiry to a body, independent of the Government, with the power to enforce a response from the agencies involved. Some issues will always be within the political arena and a response to them dependent on legislative changes that only Parliament can deliver. But there are other issues that slip through the net, especially if they are the subject of criticism within the report, rather than matters dealt with as specific recommendations. An independent body might ensure that parties criticised do not 'get away with it' by failing to respond.

When Lord Cullen agreed in October 1999 to take charge of the Inquiry into the rail crash at Ladbroke Grove, most commentators again remarked on the suitability of his appointment. Some, however, raised doubts. Dave Whyte, an academic who has taken a keen interest in the Piper Alpha Inquiry, wrote:

Amidst the intense debate and controversy that has followed the Ladbroke Grove disaster there is one point that appears to have united all of the protagonists: Lord Cullen is unquestionably the best choice to head the public inquiry. But the appointment of Lord Cullen actually tells us more about the role expected of him than it does about his ability to produce a report that will prevent another Ladbroke Grove. Cullen was chosen to head this inquiry because he is a safe bet. He is pragmatic, business-friendly and, most of all, he can be trusted not to unsettle the agenda that has already been set by government.

At the Piper Alpha inquiry he accepted, almost exclusively, the evidence of the oil companies on the shape of the safety regime that was to regulate them. The trade unions represented at the inquiry opposed any moves toward self-regulation.

The oil companies had good reason to be pleased with the outcome of the Cullen inquiry into Piper Alpha. The trade unions, the Piper Alpha families association and the public had good reason to believe the inquiry was a stitch-up.

The inquiry, by limiting the state's response to the problem of oil rig safety to the structure of the regulatory regimen, also allowed attention to be deflected away from the possibility of a criminal prosecution.

If some pieces of evidence carry more weight than others because the inquiry is working towards some pre-determined agenda, whether this is damage limitation or finding a scapegoat, the process provides little more than a piece of theatre. In the case of the Dunblane Inquiry, it allowed establishment figures and the institutions, from the gun lobby to the police, from politicians to administrators, the opportunity to act out how exasperated they had been with Hamilton and how they weren't really to blame for anything that happened. Cullen appeared unwilling to challenge the overall status quo. The police could be criticised, but there'd be no specific recommendation for accountability. Gun safety could be tightened, but only in a way that would allow shooting to continue. With the door left ajar, it wouldn't be long before the shooters could push it wide open again.

When all is said and done the Cullen Report, the most public outcome of the Inquiry, represented the opinion of one man, albeit a fair and decent one, but nevertheless one man with an establishment perspective. Surely there is a case for having the opinions of more than one person contribute to such an important document?

We should be grateful that the aftermath of the Dunblane massacre provided one of those rare occasions when, in spite of the Inquiry's recommendations, politicians were willing to grasp the nettle and change things for the public good. It is surely time to have a detailed review of the make-up and role of public inquiries. A fundamental question to be asked will be: 'Which public do they serve?'

# CHAPTER EIGHT

# 'You Don't Know Police Procedures'

## March 1996 onwards

'If there is anything to apologise for, I will apologise to the families'
(CHIEF CONSTABLE WILLIAM WILSON, OCTOBER 1996)

There is no doubt that there were many questions to be answered by the police about their role before and after the Dunblane massacre. A few days before the opening of the Public Inquiry, a list of concerns was sent by our lawyers to James Taylor, the solicitor advocate who was representing Central Scotland Police. Falling into two main categories, our treatment on the day and the licensing of Hamilton, these were:

•Lack of information given to the parents on the day of the incident;
•Delay before parents were given information about their children;
•Social workers and others being given information regarding children before parents;
•General handling of the incident by the police – a senior police officer should have been present with the families at all times;
•The parents of the injured children not being informed immediately and allowed to accompany their children to hospital;
•Police handling of the press on the day of the incident;

• Some families receiving conflicting information from the police about injuries, which differed from that given by pathologists;
• Opinion that a review should be made of the granting of a Firearms Certificate to Thomas Hamilton.

The families and the public deserve full explanations, yet there were limitations on the mechanisms of accountability available. That this should be so, even after an event of the magnitude of the Dunblane massacre, not only reinforces the lack of accountability, but serves to entrench it.

In the immediate aftermath of the shootings I had mixed feelings about the police. I had been angry at the way we had been kept waiting in the staffroom, the constant unfulfilled promises of information in a few minutes, the lack of sensitivity shown in Insp. Ross's approach towards us and the absence of a senior officer prepared to talk to us. After my brief outburst immediately after I'd been told of Sophie's death, shock and numbness took over and it was impossible to be angry. The police had been doing a horrendous job on a terrible day. I understood that, though it wasn't long before the misgivings returned. Within days the police had attempted to block the release of my press statement and then two days later I learned from Isabel MacBeath about her visit from DCS Ogg. It still didn't sink in how controlling the police were attempting to be.

More doubts arose as the witness statements and summaries of evidence arrived, piecing together the long history of Central Scotland Police's dealings with Hamilton. These told of the dozens of police officers who had known him in their professional capacity and of some who had known him personally, getting discounts at his shop and spending time on his boat on Loch Lomond. Still there was a part of me prepared to give the police the benefit of the doubt. That changed abruptly during the first days at the Inquiry with the distortions and the attempts to change evidence. Henceforth I would be sceptical and suspicious of everything that senior officers of the force said or did.

The police wanted control, for in the aftermath of disasters whoever wins the struggle to define and control the situation decides how it is seen: their version of the situation effectively becomes *the* situation. The police response had, in my view, more to do with ensuring that they were seen to have done a 'good job' rather than establishing in full what went wrong and how things could be improved.

The Central Scotland Police force is one of the smallest among Scotland's eight forces. Because of its small size, its continued existence would be under threat in any reorganisation of the police in Scotland and its independence has always been jealously guarded. Covering an area of 1,000 square miles and with a population of some 273,000, it had 568 officers and 205 civilian members of staff in 1996. In response to a report on a review of Scottish policing in April 1998, Chief Constable William Wilson defended his force by stating that:

> Dunblane aside, we have shown that we can cope with any major incidents . . . As long as there is sufficient expertise at the top, smaller forces can cope with most situations.

There is no doubt that in many areas of policing the Central Scotland force does perform well – its clear-up rates are good, for example – but that certainly doesn't provide an excuse for allowing major shortcomings, including those relating to the Dunblane massacre, to be overlooked or brushed under the carpet.

William Wilson had been Central Scotland's Chief Constable since 1990. In his submission to Lord Cullen, he wrote, 'I welcome your Inquiry and my officers have worked hard to provide as much frank, open and honest evidence as we could for your consideration.' That, of course, was the very least that would be expected. Yet to deflect and minimise criticism of their operations, the officers within his force closed ranks and attempted to 'manage' the information that came out, setting the parameters of the debate. A Public Inquiry should have been able to shift the parameters away from those of the force and provide explanations for the shortcomings of the police. This was not going to be helped, however, by the fact that Central Scotland Police was to play a dual and perhaps incompatible role at the Inquiry. Not only would it have to answer for its responsibilities in the events surrounding the massacre, but it had also been entrusted to carry out much of the related investigation. With a vested interest in portraying the force in a good light, it is possible that police officers may also have found that organisational pressures, affecting future career prospects and working relationships, worked against a thorough exploration of the facts.

The public entrusts its police forces with considerable powers to undertake their various roles in law enforcement, and it is essential that the roles are undertaken in a way that benefits the society they serve. The events surrounding the Dunblane massacre argue that there is a tendency in the operation of power within police forces for too much emphasis to be placed on the maintenance of their own procedures and organisation at the expense of providing an adequate service to the public. This can lead to the subjugation of both their clients, the public, and the officers who make up the forces. In his report Lord Cullen made a number of serious criticisms of Central Scotland Police; but with the exception of Douglas McMurdo's grudging departure, there has been little demonstration that the Central Scotland force has been held to account.

I have already related the extent to which Thomas Hamilton was known to Central Scotland Police. He had been a thorn in their side for years. Many senior officers were more than familiar with the problems at his boys' clubs, they were aware that he had taken guns to a private house and they knew him as a serial complainer who was capable of throwing up smokescreens. Members of the public had, at various times, been told to leave matters in the hands of the police as they knew all about Thomas Hamilton. Central Scotland Police had even seen fit to advise the *Stirling Observer* not to publish material supplied by him. On more than one occasion they had unsuccessfully tried to bring charges against him. Yet throughout, the force had continued to renew his firearm certificate.

History has shown us that men who run amok with guns are, like Hamilton, often obsessed with how hard done by they've been. In his book, *The Jigsaw Man*, criminal psychologist Paul Britton has written:

> On a research level, we know what motivates people to murder so ways must be found to use this knowledge and to stop them in mid-

flight. The urgency of this was underlined by the dreadful shootings at Dunblane Primary School. Even in the small amount of material I have read relating to Thomas Hamilton, there were sufficient signs to have said, 'Let's keep firearms away from this chap'.

It didn't take a criminal psychologist to deduce this. A Central Scotland police officer, Paul Hughes, had reached the same conclusion and had informed his superiors in his memo of November 1991, a memo on which DCC McMurdo decided to take no action. He didn't even consider it necessary to refer directly back to Hughes. No matter how constrained by the law McMurdo thought he was in his need to undertake what he probably saw as an administrative task, he surely had a responsibility to follow up such a worrying report from one of his junior officers. Not to do so demonstrates an arrogant attitude that had put internal procedures above a duty of care to the public.

This was not the only instance where the procedures used by Central Scotland Police failed to take on board the legitimate concerns of junior officers who'd had direct contact with Thomas Hamilton. During the 1995 renewal process that allowed Hamilton's murder weapon to be held legally, PC Anne Anderson had also expressed reservations about him after visiting his flat. Her worries were dismissed by senior officers in the chain of command between her and McMurdo's rubber stamp.

Nobody's view of Thomas Hamilton could have gone uninfluenced by the events of 13 March. The tabloid press saw him simplistically as an evil loner. *Scotland on Sunday* journalists were more correct in saying he did not live in 'a void':

> He lived among us all. To write him off as an exception misses the point: exceptions are not born. They are made, by circumstance and experience, by the slow drip of alienation, isolation and paranoia . . . We must see beyond the convenient labels that describe Hamilton as a sick pervert and an evil psychopath.

The description provided by Central Scotland Police's lawyer at the

Inquiry went many stages further. According to James Taylor he was really an ordinary chap and what people were now saying about his odd behaviour could be put down to hindsight. Because he seemed ordinary the police would have had difficulty in recognising the danger in permitting his guns. This goes way beyond the bounds of credibility. Lord Cullen was not persuaded by Taylor's arguments. How many ordinary citizens come to the attention of the police as often as Thomas Hamilton? How many 'ordinary chaps' would prompt DCC McMurdo to write the following in a letter to the Scottish Office?

> Only a bitter and petty-minded individual like Thomas Hamilton could pervert such a relationship [between police officers and local Scouts] into something sleazy and dishonourable and imagine some undercurrent of corruption. I am sorry about the length of this letter but, as a comparatively recent beneficiary of Mr Hamilton's vindictive correspondence you should be aware of the background to almost four years of ever more irrational outpourings. Both I and the two chief constables have tried very hard to resolve the matter but, as always when trying to reason with a zealot, each time a point appears to have been settled he re-introduces it in another guise, adjusts the facts selectively to suit his ends and it all begins again.

Whatever the shortcomings of the law – and there were many – and the limitations of the firearms licensing procedures operated by Central Scotland Police – and again there were many – when it came to someone like Hamilton, McMurdo should have been able to shed the straitjacket he saw himself in and make some attempt to address the very real concerns of his junior officers. To hide, as he did, behind the unwillingness of the Procurators Fiscal to bring charges against Hamilton or the possibility that a Sheriff might overturn any decision to revoke Hamilton's licence on appeal suggests an adherence to procedures that gives insufficient thought to the implications of these for the safety of the public.

Lord Cullen made it clear enough what he thought of McMurdo's position, when referring to DS Hughes's memo:

Having heard, read and re-read the evidence I consider that these considerations called into question Thomas Hamilton's fitness to be entrusted with a firearm and that DCC McMurdo should have taken the opportunity of making further enquiries, and in particular in hearing what DS Hughes had to say.

A number of passages in McMurdo's evidence convinced Lord Cullen that, while McMurdo accepted he was exercising preventive police work, he had difficulty in envisaging cases in which a person could be shown to be 'unfitted' to be entrusted with a firearm where there was no previous conviction or pending court case:

> These and other passages seem to me to provide support for Mr Campbell's [Counsel for the victims' families] submission that he [McMurdo] adopted an unduly narrow approach in which he paid not much more than lip service to the idea that a person could be 'unfitted' in the absence of a conviction or pending criminal case. He undervalued the breadth of that expression.

Lord Cullen concluded, 'On balance I consider that there was a case for revocation of Thomas Hamilton's firearm certificate and that it should have been acted upon.' Douglas McMurdo departed on the day the Cullen Report was published. He continued to wear his procedural straitjacket, claiming that he still believed 'the decisions taken were the only ones open to him'. In their evidence, most senior members of the force had agreed with McMurdo's contention that Hamilton's problems were in no way linked to his firearm applications. They, too, had been locked into the procedures.

McMurdo's departure from the force has to be viewed as evidence of moral responsibility, yet as number two in the force the buck of moral responsibility shouldn't have stopped with him. McMurdo had been deputy to two chief constables, William Wilson and his predecessor Dr Ian Oliver, who at the time of the Dunblane massacre was Chief Constable of Grampian Police. Oliver knew a lot about firearms. He was one of the police representatives on the Firearms Consultative

Committee. He had also commented on the gun-control campaign and did not favour a handgun ban. Neither Oliver nor Wilson gave evidence on the stand at the Inquiry. The role of these two men as head of the force was never scrutinised directly. I've been told that Oliver had resisted changes to procedures that some experts consider would have prevented Hamilton's licence being granted. Wilson provided a submission to Lord Cullen, but only after almost all of the evidence had been heard. There was little attempt to assign responsibility for what had happened.

Strathclyde's DCC Richardson was asked by the Inquiry to look at the administration of firearms applications by Central Scotland Police. He concluded that in comparison to those used by other forces, including his own, the procedures left a lot to be desired. A particular problem with form RL3a had already been highlighted. This was the form completed by the investigating officer during a renewal or variation. In the 1980s the form consisted of six simple questions to be answered 'Yes' or 'No'. For example, the police officer was to indicate by 'Yes' or 'No' whether the applicant was suitable or not to hold a firearm certificate (question 1) or if he/she had or didn't have a good reason for requiring the firearm or ammunition (question 2). There was no scope for raising doubts of any kind, unless the officer was absolutely certain of a lack of suitability or good reason and could give a categorical 'No' as an answer. In the case of all Hamilton's forms every answer was 'Yes'. By 1992 the form had been changed and more detail was required in some of the answers, but it was hardly a major revision following the post-Hungerford legislation. Question 1, on suitability, still required only a 'Yes' or 'No' answer. There was also no need for the officer to document whether a check had been made on the applicant's membership of shooting clubs. Under the guidance followed by the police, a firearm certificate should not have been granted for target shooting unless the applicant was a member of a gun club. Although in evidence to the Cullen Inquiry the various officers who were questioned all indicated that such checks would have been made, these were never recorded.

The Inquiry had also heard of various shortcomings in the maintenance of firearms files and criminal intelligence records relating to Hamilton. Senior officers maintained that, had all the information on Hamilton been collected together, it would still have made no difference to the outcome of his applications. One question, never adequately addressed by the Inquiry, has since been raised in a variety of guises. Was there anything exceptional about the way in which Hamilton's firearms applications were administered – either because the police wanted to avoid the consequences of his complaints, or for more sinister reasons? To set aside any doubts about special treatment, the Inquiry should have established whether any of the lapses revealed with Hamilton's applications, such as incorrect recording of serial numbers, wrong names given for shooting clubs or information absent from files, were commonplace and apparent with the applications of others.

Through comments to the press, on Internet sites and in parliamentary questions, members of the gun lobby have at various times suggested that Hamilton had masonic connections with senior officers of the force, that he was a police informer, or even that he was part of a paedophile ring involving police officers. Any masonic link was summarily dismissed by Lord Cullen. The Grand Master has denied in the press that Hamilton was a mason, though it is known that his grandfather, his adoptive father, was. Masonic connections were thoroughly investigated by reporters of at least one Scottish newspaper who came up with nothing. It is easy to understand, however, why public scepticism will continue in this and other cases as long as police membership of the masons continues and continues in secret. I doubt that there was any sinister connection between the police and Hamilton. Any truth in these allegations would have been unearthed by vigilant reporters. Hamilton himself would surely have mentioned or alluded to any direct link with the police somewhere in his prolific correspondence. In fact he asserted at one time that the police were biased in favour of the 'brotherhood of masons'. Many of the rumours only began to circulate after the Government had announced its intention to ban some handguns, rumours often passed on by politicians with known pro-gun sympathies at a time when the gun lobby wanted to inflict the maximum damage on Central Scotland Police. Their argument is that without some hidden link between Hamilton and the force he would not have received his licence. In other words, only with special favours would an unsuitable person be allowed to keep guns. Legislative changes were unnecessary as all the blame could be put on the police. I believe it more likely that the police culture of sticking rigidly to self-imposed inadequate procedures was at the heart of the Central Scotland Police's continued licensing of Hamilton. Underlying that was a law that gave the benefit of the doubt to men who wanted to own guns.

In 1999 Colin Greenwood submitted a paper in evidence to the Home Affairs Select Committee during the Committee's consideration of the Control of Firearms. He listed many aspects of the police procedures that he believes the Cullen Inquiry had failed to address. In particular he raised questions about Hamilton's gun club membership. Greenwood contends that Hamilton persistently lied about club membership in order to own higher-calibre guns he was not permitted to use. He argued that the police should have known this:

> The picture is either one of institutionalised negligence and incompetence in dealing with all firearms matters or of special treatment accorded to a person who was well known to be a trouble-maker, likely to complain persistently if he did not get his own way.

While there is some substance in what he has to say about the faults in the Central Scotland Police system, Greenwood's credentials as an objective observer are flawed. He has repeatedly criticised anyone from the Government to GCN who has dared to support tougher gun laws.

With regard to firearms licensing, my case against the police is that they were hidebound by procedural considerations, and in doing so they failed to pay sufficient attention to any duty of care to the public. They could have applied themselves harder to the task of keeping dangerous weapons away from a dubious man. Furthermore, I have no doubt that their concerns about how the public would react to these earlier dealings with Hamilton subsequently deflected them from their duty of care on the day of the massacre.

The Dunblane massacre was an unprecedented incident in Britain for which no individual or agency could ever be expected to be totally prepared. Nevertheless, most would be expected from the agency that takes overall charge after an emergency – the police. If the police fall short of providing an adequate response then it is almost inevitable that some or all of those involved will suffer. To improve the response, lessons must be learnt from each incident, but this can only be achieved if the inadequacies are admitted and scrutinised. Not to do so is to compound the failures by allowing them to go unrecognised and be repeated on another occasion.

Chief Constable Wilson wrote in his submission to Lord Cullen that 'an early priority was to identify the dead and the injured, so that relatives could be informed'. The priority, especially that of providing information to relatives, might have been an early one but cannot have been the most urgent one. To inform the relatives three tasks were necessary. First, the victims had to be identified. Second, their relatives had to be contacted. Third, someone had to inform each set of relatives. As lead agency the police were in charge of all of these tasks. The police had many other operational duties that day, including a criminal investigation, press liaison and the cordoning off of the school. Informing relatives did not appear to receive priority over these. The criminal investigation swung into action with forensic experts summoned straight away. An officer from another force, Supt Munn, was immediately called in to deal with the press and Supt Holden was given the task of cordoning off the school, ahead of his role in informing relatives. If the police couldn't give priority to the relatives then the responsibility should have been delegated to another agency, for example the local social services department. This would have had the double advantage of providing an agency that was fully focussed on the task and staff who were better trained to deal with distressed people.

How were the individual tasks handled by the police, and how could they have been improved? Difficulties with identifying the child victims undoubtedly contributed to the delay. The only adult who knew the names of all the children was Gwen Mayor and she was dead. One problem was that two children were absent from the class. Because the register hadn't been taken their names weren't known, though at least one set of parents had phoned in early to confirm their child's absence.

As it was essential to get the survivors to hospital as quickly as possible, the police made a decision not to ask any of the injured children their names, but it is difficult to understand why it wasn't possible to ask some of them who they were. A vital opportunity to eliminate some names from the list of those who'd died was lost. This inflexible decision was made worse by communication difficulties.

Initially the police at the school could not make contact with Stirling Royal Infirmary. When the survivors' names were known to hospital staff, the information was not received by those in charge of identification. The details were not passed on until after midday. Even then only two or three names were received from the hospital at a time. The communication problems were due to the limitations of the telephone land lines, which had become overloaded, and a police decision not to use mobile phones because of the possibility of eavesdropping by the press. No one appears to have concluded that in order to avoid delays it might have been possible to use phones in a neighbouring community where the phone system was not saturated, or for a police officer to drive to and from the hospital to collect the information. Even without blue lights this would have taken less than half an hour.

The task of identifying the murdered children involved staff from the school nursery. Most of the children had attended the nursery a year before, though some, like Sophie, would have been unknown to the teachers. Nevertheless the majority of them should have been identifiable by name tags on their clothing. Looking at these would have been a very difficult job, but would probably have provided most names. There was some confusion because one child wore clothes with two different name-tags, but I understand it was a sibling's name, not that of another child in the class. There were particular problems when the possibility was raised that a dead child in the gym might be Mhairi MacBeath. Mhairi had died on her way to Stirling Royal Infirmary. The hospital staff had no doubts about her identity, but the confusion at the school prompted a decision to repeat the whole identification process.

Notwithstanding these difficulties there was one group of people who could have helped, but one that the police decided not to turn to. In the vicinity were people who knew most about the children, who could provide intimate details and describe them exactly as they'd been that morning. Their families. The police decided that none of us would be told anything until after all the children had been identified. No matter how unequivocally any child's identity had been established, none of us would be told a thing until every problem had been resolved. So our assistance would never be sought. It was obvious that we had learnt directly or indirectly from the media that there had been a shooting and that there were injuries and fatalities; Supt Holden had been asked questions about this around 11 a.m. It would have taken courage to ask us for details and the process would have been painful, but if the police had told us that information was needed to help identify those injured and killed, I am sure our wait would have been shorter. If the police didn't have the resources available to take the information, there were others, such as the social workers, who could have done so. They had been called to the school but, like us, had also been left waiting around with no information.

It seems likely that all the children had been identified by 1 p.m., although it was never clear to what extent the identification process was affected by the scare about booby traps and the apparent evacuation of the gym. According to evidence given at the Cullen Inquiry, the gym was evacuated around 12 noon and the all-clear wasn't given until 3.30 p.m. If identification was not completed until after noon, some access to the gym must have been possible during that period. If identification was completed before the evacuation then there was absolutely no excuse for the delay in informing relatives. Whatever happened, the danger must have been minimal, as the police took us into the school between the times of evacuation and the all-clear.

There is no doubt there were identification problems, at least some of which could not be blamed on police procedures. However, when it came to contacting the victims' relatives the police approach appears to have been incredibly negligent. The class involved was known immediately. The school kept record cards that should have included telephone numbers for contacting relatives in emergencies. The police did not use them for this purpose. Instead they relied on the media and word of mouth to alert the relatives that there had been an incident at the school. Even when the news reached me, well over an hour after the police had arrived on the scene, I had to make my own decision about whether I should go to the school. I could have delayed going, uncertain about the seriousness of the incident. If the reason for lack of direct contact was the problem with telephone lines then the emergency contact numbers should have been delivered to Police Headquarters in Stirling, which like the hospital was no more that fifteen minutes' drive away. That, of course, presupposes that contacting the relatives was a priority. Some relatives went to Stirling Royal Infirmary where they only learned details from overheard conversations. Eileen Harrild's husband Tony was called to the hospital and, although reassured that Eileen's injuries were not life-threatening, he was not told which class had been involved. Eileen and Tony's two youngest children were pupils at Dunblane Primary and Tony had no idea whether they'd been involved too. Even so, he couldn't get information from the police. It was three hours before he overheard that it was a Primary One class and therefore his children were likely to be safe. The police couldn't even reassure a victim's husband about his children.

This brings me to the way in which the victims' relatives were eventually informed. Chief Constable Wilson had the following to say in his submission to Lord Cullen:

> Our strategy also involved using Family Liaison Teams combining the skills of police officers and social workers who required accurate briefing before being tasked.
>
> I believe this approach [Family Liaison Teams] ensured that families were treated sensitively. All received accurate information. The price of that exercise, however, was that it took time.
>
> While the parents and relatives of the victims waited for information regarding casualties they were accompanied by police officers who, despite their professional experience, found difficulty in comforting or consoling them.

There are a number of issues here. The first is whether the exercise of involving family liaison teams in informing the families was worth the time it allegedly took. Wilson's comments imply that it was more important for the police officers and social workers to have accurate briefing than it was for the relatives to be informed. He claims that the approach ensured that we were treated sensitively, but this was several hours too late. The families had been left in the charge of a brusque police inspector and two young women police officers who seemed totally out of their depth. We had been shouted at, lied to about when we would be given information and trapped for hours without access to Supt Holden, the man with overall responsibility for informing us. When our request to see a senior officer was raised at the Cullen Inquiry, Central Scotland Police's lawyer suggested that such a request should have been satisfied by someone of the rank of inspector, in other words Insp. Ross. It was, he implied, our fault for not knowing, under the most harrowing of circumstances, what a senior officer was. We assumed the request was for someone who could tell us what was going on. To be pedantic about something like that reflected precisely the lack of sensitivity we got from the police force as we waited.

As for Wilson's officers finding difficulty in comforting or consoling us, I saw no attempts to do either during our wait. This is understandable if the officers concerned weren't trained for such a job, but there is no point in pretending afterwards that they were. To claim, as well, that all members of the family liaison teams were appropriately experienced is misleading. Many were thrown in at the deep end, as much out of their depth as the families they were tasked to tell. With no disrespect to my policeman Derek, a man I came to admire, he had no special expertise for his role that day. He'd been called away from a desk job and plunged unprepared into telling a parent of his child's murder. Other families were also told in a very formal manner, hardly what we'd spent hours waiting for. As my liaison team wasn't given access to the record cards, they knew less about me than others who could have told me a lot earlier.

However beneficial the family liaison teams were to be later – and unreservedly I can say mine was – the families should not have been made to wait simply so that the teams could be assembled. When the teams had been briefed, by 1.45 p.m., we were made to wait longer, some families for another hour and forty-five minutes. So, even after the identification problems had been resolved and the teams assembled, we couldn't be told immediately. Dunblane Health Centre staff had sat in the library, prepared to tell us before midday.

At the heart of the delays, I believe, lay police attempts to keep tight control over everything. Making us a priority would have meant telling the relatives before the police had control of the information given to the media. Rod Mayor's story raises many questions about the motives of the police. Rod drove to the school after phone calls from a friend and one of his daughters. Arriving sometime after noon, he was put in a room on his own and left for over half an hour with no information. There could never have been any doubt that Gwen Mayor was one of the victims, so there should have been no necessity to keep Rod waiting. Yet he was denied any information until he threatened to leave the school to talk to the press. Only after this was he told that his wife had been killed. This can only be interpreted as a deliberate attempt to delay telling him for as long as possible.

No one in direct contact with the victims' families seemed able to take any initiative that would help us. Orders were coming remotely from the top. Supt Holden's evidence at the Cullen Inquiry indicated that he had to go to his boss, DCS Ogg, to check whether he could pass on any information. We suffered the long wait, not because of any caring attitude towards us, but to allow the police to maintain their control over the situation. Once control was achieved, the police version no doubt required the official release of information to the press, through Louis Munn, to coincide with the families being told. The truth was that Chief Constable Wilson had talked to the press much earlier and the families weren't told anything until much later.

Why did they need such control? I have no doubts that the senior officers were distracted by concerns about the criticism they were likely to get about the licensing of Thomas Hamilton's guns. Louis Munn's arrival seemed to have as much to do with ensuring that the right spin was put on everything as it was about passing on information. Even the press briefing he organised the next day, at which William Wilson told reporters that he was a Dunblane resident and that he knew some of the children's parents, seems retrospectively to have been a neat piece of stage management, organised to gain sympathy for the police at a crucial time. Sympathy for the police was used to deflect criticism on later occasions. In response to the questions about why Police Board members failed to raise the issue of Dunblane in July 1996, the convener Jeanette Burness said, 'They [members of the force] have got kind hearts. They really feel so down at the moment. They have had a tremendous shock.' No one can doubt the sorrow experienced by the force, nor the humanity shown by many of its officers; nevertheless this does not provide an excuse for not raising questions about accountability.

Central Scotland Police took their control a stage further, firstly by claiming that they were unaware of families' complaints until just before the Cullen Inquiry, and secondly by distorting the times we were told of our children's deaths. On the day of the massacre members of the liaison teams would have been well aware of the parents' feelings. Insp. Ross would have to have been deaf and blind not to know that we were upset about the lack of information. Yet the police maintained that they didn't know of our concerns until a formal letter had been received from our lawyers in late May. Police procedures allowed them to believe that a complaint is not really a complaint unless made official by a lawyer's letter. They could conveniently forget what Isabel MacBeath had said to the Prime Minister on 15 March and DCS Ogg's subsequent visit to her.

At the Cullen Inquiry, the times at which the police claimed we were told that our children were dead bore no relation to the truth. This may seem a minor matter in comparison to everything else that had happened, but to me it sums up the controlling attitude adopted by the police. To get the times wrong the police had either ignored or changed statements. When Isabel MacBeath accessed her file, she found that the police claimed she was informed at 2.10 p.m., not the correct time of 2.40 p.m. Other parents describe being approached by their police officer at the Inquiry and being told they were mistaken about the time. One relative said, 'the police just stood there and lied on oath – sticking to bizarre time-scales'. Another said:

> Rather than just admitting they were human and were not looking at their watch . . . they were totally insistent that their timing and their version of everything was right.

These 'bizarre time-scales' were shown to be incorrect by social worker Margaret Aland's evidence that the Dunn family had not been informed until 3.30 p.m., an hour later than the police admitted. No police officer was asked to explain the discrepancies. What was the point of lying about the times if there were legitimate reasons for the delay? Chief Constable Wilson believed there were good reasons; so why the concerted effort to distort the times? The answer is, I believe, that it didn't fit the police version. In trying to preserve their version of events the force had trapped junior officers into pressurising bereaved parents.

On the families' being informed of the fate of their children, and in particular the time that it took before the families of those who had been killed were informed, Lord Cullen was to say:

> These delays were entirely unacceptable, especially when they were combined with the distressing effect of lack of any information, even an explanation that there was a problem and something was being done about it.

They were most definitely 'entirely unacceptable'. Lord Cullen's words are strong enough, but he didn't follow them up by censuring the police for their attempts to gloss over the delays.

Central Scotland Police have continued to wriggle out of their responsibilities for the delays ever since. On the day the Cullen Report was published, the Chief Constable gave a press briefing. If television reports accurately reflect its content then Wilson's main concern was over the departure of Douglas McMurdo, a man for whom he had the greatest respect 'both as a professional and a friend'. Wilson's response to the criticisms in the Report was less open. All he would say was that 'measures are in place to overcome all areas of concern'. How did the public know?

A week later the Chief Constable and DCS Ogg met with the Central

Scotland Joint Police Board to discuss the Cullen Report. The Board is the body responsible for overseeing the local force. Made up of local councillors, it appoints the senior officers and determines the budget. It should have provided a mechanism for holding the force to account. When Wilson had presented his annual report to the Board in July 1996, reporters were shocked to find that 'references [within the report] to a tragedy unparalleled in Scottish criminal history are brief'. The subject of Dunblane was not even raised by the Board at that time. There were assurances of questions to come and the Chief Constable promised an internal investigation: 'It will not be a whitewash – the Police Board will be told everything, warts and all.' The vice-convener, Cllr Ian Wyles, said he would call for another agency to assess the police role if that proved necessary to allay public concerns about officers investigating themselves. The convener, Cllr Jeanette Burness, said that there would be an open discussion on Mr Wilson's internal report, which would be made public. It never was.

When the Board met Wilson and Ogg in October 1996 it was behind closed doors. Although Jeanette Burness claimed that the two senior police officers were given a thorough grilling, it was revealed that a number of the Board hadn't even read the report before the meeting. At a press conference afterwards, Burness said that the Board had complete confidence in the Chief Constable. In spite of criticisms in the Cullen Report, the public concerns expressed in the media and the distress of the families, the Board was satisfied that Central Scotland Police had nothing to answer for. The Board, however, hadn't consulted the families and had given our lawyers little notice of the press conference. When it came to local accountability, those with direct experience of the shortcomings of the police were not to be counted.

At the same press conference Chief Constable Wilson offered a private meeting with the families. The offer was made in answer to a journalist's question, not directly to the families. Even if we'd been approached formally the offer would not have been taken up. We wanted public explanations for what had happened and why the police hadn't been prepared to tell the whole truth. We'd assumed that everything would be aired at the Inquiry, but the police had failed to take that opportunity to be totally open. We couldn't trust them to be open at a private meeting either. The least we wanted was an apology from the police force that had licensed Hamilton, had failed to provide proper care on the day of the massacre and had distorted the truth afterwards. A meeting would have been a tactic to avoid making a public apology. Wilson suggested that if there was anything to apologise for he would. He never did. Wilson once said that he understood why we might be angry with the police. These words – spoken months after the event – weren't good enough, just as reassurances that everything was now in order meant nothing if there was no acknowledgement that things were wrong in the first place. At the start of his submission to Lord Cullen, the Chief Constable wrote that his force was

> committed to upholding the rule of law, exercising the policing functions efficiently and with courtesy, integrity and fairness . . . We always aim to foster good relations with the public and improve quality.

To improve quality someone must take responsibility if that quality is lacking. Lord Cullen was in no doubt that quality was lacking. If no one can be held to account for mistakes then how can the public ever be assured that incompetence won't continue?

The police appear to maintain a wish to be immune from the rigours of public scrutiny. Chief Constable Wilson, speaking in October 1999 at a time when the setting up of an outside body to investigate police complaints was being discussed, rubbished the idea, claiming that 'anyone who investigates complaints against the police needs to have years of police experience to understand what is happening'. One body that meets the Chief Constable's requirements is Her Majesty's Inspectorate of Constabulary (HMIC). How did they deal with the criticisms of Central Scotland Police after Dunblane?

The HMIC report on the Central Scotland force released in 1997 deals with the massacre in a mere two pages. It was a whitewash. The report considered that most matters had been dealt with in Lord Cullen's report and that the force and its Chief Constable were to be commended for putting new measures in place to remedy problems highlighted by Cullen. These measures were not specified. On the matter of the entirely unacceptable delay in telling the families, the report says, 'The procedures were applied with the best intentions, but the force now recognises their shortcomings and has acted appropriately.' Appropriate action didn't include admission that things were handled badly, or an apology. The Cullen Report should have prompted thorough and transparent changes. The ability of Central Scotland Police to deal with the outstanding matters so swiftly raises the question why these measures weren't in place before. As far as HMIC was concerned, it didn't seem to matter that there had been faults before the massacre, or on the day. Could we really have expected any more from the police checking on themselves?

At one point Chief ConstableWilson speculated that a major barrier had been placed between the senior management of Central Scotland Police and the families most deeply affected because the force's authorisation of weapons was to form a major part of the Cullen Inquiry. The reality is that a rift appeared on the day of the shootings, which was deepened by the contemptuous attitude of certain officers at the Inquiry. It was the culture apparent among senior officers that had come between us. The police thought they knew best and considered their rigid procedures appropriate. That was what caused distress and nothing had changed by the time Wilson made those comments. Who was ultimately responsible for all the operations of Central Scotland Police? It was the Chief Constable. He was morally accountable and ought to have resigned.

Les Morton tried to get answers by writing to the Central Scotland Joint Police Board. A body that included elected representatives should have been under some obligation to make their local force accountable. Les's first letter to the convener Jeanette Burness, written on 16 December 1996, posed nine questions, each of which arose from criticisms of Central Scotland Police made in the Cullen Report. Dismissively, Cllr Burness considered that a letter from a bereaved father merited a reply of less than four lines. The Board, it seemed, were to be as indifferent to our concerns as the force itself. Les sent two more letters before he received a reply of any substance. The letter read as if it came from the police, not from an independent committee. The gist of the letter was that Cullen had not actually criticised Central Scotland Police and anyway the force was doing a fine job. The Board had every confidence in the Chief Constable. The Board appeared unwilling, perhaps unable, to take an objective stand.

Les eventually sought the help of Stirling's MP Anne McGuire. She communicated with the Board. They were only prepared to discuss matters with Les if he gave them advance notice of the questions he would ask. The discussion would be limited to those questions. Such conditions, enforced by a public body on a bereaved father, were totally unacceptable. So much for the promised open discussion.

It is no surprise that the Joint Police Board lacks teeth. When it comes to running police forces in the UK, the chief constable has almost complete control. The 1962 Royal Commission on Police Powers and Procedure judged that chief constables were effectively accountable to no one and subject to no one's orders in a wide range of matters. It concluded that chief constables 'should be free from the conventional process of democratic control and influence'. The problem of controlling the police can 'therefore be restated as the problem of controlling chief constables'. A police board has no operational control, and only in exceptional circumstances has there been any attempt for one to enforce political accountability of police operations. Rarely has a board stood up against its local chief constable, even when there has been public support to do so. Some members of the Merseyside Police Authority attempted to do it in the 1980s after the Toxteth riots; and in a rare success the Grampian Police Board were able to call their Chief Constable, Ian Oliver, to account after the mishandling of the Scott Simpson murder case in 1998. Oliver took early retirement. After Dunblane, however, the Central Scotland Police Board tamely accepted the police version of events, acting more as a ventriloquist's dummy, controlled by the police.

Their attitude reflected that of the force that was supposed to account to them: it was one of arrogance. The police always knew best and we the public must effectively take this on trust, no matter what. As both relatives of victims of a preventable horrendous crime and victims ourselves of the police handling of the events, we appeared to have no right to challenge this view. 'As long as it is reasonable to believe that the police have acted in good faith' observes Phil Scraton in *The State of the Police*, 'then the public must bear the brunt of any mistakes. The distinction between an "honest mistake" and "deliberate abuse" will be very difficult to draw.'

My frustration at the lack of accountability prompted me to write to *Scotland on Sunday* in April 1998. Grampian's Chief Constable Ian Oliver, William Wilson's predecessor as head of the Central Scotland force, had been severely criticised for his force's investigation of the murder of a young Aberdeen schoolboy, Scott Simpson. An internal report had cleared the force, but a subsequent investigation by an outside police officer, Lothian's DCC Graham Power, had been highly critical of Grampian Police and their attempts to minimise criticism. I wrote:

> How often have police 'become involved in an attempt to cover their tracks to ensure their version of events was not challenged' (Toll of mistakes in murder hunt, April 19th)? Chief Constable Ian Oliver appeared satisfied that Grampian police officers had presented the facts correctly in their internal report. However, my own experience of the Dunblane tragedy lends support to the view that police are prepared to write reports primarily to satisfy themselves, rather than the truth.
>
> My daughter was a victim at Dunblane Primary School. We were promised that the Cullen Inquiry into the events would seek to establish the truth. Evidence was to be examined in full so that every possible lesson could be learned. We were to be sadly disillusioned within hours of the opening of the Inquiry.
>
> The police were well aware that on the day of the tragedy we, the families, were upset at the way we were treated. In particular, the police knew of our criticism of the length of time it had taken to inform us of our children's fate, up to five hours in some cases. Later, we learned of some of the operational problems that might have contributed to the delay and accepted that some of these may have been unavoidable.

But were Central Scotland Police open about this, and prepared to learn lessons? No, they'd obviously decided their own version of events. On oath, they stated that we had been told significantly earlier than we had. That was only part of it. Families were told that they had got the times wrong in their statements. There was an echo of this in Grampian's DCC Beattie urging Graham Powell to change his report.

Our own indignation at Chief Supt Ogg's testimony was recorded at the time by many of the journalists present (*Scotland on Sunday* described it as 'the loudest rumble of discontent . . . a burst of sighs and expressions of disagreement'). Only after a social worker, who was also present when a family was told of their child's death, was called to the stand and subjected to an unnecessarily harsh grilling was it clear that the police version was wrong.

Why did they do it? Why is there a culture of arrogance that allows the police to spin their own version of events to avoid criticism? Was it part of the ethos Central Scotland Police had inherited during the time Oliver was in charge prior to his move to Grampian?

The more serious question for the Dunblane families is this. If the police are unwilling to be accurate about something as clear cut as the times when families of murder victims are informed of their loved ones' deaths, then how can we trust anything else they say, for example in relation to their dealings with Thomas Hamilton?

Just as is happening now with Grampian Police, the attitude of senior officers of Central Scotland Police has left a legacy of mistrust. And like Ian Oliver, Central Scotland's Chief Constable William Wilson never wanted the buck passed to him. One of Scotland's most heinous crimes took place on his patch, his force failed, and still they chose to distort what happened. The buck should always stop with the man at the top. If this is appropriate when there has been incompetence over the murder of one child then it must also apply when there has been incompetence leading to the murder of sixteen children and their teacher.

The letter prompted follow-up articles in a number of other papers. Most focussed on my suggestion that the buck stopped with the man at the top and assumed I was calling for his resignation. I probably was. It was something that Les Morton had called for in his letters to the Joint Police Board.

The *Stirling Observer* sought comments from Cllr Burness, who maintained her full support for her chief constable. I wrote to her, expanding on the points I'd made to *Scotland on Sunday*. I concentrated on three matters, asking why the police had given a distorted version of events at the Cullen Inquiry, telling her of the legacy of mistrust this induced and raising the question of how a police force can be held accountable. Les Morton had not received any sensible answer to his questions about firearms licensing and so I didn't raise these matters again. I explained to Cllr Burness that reading Les's correspondence with her had already led me to conclude that the Board was unwilling to ensure transparency in matters surrounding the Dunblane massacre. I told her that Chief Constable Wilson had been somewhat equivocal in relation to how he felt about the relatives' treatment, saying that on 13 March the primary concern of himself and his officers was for the feelings of the families, yet this had never been apparent in the actions of some of his senior officers. I went on to say:

> No matter how well intentioned, the police got it wrong. Our wait in the staffroom was a living hell that none of us can ever forget.
>
> It might have helped if Mr Wilson had communicated directly with us to tell us why we had to wait. I find it difficult to comprehend why the police, so concerned about our feelings on the day, felt under no obligation to give us a formal explanation.
>
> If Mr Wilson really cared, why did one of his most senior officers ride roughshod over our feelings at the Inquiry? It was hard enough listening to evidence about our children's deaths, without having the actual events arrogantly distorted by DCS Ogg. It is little wonder that we still feel aggrieved two years on.

I questioned how the Police Board had dealt with the Cullen Report:

> You appear to be satisfied with this; I am not. This should have been your opportunity to reflect as openly as possible the concerns of the people of Central Scotland. In your comments to the *Stirling Observer* you say that both Mr Wilson and DCS Ogg were thoroughly grilled by the board. However, at the subsequent press conference it was revealed that the majority of the police board hadn't actually read the Report at the time. What kind of grilling was it? Did you raise any of the families' concerns? I assume not as you never contacted us either before or after. Presumably you felt it was nothing to do with us.
>
> According to last week's *Stirling Observer*, 'They [Wilson and Ogg] did not deny criticisms levelled at them'. So they did admit faults. What were they and how were they made accountable for them? We don't know, because the first thing you did at the meeting was to vote to exclude the press and public (*Scotsman*, 25th October 1996).

I concluded:

> The aftermath of many recent tragedies has often been notable for two things: the realisation that the police version of events has been found wanting and the resolute way in which the victims' families have sought to establish the truth and the accountability of those in charge. It ought to be the responsibility of the police board to ensure that no stone has been left unturned, but in our case we just don't know whether that has happened or not.

Burness's reply was nevertheless in the same vein as some she'd sent Les Morton. I was told that the police weren't arrogant. Ignoring the details I had presented to her, she suggested that the discrepancy between the police version and our version of the times we were told of our children's deaths could be explained away by simple mistakes. I had told Cllr

Burness about Isabel MacBeath's visit from the angry DCS Ogg. Burness said she couldn't comment on this as she didn't have the facts. I'd just given her the facts, it was hardly something I was going to make up, but she showed no concern about it.

I wrote a second letter, emphasising that I failed to see how the attitude of Central Scotland Police could be interpreted in any other way but arrogant. On Ogg's visit to Isabel I commented:

> To treat a bereaved mother like that smacks of arrogance to me. How is it possible to have any other view? I realise that information on this was not available to you but surely it is of some concern to the board that the senior officer dealing with the aftermath of the tragedy could behave so crassly to one of the victim's relatives.

I again questioned the role of the Joint Police Board:

> Because of some of the things you wrote in your letter I have to say that I am now somewhat puzzled about the role of the Police Board. On the one hand you were prepared to give the chief constable your full support after the publication of the Cullen Report, yet imply that only the Secretary of State for Scotland could have dealt with matters contained within it. You said that Mr Wilson and DCS Ogg were given a grilling before the press conference, but if you had no responsibility for following up the report then what was the point of this?
>
> I am still very dissatisfied. I continue to believe that senior officers behaved in a high-handed and arrogant way. You gave me no reassurance that I had misunderstood their actions. We do know that there are many good officers in the Central Scotland force. Many of us have nothing but praise for our liaison officers, and so I would be grateful if you would not view my comments as a criticism of the force as a whole. The problems lie at or near the top. What continues to be lacking is any sense that there is a need to be accountable for mistakes, misjudgements and the neglect of the duty of care to the general public.

You can rest assured that I shall not be letting this matter rest. I still find it incredible that, save for the resignation of the hapless DCC McMurdo, no one in Central Scotland Police has been shown to be publicly accountable for the mistakes made.

In her letters to both Les Morton and myself, Cllr Burness attempted to belittle our concerns. There were also implications that we had brought some of the problems with the police on ourselves. Some of her comments pre-empted or repeated those of Chief Constable Wilson. She talked about the gulf that had grown between the families and the police before the Cullen Inquiry because of firearms licensing and suggested that the police were unaware of criticisms until receiving a formal note from our lawyers. She mentioned our refusal to meet with the Chief Constable, referring (it is worth reiterating) to a meeting which was offered not directly to the families, but in reply to a question at a press conference to which none of the relatives had been invited. Most relatives remained unaware that an offer had been made.

Despite occasional press reports to the contrary, the relatives never took legal action against Central Scotland Police. For a time this course of action wasn't ruled out, but the courts were not the place to redress all the outstanding issues. A legal mechanism, which could only involve seeking financial compensation for loss, would become too murky and lengthy to ensure that truth and justice came shining through. A public inquiry had failed to do that, so why should a law suit? We had wanted a guarantee that those such as senior police officers, who are entrusted to do a job in the public interest, didn't use their procedures to justify inappropriate practices that cause the public harm. This could only be achieved if they took on the moral responsibility as well as the legal responsibility demanded by their position.

There are those who react to any criticism of the police as if it undermines the whole fabric of society. But to place the police force in a position where they are beyond criticism is a recipe for disaster. Criticism of individual officers or, indeed, police procedures is not a criticism of every officer in the force. Bad practices and incompetence must never be hidden because of a misguided hope that all policemen and policewomen are wonderful. Police officers are not infallible, nor should they be beyond reproach. As in any other profession, if they get things wrong they should be held to account. There have been too many examples in recent years of police misconduct, involving failure to investigate cases, dereliction of duty or blatant distortion of evidence, to be able to give the police unequivocal support.

Her Majesty's Inspectorate of Constabulary had found little to criticise in Central Scotland Police's operations. Political accountability was also lacking. The local politicians, through the Joint Police Board, seemed powerless or spineless (probably both) and didn't want to raise difficult questions on behalf of their community. Cullen's words were sufficient – no action was needed. National politicians also have little appetite for criticising the police, as their desire not to undermine the credibility of the forces of law and order makes them turn a blind eye to behaviour and attitudes that would not be tolerated in other walks of life. The police cannot continue to believe that they deserve the respect and, more importantly, the support of the public, if they adhere to the position that their own procedures are flawless.

The shootings at the Primary School were a unique event, but the failings of the police and their attitude towards criticism were not. It has exposed the shortcomings of the police and the difficulties in getting the police themselves to recognise them. It is incumbent on everyone – the police, the politicians, those who have been affected by police inadequacies and even those who have not – to push for greater accountability.

CHAPTER NINE

# Whose Tragedy Was It?

## From 13 March 1996

'We will pull together, we will be there for those families not only in the short term but I know in the long term as well, it's that sort of community'

(PROVOST PAT GREENHILL, MARCH 1996)

In March 1996 the word 'Dunblane' took on a new meaning. Once just the name of a Perthshire town, meaning 'hill of Blaan (St Blane)', it would be used henceforth to describe the actions of men with guns, gun legislation and anti-gun campaigns. The newspapers told of men who threatened to 'Do a Dunblane' or 'Repeat Dunblane', as the *Daily Mail* and *The Guardian* did when writing about a prisoner who had a grudge against two London schools. The first Firearms (Amendment) Bill was described as the 'Dunblane bill' and the outlawing of pistols and revolvers viewed as the 'Dunblane handgun ban'. There was a new period in British history, 'Post-Dunblane', a time of stricter gun controls. Dunblane would be linked with guns for a long time to come. The families of the victims had become the Dunblane families or the Dunblane parents.

There is still frequent reference to Dunblane in the press. The *Guardian Unlimited* web site, for example, reveals that Dunblane was mentioned in fifty-four separate articles in *The Guardian* and *The Observer* during 1999, all but a handful referring specifically to the massacre, the trauma it caused or to changes implemented in its aftermath. I can understand why some Dunblane residents are sensitive about the name of their town being hijacked and the impression the press can sometimes give that, when the victims' families say something, we are speaking for the whole town.

The community seemed undecided about whether they wanted people to come to the town or not. Tourism in the town decreased dramatically in 1996, but it was unfair to blame the victims' families for that, as some appeared to do after the Council distributed a leaflet entitled *Important Information to Summer Visitors from the City of Dunblane*. This contained a welcome message but asked for understanding, requesting that townsfolk weren't questioned about the tragedy.

So whose tragedy was it? It was a tragedy that had an impact on everyone in Dunblane, although that impact was unequal, and the ripples went far beyond the town. When I watched some of the post-massacre interviews I got the impression that this focus on the community tragedy, though valid, failed to recognise that those most affected didn't all live in Dunblane. It presupposed that a resident of the town, with no connection to a child at the school, was in some way more affected than, say, a grandparent from another area. Later, when people from outside the town wanted to campaign for gun control, they were treated with suspicion. Moreover, because the families attracted attention from outsiders, we were accused of publicity seeking. At times it felt as if local critics considered that we, and not Thomas Hamilton, were responsible for drawing the world's attention to the town.

In November 1996 the community of Dunblane was awarded the *Sunday Mail*'s Great Scot of the Year award. Presenting the award to the Cathedral's minister Colin McIntosh at a ceremony in Glasgow, Lord McLuskey said on behalf of the judges that 'if there is one aspect of this tragedy that has humbled us all, it is the dignity with which the people of Dunblane have borne their suffering'. By Christmas the façade of dignity had been shattered.

I understand how hard the reminders of the massacre might be, especially for those who don't have to live with them constantly. However when memories were rekindled by the reappearance of the media or the mention of Dunblane in the news, the reminders sometimes led to resentment that was turned on the families. Much of this, I think, had to do with Dunblane's image. Some wanted it both ways, complaining that the town was never out of the news, but willing to contribute a word or two to journalists whenever required. Nothing seemed to fuel resentment more than the differing opinions over the gifts and money.

## FUNDS

'The community, drawn together by a tragic event could easily be pulled apart by the distribution of these funds'
(DUNBLANE PRIMARY SCHOOL BOARD UPDATE NEWSLETTER, MAY 1996)

Commentators can be very judgemental about the donation of money to disaster funds. Some decry the response as unnecessary and uniquely British. Others have gone further, claiming that the victims or their families don't deserve anything. This certainly happened when the victims were 'drunken' Liverpool fans at Hillsborough or 'hedonistic' party-goers on the *Marchioness*. The 'innocence' of our children ensured that such thoughts were less prevalent after Dunblane, but it didn't stop the questions about whether the money was deserved. Perhaps it was considered unseemly for anyone to 'benefit' from a tragedy and that the victims' families shouldn't be thinking about money, that no one should. Nonetheless there were claims and counter-claims about why money had been sent. Was it for individuals or the community, the families or the school? Was it for dealing with immediate problems or for the benefit of future generations?

The families themselves never requested money. For those of us who lost our children no amount of money could substitute for them. Every parent would have swapped all they own to have their child back in their arms. The donations reflected a wish by others not to replace the loss, but to do 'something'.

The Dunblane Fund was set up by the local authority and, because of the expertise and experience available among council officials, this ought to have become not only the main fund but ultimately the sole fund. A news release, issued on 18 March, clarified the mechanism by which donations could be made. The trustees followed the guidelines of the Disaster Appeal scheme and accepted donations through UK clearing banks and the local sorting office. There was no attempt to have fund-raising schemes, although some groups and individuals who contributed to the Fund did collect money in this way. It was not set up as a charitable trust, the tax advantages of charitable status being outweighed by the restrictions this placed on what the fund could do with the money. By the time the Fund stopped taking in donations, in March 1997, money received had amounted to £5,021,668.

Nonetheless some difficulties arose. Interim trustees were appointed by the end of March 1996. According to the minutes of the Stirling Council meeting of 11 April 1996, the Council discussed the Fund with representatives from the Primary School and the Dunblane community on 2 April. The Council wanted to appoint seven permanent trustees and thought that these should be drawn from the Primary School and the wider Dunblane community, with one each from the following: Dunblane Primary School Board, Dunblane Primary School PTA, Dunblane teachers, Dunblane churches, Dunblane community council, Stirling Council and the Chief Constable. It was a set-up that included many vested interests. Some were representing potential beneficiaries. The Primary School Board and PTA even had a separate fund. Already a discussion had begun on the letters page of the local paper about how the money should be spent. No one, though, had asked the victims' families what they thought. Rod Mayor wrote to the *Stirling Observer* (24 April), voicing his concerns over decisions taken without consultation with the families.

The families learned about the Dunblane Fund indirectly and decided to seek more information. We didn't want to be trustees. That was neither appropriate nor possible. What we did want was some involvement in the discussions that the rest of Dunblane were having. Two of the bereaved fathers, Duncan McLennan and Kenny Ross, accompanied by Duncan's lawyer brother, went to a meeting of the interim trustees held in Dunblane on 16 April, at which the permanent trustees were to be selected. They felt as if they'd gatecrashed an exclusive get-together. Duncan and Kenny's appearance did prompt a change of mind and the selection of trustees was postponed until the families had been given an opportunity to express their views.

We were able to do this at a meeting held on 8 May in Dunblane's Victoria Halls. The atmosphere was tense. The families had recently heard more about the money that the Dunblane Primary School Board and PTA had gathered in, at that time reported to be over £500,000, and that their intention was to keep it separate from the Dunblane Fund. We were concerned that the independence of some School Board and PTA members was compromised and we were angered by their wish to have representation on the board of the Dunblane Fund as well as holding their separate fund. At the Dunblane Fund meeting, we challenged their right to become trustees and argued forcefully for independent trustees.

The argument against vested interests won. The interim trustees were replaced by five largely independent trustees: Lt Col James Stirling of Garden (Lord Lieutenant of Stirling), Sheriff Robert Younger (Sheriff of the Sheriffdom of Tayside, Central and Fife at Stirling), Pat Greenhill (former Provost of Stirling District Council and one of the interim trustees), Cllr Pat Kelly (Stirling Council) and Ian Ross (former Director of Social Work, Central Regional Council). Pat Greenhill provided a link to another fund, the *Stirling Observer* Dunblane Help Fund, of which she was Chair. Her presence on the board of the Dunblane Fund was not contentious at the time, as she was no longer an elected representative for Dunblane, but some of us thought her independence may have been compromised after she won back her Dunblane West ward in a by-election in June 1998. She continued as a trustee. Two Council officials who'd served as interim trustees, Bob Jack and Bill Dickson, retained their involvement with the Fund, as secretary and treasurer respectively.

The Dunblane Fund got on with its work efficiently. Its primary purpose was to 'use the funds and any income accruing to make provision for the relief of loss suffered by those affected by the tragedy'. Although initial provision was for those families who were directly involved in the tragedy, payments were not confined to the families. There was no direct contact between the trustees and beneficiaries: information was collected by fund manager Maurice Pettigrew, who prepared reports from which the names of potential beneficiaries were omitted.

The Trust Deed had set out subsidiary purposes, including provision for a suitable memorial and provision for the benefit of the community. Together with the *Stirling Observer* Dunblane Help Fund, the Dunblane Fund supported the design and construction of the Memorial Garden and the production of the two commemorative roses. It also helped with the installation of play equipment donated to Dunblane by the Association of Play Industries. When the Fund closed in 1999, the residual balance was passed on to the Dunblane Community Trust, the primary purpose of which is to fund and support the Duckburn Youth Centre Project in the town. The Trust also received the balance of the *Stirling Observer*'s Fund, around £1 million.

The *Stirling Observer* Dunblane Help Fund was set up as a charitable trust that allowed tax advantages but placed more restrictions on its aims. Each week the *Stirling Observer* proudly displayed a thermometer, rising as the funds came in. The Fund eventually totalled £2,032,700. It was used to provide some support to the families for unexpected expenses and contributed to the payment for the victims' headstones. It also became closely allied to calls for a community project. As early as April 1996 there was undue haste to get money allocated to a major project. A questionnaire, 'Your View', was sent to all Dunblane residents, asking what they would like the money spent on. Listed options were Community Centre/Sports Centre, Swimming Pool, Memorial Garden, or options involving sharing money between the community and the families or just among the families.

Within six weeks the community was being asked if, as a result of our children being killed, they'd like a swimming pool. And a lot of people did, apparently. Some of the parents who'd grown up in Dunblane have told me how in the past volunteers had tried to raise money for similar ventures but had never gained sufficient support within the town. Now, because of these donations, some in the community had decided it was a good time for a swimming pool or community centre. Correspondents to newspapers wrote that it would be an appropriate memorial to the children. Families of victims of previous disasters have also found that a community's wish for a community centre has been given a priority. Eleven years after the Lockerbie disaster, the victims' families were angered by a decision to use fund money for a leisure centre and swimming pool in the town, rather than to provide financial help for the families to attend the trial of the two Libyans accused of the bombing of Pan Am Flight 103.

The Revd Colin McIntosh responded to the unease being felt in the town with an insightful letter to the *Stirling Observer*:

> It seems to me that discussion on how the various Funds are spent and what further steps need to be taken are issues which can wait. We are not ready to bear them yet.
>
> The greatest mistake we could make would be to imagine that we are actually serving the community or our families by being seen to be busy on their behalf . . . The one thing we have plenty of in Dunblane at the moment is time.

The families themselves had differing views about whether a 'bricks-and-mortar' project would be appropriate, but all of us were horrified at the rush. If a new facility were to be created, in my view it had to be something for the children of the town. The decision to go ahead with a youth community project appears to be an appropriate one.

Other funds were set up with more specific aims. In recognition of the hospital's role on the day of the massacre, *The Sun* raised money that was used to construct a playground at Stirling Royal Infirmary. The Stirling University Graduates' Association set up a Dunblane Primary School Fund, which makes an annual donation to a charity: the first recipient was the Children's Hospice Association of Scotland. The Dunblane Bereaved Families Fund provided the families with immediate help. Other groups collected money, cut through the protective red tape that was sometimes placed around us and made direct approaches to the families. We thank them especially.

In spite of the initial communication problems with the main funds, and the disquiet that some of us felt about the type of ventures suggested, they were at least open and accountable. Regular updates were provided in newsletters and personal correspondence. If only this had been the case with money held by the Dunblane Primary School Board and PTA. A few weeks after the massacre, the families heard stories about a bank account containing hundreds of thousands of pounds in donations set up by representatives of these two bodies. Puzzled as to why this wasn't part of the Dunblane Fund, we were offered an explanation from Gerry McDermott, a member of the School Board who came to one of our joint meetings in early May. He told us that the money had been sent specifically for the school. We told Mr McDermott that we were concerned that they might cause a split by holding on to the money. Mr McDermott promised to inform the other members of the Board and PTA of our concerns, but I understand that few were told. Our reservations deepened when, a few days later, we discovered that details about the School Board/PTA fund had been published in the press within two days of the massacre. Some of the details gave the impression that it was the main fund.

At the Dunblane Fund meeting on 8 May, we heard more when a PTA member explained that they were keeping 'their money' as they 'didn't want the Council to get their hands on it'. We continued to seek information about the money through the officials of the Dunblane Fund, helped by a solicitor friend who provided invaluable assistance. None of the victims' families spoke to the press about the money. Others were less reticent. Gerry McDermott and the School Board's Chairman Mike Robbins both provided comments as the press sensed a split in the community. 'FATE OF £1M SCHOOL FUND SPLITS DUNBLANE,' wrote the *Sunday Times* on 26 May, 'DUNBLANE CASH SPLIT,' said the *Mail on Sunday* a week later. It is probably not a coincidence that the stories appeared just after Rod Mayor and I had both written critical letters to the School Board.

The School Board had eventually sent the families a document entitled 'Update Newsletter'. It was the first solid information we'd been given, but was incomplete. Obsequious in tone, it urged us to work with the Board. I wrote a letter to Mike Robbins on 20 May and asked him to pass on these comments to all the members of the School Board and PTA. I understand that very few saw this letter:

It is with great sadness that I feel compelled to make critical comments about the way in which this Fund has been dealt with. The views expressed below are my personal ones, but I know that many of my fellow bereaved parents share a lot of similar misgivings. I list below a number of points to which the parents and the community deserve a full response.

In the Update Newsletter you emphasise that advice was offered that 'money would pour into the town, and that the community, drawn together by a tragic event, could easily be pulled apart by the distribution of these funds'. Setting aside whether it was appropriate for the School Board/PTA rather than the Council to be receiving advice on funds from Lockerbie and Hungerford, it seems to me that the School Board/PTA followed what was potentially the most divisive route possible by setting up a separate fund. Surely the best decision for the community would have been to aim immediately to have one fund which could then be administered by independent trustees along the lines now adopted for the Dunblane Fund? No matter how well you think you had informed the general public about the likely aims of the School Board/PTA fund, it was inevitable that the aims of different funds would appear ambiguous and not clear-cut to a large number of potential donors.

I would have thought that the best response to the tragedy would have been for yourselves and the Council to have got together, and acted together, straight away. I sense that past friction between the School and the Council has had too much influence on the decisions that were taken. You and the Council owed it to our children to have done everything possible to work as one. I feel that the comment about not wanting the Council to get the money, made by your PTA colleague at the meeting of 8th May of the interim trustees of the Dunblane Fund and reiterated in the Newsletter, is all too revealing. I find it very hard to believe that, at a time when the whole country was grieving over what happened in Dunblane, 'many people' took the trouble to say specifically that their donations were 'made on the understanding that the money was not paid into a Council-controlled fund'. Why did they do this? The community should be told exactly how many is many.

I take issue with your statement that the existence of the Fund was announced locally but donations were neither invited nor solicited. This is not the impression I now get from press cuttings of 15th and 16th March passed on to me. The address of the Bank of Scotland was in *The Times* and the English edition of the *Daily Express*, hardly local. There was no need to publish the name and address of the bank if you were simply receiving cheques or answering phone enquiries. However, the most blatant example I have seen is something which looks like a classified advertisement that appeared in the *Daily Express* on 16th March. I reproduce the text in full:

'DONATIONS to the Dunblane appeal fund can be addressed to: The Bank of Scotland, 63 High Street, Dunblane FK15 0EJ. Make cheques payable to PTA School Board Fund. Deposits can also be made at any branch of the Abbey National payable to account number X10985592 DUN.'

If this is not inviting or soliciting funds I don't know what is. There is no mention here of the funds being for the school only, and the words Dunblane appeal fund are certainly at odds with what is now suggested to have happened. Anyone sending money to the Bank of Scotland or the Abbey National would not necessarily have sent an accompanying letter, and so you could not know whether or not he or she wished to avoid contributing to a Council-run fund. You could have had no idea where every donor intended the money to go.

At no time until recently did anyone try to explain to me or the other parents what was happening about the funds. Initially we had to go out and find the information for ourselves. Never forget that this money would not have been sent in the quantities that it has been had our children and their teacher not been murdered, something which is never touched on in the Newsletter. It would have been courteous to have provided an explanation very early on as to what you were doing and why. I find it difficult to understand why the School Board/PTA were apparently willing to go against Council advice on the matter of funds but were content to follow implicitly their apparent instructions that there should be no contact with the families. I was delighted when a few weeks ago Nora Dougherty introduced herself to me in the street, and I would have been pleased to see anyone else from the PTA or School Board. The fact that no one came or has come since I learned more about the various funds has heightened my curiosity about what is actually going on. My concerns have been compounded by the impression I get from reading the newspapers that some members of the School Board are all too willing to be quoted as if they represent the parents most affected by the tragedy. So why no contact until now to find out what we really feel?

I share your desire to do everything possible to help the children, staff and parents at Dunblane Primary School. However, to request us, as you did in the letter, to join you in achieving this ideal asks rather a lot from a group who until now have been bypassed, at least at the formal level, by the School Board/PTA. My initial view is that there are some children who ought to have special help (Primary 1 children who have lost numerous friends, Primary 4 and 7 children who were shot at) and the same goes for many of the wonderful teaching staff. The more grandiose, and to my mind gratuitous, plans (e.g. university scholarships suggested in a trust document I have seen) should not be considered for many months to come. With the Public Inquiry about to start, few of the bereaved parents are in an appropriate state to give objective opinions on what should happen to the money in the long term, and neither, in my view, is the community. It would, however, be an insult to go ahead with anything significant before the parents can give an opinion based on a full account of how and why the Fund came about.

In summary, my suggestion is that you immediately provide more explanation about the Fund. The first priority should be to announce, at an open meeting, how much money is in the Fund (an important fact omitted from the Newsletter) and present a breakdown of how the money arrived (personal letter, direct to bank account etc.) and a clear indication of how much was actually sent to the school specifically for the purposes you have outlined. Any donations over which there is any doubt should be transferred to the Dunblane Fund. This, more than anything else you can do, will help heal any possible rifts in the community. Were you to do this, I for one would certainly give wholehearted support to requests from the School Board/PTA to the Dunblane Fund on behalf of all those pupils, staff and parents affected by the tragedy.

Please, please remember what happened that day to my daughter and her friends. You owe it to their memory and to those of us who grieve for them to be completely open about the Fund. I have to say that when questions were raised about the Fund at two meetings I have attended the responses were all too evasive. The Newsletter provides very little of the detail needed to make me feel comfortable that the nature of the Fund fits with its aims.

There was no reply, not even an acknowledgement. There is no record in the School Board minutes that my letter was received, although the School Board/PTA Fund was discussed at a meeting the week after my letter was sent. Rod Mayor's letter also went unanswered. After the press articles it had seemed as if the School Board preferred to talk to journalists than to write to bereaved families. I wrote to Mike Robbins again. This time it prompted a phone message from Gerry McDermott offering me a visit, but by that time I wanted written details of what was going on.

The matter rumbled on. For months no one accounted publicly for the £1 million now sitting in the School Board/PTA account. Matters came to a head in October when leaders of the Scottish School Boards Association (SSBA) learnt of the families' disquiet. In December I went as an observer to a School Board meeting. Four members resigned, three of them over the failure of two other members of the Board to keep them informed. Complaining about the intervention of the SSBA, the wife of one of the remaining members wrote to the *Times Educational Supplement*:

> I am not suggesting that the leadership of the parents [School Board] has always got things right. But it has not been prepared to succumb to pressure from a vocal group of families. It is sad that others have, because the losers, at the end of the day, will be the children.

Why would calls for accountability and transparency in their dealing prompt such a response? I assume the 'vocal group of families' was the victims' families. Which children were the losers, I wonder? The money remained at the school, with responsibility passed into the capable hands of PTA representatives. The PTA immediately invited the victims' families to a meeting at which various misunderstandings were aired and explanations provided. It gave me a better picture of how the fund had come into existence. The PTA said that they didn't know how most of the details had got into the national newspapers, although the press office of the bank was responsible for one advertisement. A retraction had been requested. There were, however, still unanswered questions about the speed at which details of the School Board/PTA account had appeared. We were asked to accept their word that everything possible had been done to ensure that all donations over which there'd been doubt had been redirected to the Dunblane Fund.

Half of the money in the account was distributed between the three local schools, Dunblane High School and the two Dunblane primary schools (a second primary school, Newton Primary, had opened in the autumn of 1996). Provision for the High School was essential, as most of the pupils who had been at the Primary School on 13 March would attend there in later years. A donation was also made to the Gwen Mayor Trust. The rest of the fund's money was used in September 1998 to set up the Dunblane Primary School Charitable Trust, whose aims are to relieve the distress of children, their families and the staff who were affected by the tragedy and to help to provide education, leisure and recreation facilities for the young people of Dunblane. Applications were still being invited in February 2000.

Dunblane Primary School had been the recipient of many generous donations of equipment and there had been many gifts and offers for the pupils. Money was also sent directly to headteacher Ron Taylor. There had been no shortage of generosity to the school.

I am grateful to all those who donated money to the funds. They helped all of us deal with situations for which we could never have planned, increased expenses, absence from work and uncertainty about the future. Nobody was 'personally enriched'. If the public wishes to display its care through the donation of money, this should not be rejected or resented.

Coming out of this conflict around the funds I believe there are salutary lessons. At times of tragedy we want unity not division. With the exception of small funds, like the Dunblane Bereaved Families Fund, which provide immediate aid to those most directly affected, the aim should be to have one fund and one fund alone. This avoids potential disputes during a period of heightened sensitivity. The setting up of distinct, and possibly rival funds, fuels divisions. Members of the public won't know all the details relating to the tragedy and may send their donation to the only address they know, the site of the tragedy, the local authority or a help centre, which doesn't necessarily reflect their precise intentions. The wishes of the donors are best assessed by independent trustees. Transparency and accountability are vital and so all concerned parties should be kept fully informed about developments. Communication problems certainly contributed to the families' worries about the School Board/PTA money. Funds shouldn't be set up or administered by amateurs who happen to find themselves in particular positions when disaster strikes, but have no appropriate experience to deal with the circumstances and outcomes.

The Dunblane Fund took the wise decision not to be a charitable trust. The limitations placed on a charitable fund have led to insurmountable problems with other disaster funds. To cope with all possible requests, and the variety of wishes of the donors, as much flexibility should be built into the purposes expressed in the trust deed.

An independent body which can oversee the setting up of the fund immediately after the disaster would be invaluable. I understand that the Red Cross offers such advice. Outside assistance shouldn't be assumed to be interference. It may be a means of helping at a difficult time and defusing conflicts within an already shattered community.

The press still interview individual parents who are unhappy about the money they've received from funds or the Criminal Injuries Compensation Board, cases that should never have been discussed in public. The critics say the money sent to Dunblane caused problems. The money sent to Dunblane did not create problems. The problems were created by the lack of transparency and accountability of some of those involved with the funds.

## CLLR DICKSON'S COMMUNITY AND THE FIRST CHRISTMAS

'For nine months we've been making allowances for them'
(CLLR ANNE DICKSON, DECEMBER 1996)

We might have guessed how the gun lobby would behave and in the end I realised that there were shortcomings in the Central Scotland Police; but the attitudes of a few in the community came as a real shock. We'd been badly let down, and just as we'd wanted the Inquiry to restore our faith in the system, the police and the politicians, so we needed the community to keep its promises of help for as long as we needed it. One of Thomas Hamilton's complaints had been of rumours being spread about him in Dunblane. It is deeply ironic, but perhaps not unexpected in a small town, that it didn't take long for a few rumour-mongers to start on the families of his victims. Perhaps it was the money that sparked it all off. It wouldn't have been surprising if we were over-sensitive to criticism, we were a group still struggling to come to terms with the awfulness of what had happened. Yet there seemed more to it than that, as if there were a sustained attempt to minimise what had happened so that the town could 'recover' and the whole incident be forgotten. The most telling examples of this are found in the words of

Cllr Anne Dickson. These are the opposite of what you'd expect from a community that says it cares.

Mrs Dickson is the Conservative councillor for the Stirling Council ward of Dunblane East. At the time of the tragedy she was a member of the ruling Tory group on Stirling District Council. She took upon herself the role of leader of the 'moving-on tendency'. When Chris de Burgh's concert was announced at the beginning of July, Cllr Dickson, claiming to be a fan, said he shouldn't come, describing to *The Scotsman* how

> a topic on the streets of Dunblane is that there should be a cut-off date, when life can move forward again. Quite honestly *we're* [my italics] in danger of being swamped with funds and offers – all told, in the various funds we have over £5 million now, a vast amount of money.

Who was being swamped? Mrs Dickson was much involved in dealing with the mail that had flooded into Dunblane, but she speaks as if it all belonged to the town of Dunblane and that the town was homogenous. At the next Thursday meeting the families discussed her comments, and Pam Ross volunteered to phone Anne Dickson to express our concerns about what she'd said and to ask her on what basis she was saying it. Our Newsletter from 23 July records that

> Pam's call to Anne Dickson was 'unsatisfactory'. It does seem from what Anne Dickson says, what others have picked up around the town and what appeared in the press on Saturday that there are some rather resentful people around. Do we just ignore it or do we make a collective response at some time?

When the Cullen Inquiry came to a close, the families spoke to the media for the first time, a first opportunity for most to express how they were feeling. Although the interviews were primarily about Dunblane it was inevitable that the reporters would ask about the previous day's machete attack on a Wolverhampton nursery class. The next day, 10 July, the *Stirling Observer* reported:

Cllr Dickson said that the almost immediate response of the national media to talk to people involved in the Dunblane tragedy was disturbing. 'It brought home to me straight away that *we* are never going to get away from what happened on March 13.'

It would have been surprising if another attack on young children had passed unmentioned during the families' interviews.

After Ann Pearston's speech at the Labour Party Conference, Mrs Dickson offered these unsolicited comments which appeared in *Scotland on Sunday* on 6 October 1996:

> After the Labour party speech I got quite a few calls from people upset at what she was doing. Ann Pearston does not even live in Dunblane. She does not know about the weariness people living here are suffering from. She is a campaigner. When this awful thing happened I was optimistic Dunblane was the kind of place which would eventually get over it, but I failed to take into account that certain people don't want *us* to get on with our lives. They tag Dunblane to their causes because it will get publicity.

She had apparently become a focus for the discontent in Dunblane, a call-centre for complainers. I responded:

> I am writing to say that I found your reported comments on Ann Pearston in today's *Scotland on Sunday* an unwarranted insult. Let me tell you what I, as one of the local community most affected, think about Ann and the legitimacy of her involvement. Ann's children knew my daughter, Ann had lived in Dunblane and she has always had the full support of the parents most affected, those whose children were killed, and has consulted us throughout the duration of the Snowdrop Campaign. She has made a courageous stand against an evil which you appear unwilling or incapable of facing. None of the parents has been coerced into joining campaigns against guns. We are campaigning willingly.

You are often quoted in the papers as speaking for Dunblane, but it is a Dunblane which I continue to have difficulty in recognising. From your comments it comes over as a community full of heartless people who wish to sweep the consequences of the 13th March under the carpet. It is a Dunblane in which those less affected must be sheltered from the full horror of the events and don't care to cope with the grief felt by those of us who have suffered most. In short, it is a Dunblane which appears prepared to leave us behind.

I am sorry that some people in Dunblane are so anxious to draw a line and have such problems dealing with the campaigns and all the other reminders. I hope that those for whom you appear to speak survive their lives without the need for the support, sympathy and understanding which others in Dunblane are giving so readily to us. I am reassured that their help will continue to be provided even when your minority of the Dunblane community has moved on.

There was no reply. We were not the only ones offended by her remarks. The next day Ruth Wishart wrote in *The Herald*:

I haven't met Cllr Ann [*sic*] Dickson from Dunblane, and that's the way I'd like it to stay if reports of her latest utterances are at all accurate. It is reported that Ms Dickson has suggested that the women involved in the Dunblane Snowdrop Campaign have capitalised on local grief for their own ends. It's difficult to think of a more crassly offensive suggestion, and impossible to imagine on what basis the allegation was made.

When the Cullen Report was published on 16 October media interest was intense, though no more than justified. Anne Dickson was interviewed on Grampian TV's *North Tonight* and repeatedly spoke of the weariness in the town: 'When will it end?' She said that people from the town had been away on holiday and been ashamed of admitting they were from Dunblane – instead they would say they were from near Stirling. 'When will life get back to normal? People have never enjoyed a holiday so much.' She complained that there was no fighting spirit left and that the longer things went on, the longer it would take to get that fighting spirit back. The impression she gave was that people were upset, not because there'd been a mass murder at the school but because Dunblane was in the news.

She probably didn't expect anyone from Dunblane to see her interview. Grampian TV covers a region to the north of Dunblane. However some of the Dunblane mothers had travelled to Aberdeen to appear on another Grampian programme, *The Time and Place*. They saw the interview and were furious. Pam Ross and Liz McLennan immediately phoned Anne Dickson and told her how hurt they were by her remarks. They asked if she had any idea what it was like for those who had been bereaved. They weren't listened to; it was as if it didn't matter what the victims' families were feeling. Asked about the interview by John Stapleton on *The Time and Place*, Alison Crozier gave plenty of examples of the fighting spirit being shown by people. Had Anne Dickson not seen the families at their press conference that day? We too were weary, but we were still fighting.

After two phone calls, my letter and the press comment about her, Mrs Dickson should have had no doubts that her comments were causing distress to the victims' families. Just before Christmas she let rip again. It was over a Christmas tree. I can provide no better summary of our side of the Christmas tree story than the press statement that the bereaved families released in December:

> The idea to place a simple Christmas tree with seventeen white lights by the graves of our children and their teacher was first proposed and then passed on to Stirling Council for approval in early October. It had always been our view that if anyone with relatives in Dunblane Cemetery considered the idea inappropriate we would not wish to pursue it. Until last week we understood that the tree had the blessing of the Council and so were surprised when we were informed at this late stage that it could not be sited in the cemetery. The reasons for this decision were not adequately explained in the letter we received. Only after further inquiries were we told this week that a survey had

been carried out and that some objections had been received. The bereaved parents would have been willing to have discussions with the councillors involved in taking the decision at any time since October, but no one had contacted us. We feel that the Council have handled this matter badly and that communication with us should have been better.

The tree was to symbolise peace and hope and to help our families through this first Christmas without our children. However, we would not want our wishes to be fulfilled at the cost of dividing the community. At last night's meeting of the bereaved parents it was decided unanimously that we no longer wish to have a Christmas tree at the cemetery.

A few days after the Council had sent its letter to the bereaved families, the story was picked up by the media. When asked to comment, some of the families expressed their disappointment, mostly with the way the Council had handled the matter. Mrs Dickson, it seemed, had been waiting for this opportunity to criticise the parents:

> I certainly am not callous. Up till now I have fully supported the parents in what they have wanted and what they are doing, and so is the community. *We*'ve put a shell round ourselves, *we* have kept ourselves very much to ourselves but I'm afraid on this issue *we*'ve got a division. It had to happen. And it's regrettable that it's happened over a Christmas tree. But I would say that the Christmas tree is a symptom of what is wrong in Dunblane. (*Reporting Scotland*, BBC Scotland, 10 December 1996)

She claimed that 'it had to happen', though it's not clear why. As for her full support she says she gave us, there was no sign of that in her comments about Ann Pearston, nor in the way she'd dealt with the letter and phone calls.

> People feel the parents have gone too far this time. There comes a time when they should consider other people. Everyone has

been too frightened to say anything because emotions run too high, but Dunblane has been simmering and now this issue has been the crunch . . . I knew it would come to this eventually . . . This is the first time the parents have had No for an answer and a lot of people have lost loved ones this year, not just the families at the school. (*Daily Mail*, 11 December 1996)

*We*'ve been making allowances for the families for nine months. But there comes a time when they should consider other people. (*Daily Express*, 11 December 1996)

'*We*'ve been making allowances.' But wasn't that exactly what everyone might have expected from a caring community?

But *we* have protected the families of the victims for too long. The bubble was going to burst, and the tree issue has done that. (*The Scotsman*, 12 December 1996)

She presented herself as part of that caring community – '*we* have protected them'. We'd received no protection from her.

For nine months a whole lot of people have suppressed how they are really feeling. *We* have supported the parents with an outward show of solidarity . . . However I only spoke out because I knew I had such widespread support from the community which I represent . . . *We* have been subjected to a bombardment for the last nine months and it was only a matter of time before the bubble burst. The council has bent over backwards for the parents, offering every help and service it could . . . Can you imagine that? The cemetery will be full of well-meaning people laying teddy bears and the like, but *we* have had enough of well-meaning people, *we* need to be left alone to get on with life. (*Daily Mail*, 12 December 1996)

Her remarks about us not considering other people were particularly spiteful. In the *Daily Express* Dorothy-Grace Elder wrote of Anne Dickson's 'dunderheid comments'. Joan McAlpine of the *Sunday Times* picked up on what she'd said and, in an article entitled 'The two faces of douce Dunblane', made these pertinent comments:

> That insistence on enforced normality is evidence enough that 'the community as a whole' does not suffer equally. This is certainly the impression conveyed by the uncaring comments of Ann [*sic*] Dickson, the local Conservative councillor. She claims she has widespread support when she says: 'Enough is enough. We've been making allowances for the families for nine months.' Dickson and others appear to be irritated by the publicity which the families have received. But the parents only exposed their pain to change the gun laws. They learnt, as all effective campaigners must, that journalists need more than slogans to sustain a story . . .
>
> But douce has a wider, colloquial meaning: repressed, even a bit snobbish. This would appear to be Mrs Dickson's Dunblane – where you sweep inconveniences under the carpet, no matter the cost to others. We should not be surprised that this place, whose 'collective grief' journalists have misguidedly highlighted, has its selfish side . . .
>
> Mrs Dickson gave a real insight into this side of the town when she complained about making allowances for the families for nine long months. That long? Nine months takes us right back to March 13. I wonder what it was they were tolerating in those dark days? Perhaps, as the decent people of the town sat in shock with the rest of the country, douce Dunblane was worrying about the effect of the publicity on their house prices.

Anne Dickson's pre-Christmas outburst opened the floodgates. Others in the town wanted to have a go. Reporters sought out criticism of the families from the community and found some. We'd been warned that there might be people in the town on retainers from reporters looking for stories about the families. An anonymous person who was 'close to the school' divulged to the *Daily Mail* a section of a confidential letter we'd sent to the School Board. The same person criticised the Christmas tree, and like many others exaggerated its size and brightness beyond all recognition. Another critic, who didn't want to be named, moaned about our behaviour in the pub. I think this referred to an evening when we'd asked if we could watch David Scott's response to Prince Philip on the television set in the bar. In stepped the Revd Moira Herkes, the associate minister at Dunblane Cathedral, saying how we'd not dealt properly with our grief. She later claimed not to have spoken to the press, though her colleague Colin McIntosh was so concerned that he came round to the house to apologise to me.

The media turned the Christmas tree issue into a public debate. People far and wide pitched in, their understanding distorted by the exaggerations of our Dunblane critics who had doubled the size of the tree and had added flashing coloured lights. To gauge local opinion, Stirling Council conducted a poorly promoted telephone poll within Dunblane. The families had already withdrawn the idea and prepared the press statement before the result was known. The vote was heavily against the tree, though it's hard to believe that the few hundred who voted were representative of the whole community. Without all the publicity, whipped up by Anne Dickson and others, what harm would have been done by a simple tree, tucked away in one corner of the town's cemetery, a gesture for a group of families who were not just suffering individual losses but bearing most heavily the load of collective loss?

Anne Dickson claimed that her phone had been red hot with people calling to give her their support. Yet when others tried to contact her, the phone at the Council went unanswered. David Scott was one bereaved parent who phoned, anxious to know why she was so critical. After failing to contact her, he attended one of her surgeries. She wasn't there. He managed to catch up with her at the next surgery after Christmas. It was a depressing experience. Try as he might, he couldn't get through to her or make her understand how the families might be feeling. She was only concerned with herself and the community: 'Didn't he know how hard a year it had been for *us*?' He left, thanking her for not listening.

I reacted badly to Mrs Dickson's comments and became disturbed that there might be a significant section of Dunblane who agreed with her. Alan Rennie, the *Stirling Observer*'s editor, had written

> That Anne Dickson, a genuinely kind and warm-hearted person should somehow be cast in a villainous role at this stage in the whole post-Dunblane scenario is desperately unfair. What she has said is what I have heard on countless occasions since about May or June this year.

This was a surprise. In May and June none of the families had spoken in public. It must have been our private comments about the money that had upset the town's establishment.

I began to think about leaving the town and said so to the *Daily Express*. The day before Rennie's editorial, *The Scotsman* had published two letters, one from Allison Irvine, whose son Ross had died in the gym, and one from my then girlfriend Sandra. Allison wrote that 'the rest of Britain and the world, in fact, remember us and our dear ones who died. But, regrettably, it seems most of Dunblane has forgotten.' Sandra described it as 'a shameful week for Dunblane'. In fact I was relieved to find that many people went out of their way to dissociate themselves from Anne Dickson's comments. After my interview with the *Express* I received letters of support and flowers were brought to my door. Others in Dunblane wrote letters to Anne Dickson, but received no reply. 'Your remarks have done more damage to the plight of Dunblane and to the morale of those directly involved than I care to imagine,' wrote one. 'What we are witnessing,' wrote another to a friend, 'is human nature at its lowest – at its most un-Christlike. But what should we expect from unregenerate people?'

There is no doubt that some people had become unhappy that Dunblane was not just in the news but also in the charts. A local musician, Ted Christopher, had rewritten the words of Bob Dylan's 'Knocking on Heaven's Door' and, with a band made up of local musicians, ex-Dire Straits guitarist Mark Knopfler and the voices of a group of Dunblane children, he recorded the song at EMI's Abbey Road studios. The children were siblings and friends of the dead children and were uplifted by the experience. Initially it was a contribution to the anti-handgun campaign, though there were times when the project got lost in hype, especially when the tabloid press seemed more interested in whether the record would top the charts – in particular whether it would be the Christmas Number One. It did get to Number One, but a week too early for Christmas. The record got mixed reviews, reflecting varying opinions on the appropriateness of a song linked to tragedy. Whatever one's views, however, the record was a success in that it increased the profile of the anti-handgun campaign and raised £500,000 for charity.

As Christmas approached I wrote about my feelings in an article for *Scotland on Sunday*. They had asked me to comment on what had been happening in the town and whether I wanted to add more to what I'd said to the *Express* about leaving Dunblane. I decided I'd rather write a piece myself about grief. Here is part of that article:

> Two weeks ago, after much delay, I summoned up the strength to make arrangements for my daughter's headstone, believing that things were perhaps moving on, albeit very slowly. I didn't know that this would also be the week that the parents found themselves on the receiving end of callous and heartless attacks in the press and on TV, accusations from within the community that we weren't dealing with our grief appropriately and were imposing on the community by not doing so.
>
> How does one deal with this kind of grief appropriately? During the year various advice has been offered to me. Those who cared about me, friends, social workers, doctors and nurses, shared my grief and have been a great support. Others, who have never visited me, preferred to dictate the grieving process in public statements. It hurt me, and I'm sure many others, that these people, speaking on behalf of Dunblane and priding themselves in the public image of a caring community, failed to visit me and other families to find out how exactly we were coping. Nevertheless they have felt free to pontificate about when and how to grieve.

This public advice seemed to be based on a number of misconceptions about grief, most notably that there is a 'standard' grieving process which lasts for a set time. The Dunblane experts set their stopwatches going on 13th March. When a few months were up, or once events such as the Memorial Service were over, they said 'That's it, you've had enough time, we've made enough allowances, pull yourselves together and draw a line under your child's death and get back to normal.' But there is no normal for me any more.

The harsh reality of grieving in Dunblane is that a few prominent people appear unable to face the fact that one of the most heinous crimes in Scottish history happened in their midst. In rushing to heal the community, they appear prepared to leave those of us most directly affected stranded. C.S. Lewis wrote in his book *A Grief Observed* that 'an odd by-product of my loss is that I'm aware of being an embarrassment to everyone I meet . . . Perhaps the bereaved ought to be isolated in special settlements like lepers.' Unfortunately, there are echoes of his sentiments in the recent comments from a few of my fellow citizens. One local councillor would, I am sure, prefer it if we shuffled away. 'Enough is enough' she has said, but for whom? The letters and messages I have received over the last few days have reassured me that it has been 'enough' only for a minority in the city.

There has also been a collective grief. Some of my friends' children were killed or injured in the gym, and, of course, many of Sophie's friends of whom she talked lovingly were killed or injured. Even if Sophie were still alive I would be grieving deeply for them. There are many of us who share the same grief and have found comfort and strength in being together. This has played an essential role in the past few months, and the closeness of the bereaved parents group has allowed us to deal with our own grief and to face the world outside Dunblane with dignity and confidence. This has been very important for most of the parents as it has also been a very public grief.

The public deaths of our children, followed by a Public

Inquiry, made it inevitable that grieving privately would be difficult. It has been suggested that we should have left the issue of gun control to others and that we have delayed our grieving process as a consequence of our involvement. This again presumes there is a normal grieving process. I, along with the other families, knew that the death and injuries in the gym that day were the result of poor gun laws. We were in a unique position to be heard. But such is the fickleness of public opinion that I doubt we would have received such wide attention had we grieved in silence for a year and then taken up the gun issue in 1997. We believe we have done what we had to do to prevent any others having to grieve over the loss of their loved ones in such a massacre or any gun incident. Expressing our views in public is not the same as grieving in public. Most have noted the dignity with which we have conducted ourselves. The response this week to Prince Philip's crass and ill timed comments has, as always, been measured and logical. Because we are grieving does not mean we are irrational, and rarely do the public get a glimpse of the strong emotions still raging inside us. I deal with these privately.

Les Morton had summed up our feelings in many fewer words during the filming of the programme *Dunblane: Remembering our Children*. Recalling the attitude of some clergy and local politicians who wanted us to move on, he asked, 'Move on to where, exactly – to a time when we no longer remember our children?' No.

In the book *Dunblane: Our Year of Tears* Colin McIntosh wrote, 'I also have a concern that after 13 March [1997] the community as a whole will think that it's time to get back to normal. I think that will be false.' Mrs Dickson, claiming she was unrepentant about her previous comments, was one who thought it was time. Before the first anniversary, she told *The Scotsman*, '*We* have been totally swamped. *We*'re just hoping we don't get anything like the same amount of Easter eggs as *we* did last year or that teddy bears flood in again'. Her feelings about the aftermath of the massacre are still clear in more recent comments to overseas journalists.

Shortly after the horrific shootings at Columbine High School in Littleton, Colorado, in April 1999, she claimed a role in fostering community harmony in Dunblane that had eluded me:

> 'No matter what happens in the world, if some connection can be made with Dunblane, *we* are news again,' said Ann [*sic*] Dickson, a member of the region's Stirling Council and a 30-year resident of Dunblane. 'This is one of the most awful things that our bereaved families have to face. Normally, if you lose a member of your family, you are not reminded of it in such a brutal, violent way.' 'The main thing the authorities have got to get right is to involve the community,' said Mrs. Dickson. '*We* kept people busy doing things, not sitting back. From that point of view, the gripes, the bitterness, was kept to a minimum.' (Associated Press, 25 April 1999)

Canadians could read of her dislike of the public's generosity:

> 'Dunblane is a calm place again,' Councillor Ann [*sic*] Dickson said. 'It's reverted back to the same peacefulness, but I don't know how deep it is. It only takes what happened in Littleton and it comes back again.' Mrs. Dickson, the town councillor, said the funds were more trouble than anything else. 'I don't think it helps a community giving money. I think it adds to the problems of the community, quite honestly. To survive, you've got to face up to moving on.' (*Toronto Globe and Mail*, 13 May 1999)

Her resentment always appeared to be directed towards those who'd responded generously, those who'd campaigned and the families who'd suffered the most. Rather than taking us forward, moving on, what she wanted was to take us back to 12 March 1996, to a day when there'd been no massacre. We knew that wasn't possible.

Had she only spoken for herself? Judging from her claims about the red-hot phone and Alan Rennie's editorial, apparently not. I tell myself that support for her opinions was limited, though enough people in Dunblane East voted for her to continue as their councillor. In the last local elections she was re-elected with a majority of 538. When the possibility arose that the Conservatives might control Stirling Council their group put forward Anne Dickson as their candidate for Provost. The Conservatives didn't take control.

After the events of 13 March there must have been a variety of feelings within Dunblane among those who'd known Hamilton. Some local people were prepared to blame others for their harassment of Hamilton and for spreading rumours about him. This was also a view expressed by the Scottish Target Shooting Federation in their submission to the Cullen Inquiry. Other Dunblane residents may have felt ashamed of their earlier contact with him, others that they hadn't done enough to stop him. Although not a Dunblane resident, Thomas Hamilton had participated in the community for many years and had finally taken revenge on it, presumably because he resented its unwillingness to accept him. No one in Dunblane had encouraged him to murder, and whether they had supported him or opposed him no longer mattered.

Are the connections between the killer and the town a reason why some in the community want the massacre hidden away in the past? They could be, but in my opinion much of what has happened has to do with small-town politics.

As a result of the *Stirling Observer* publishing a cruel anonymous letter on the day before the first anniversary, I'd had occasion to reply to a letter I'd received from editor Alan Rennie. I wrote about the community's needs:

> In your letter you often refer to the needs of local residents and the community. Of course the wider community deserved support, but many of these people's lives go on normally. The effect on them of the events of March 1996 has been transient, especially when viewed in relative terms. I am sorry if they find it difficult to be reminded that one of the most awful crimes in Scottish history happened on their doorstep. They can always turn to another page of their newspaper or another TV channel if they really want to forget about it. I don't have that luxury. Your emphasis on the suffering of the 'community' overlooks the

fact that, with respect to the effects of the shootings, there is inevitably an enormous gulf between different groups. The bereaved families and those of the injured were always going to suffer more and for longer than the community in general. A caring community would wish to continue to share the loss with us, not attempt to brush it away under a carpet of media silence. Fortunately, in my experience only a few belong to the 'enough is enough' brigade, but they have been disproportionately vocal.

The letter you chose to publish on the eve of the first anniversary was the culmination of months of spiteful comments against those of us who had lost loved ones in the tragedy. It caused deep hurt among the bereaved families at one of our most difficult times, as you surely know. If it reflected 'sincere views held by many local residents' then you, as a responsible editor, should have chosen a less vindictive letter and, most crucially, one from a correspondent who did not hide behind a cowardly cloak of anonymity. You also had the option of delaying publication until after the TV programme had been screened instead of allowing it to be prejudged [*Dunblane: Remembering our Children* is described in Chapter 10]. The printing of the letter, together with the content of some of your editorials, contributed to the atmosphere of unsubstantiated rumours and gossip in which a few of the Dunblane 'community' had indulged for months.

My views about some of the post-massacre events in Dunblane are perhaps more critical than those of the other families, though I was never alone in feeling hurt by these incidents. These could have induced us to give up campaigning, but it didn't. There were others whose attitude towards us was far more encouraging. They contributed to more enriching events, a positive side to the aftermath that showed that the vast majority of people cared.

# CHAPTER TEN

# Memorials and Anniversaries

## October 1996–April 1998

'Forever remembered'

## 9 OCTOBER 1996

'Out of Darkness into Light'

A Memorial Service for the Dunblane victims was proposed very soon after the massacre, and certainly before any of the families could be consulted. When some of us travelled to London in April with the *Sunday Mail* petition, the journalists told us that they'd heard about a service being planned for Westminster Abbey. It was news to us and it felt as if the tragedy was being taken out of our hands. Such a service, we feared, might be full of pomp and couldn't reflect appropriately the lives of sixteen bright infants and their teacher. Fortunately other more prominent Scots had already expressed the view that if there were to be a service it should be held in Scotland. For us it could only be in Dunblane. We had a cathedral, so why did we need to travel hundreds of miles to remember our children?

Michael Forsyth, visiting us in early May, had also mentioned a memorial service. It appeared to be what the community needed so that a line could be drawn. Although there was some pressure to arrange it as soon as possible, we dug in our heels. The memorial service should wait until the families were ready. It would have to be held after the Cullen

Inquiry was over and preferably after the Cullen Report came out. During the summer a representative group of parents, Karen Scott, Kareen Turner and Kathryn Morton, met with the local clergy, and a plan for the service gradually evolved. It would be ecumenical, with each of the town's ministers participating. Because of the Cullen Inquiry and the summer holidays, there was no suitable date until October. Wednesday was considered to be the best day of the week, but we had to rule out the Second, Sophie's birthday, and the Twenty-third, when Kevin Hasell should have been six. We decided on the Ninth. As it turned out, the Cullen Report did not appear until a week after the service.

Dunblane Cathedral has room for 600–700 people, which placed severe restrictions on the numbers who could be invited. Each of the bereaved families was able to invite a handful of personal guests. We'd wanted to restrict the number of dignitaries to a minimum and differed amongst ourselves about whether a member of the Royal Family should be invited. The majority view was that one of them ought to be there. We'd hoped that the Princess Royal, who had special links to Scotland, could come, but she was already engaged. The invitation went to the Prince of Wales. Given his love of shooting sports, this was not without controversy and did not go without comment among some of the press. Only two national politicians were invited, Michael Forsyth and George Robertson. Invitations were sent to the families of the other children in the class, to the school staff and to representatives from as many as possible of the groups of people who had been directly involved. It was possible to include many thousands more as the service was relayed to other Dunblane churches and televised throughout Britain by the BBC.

The service was planned to be an inspirational occasion. There was no funereal black and the fathers sported bright ties that our children would have loved. Each of us wore a tartan ribbon as a token of remembrance and a symbol of solidarity. Joyful hymns had been selected – 'All Things Bright and Beautiful' at the start, 'Shine, Jesus, Shine' at the end. I found the music inspiring. Some of it had been composed in memory of the victims, a hymn by Jean Holloway, an anthem by Robert Steadman. But I was less in touch with other parts of the service, the lessons, the prayers and the sermon. Those worrying elements of drawing lines and moving on had crept in. The theme was 'Out of the darkness, into the light', but this was still far too early for me.

Following her reporting of the massacre for GMTV, broadcaster Lorraine Kelly had become close friends with Pam Ross and was invited to participate in the service. She read a poem, 'Little Child Lost' by Eugene G. Merryman, Jr. Then came the most moving part of the service. To the plaintive sound of 'Lament for the Children', played by lone piper Hugh McCallum, Lorraine read out the names – Gwen Mayor first and then each of the children: Victoria Clydesdale, Emma Crozier, Melissa Currie, Charlotte Dunn, Kevin Hasell, Ross Irvine, David Kerr, Mhairi MacBeath, Brett McKinnon, Abigail McLennan, Emily Morton, Sophie North, John Petrie, Joanna Ross, Hannah Scott and Megan Turner. As each name was read, family members came forward to light an eight-inch white candle on which a name had been spelt out in gold letters. There is something especially poignant about the lighting of candles to remember those who have died.

Over tea after the service I got into conversation with a somewhat perplexed Prince Charles. He asked me if I came from Dunblane. I don't know why else I would have been there with him. I decided to get away from the formality and Willie Turner and I walked across the road to the Tappit Hen. Others joined us to relax after an emotional occasion. In the evening the bereaved families met for a meal at Coll Earn House in Auchterarder, a few miles up the A9, the first of many such meals held on special occasions. Our guests that evening were Chris de Burgh and his wife Diane, with whom we'd kept in touch since his concert.

There were stressful times ahead, especially the publication of the Cullen Report, but there would also be more pleasurable things. As Christmas approached, many of the other families took up offers that their children could enjoy: a children's party provided by the Celtic Supporters Club (they were incredibly generous on this and other occasions); a trip to Finland to see Santa Claus, courtesy of *The Sun*; and another chance to see Santa in Aviemore on a trip organised by Scalliwags, the Dunblane pet shop. The latter proved to be something of an adventure when many of the families became stranded overnight in Aviemore by a snowstorm. I couldn't join in these things. I would have struggled to have been with so many children. Scalliwags generously gave me a clockwork toy collector's item instead. I helped Breakthrough Breast Cancer at their annual party in London, enjoying drawing the winning raffle tickets. They presented me with a huge box of purple crocus bulbs for Dunblane. I also sold raffle tickets at one of Breakthrough's Delia Smith evenings in Edinburgh.

The first Christmas without our children wasn't helped by the spate of public criticism that erupted in Dunblane. Nevertheless the bereaved families were able to enjoy themselves at another dinner in Auchterarder and a smaller group of us had Christmas lunch together. To show our appreciation to the many people who'd helped us in the previous nine months, we sent Christmas cards from the Thursday group. The cards showed a section of a new altar cloth from the Chapel Royal at Stirling Castle. The cloth had been commissioned by Historic Scotland, designed by Malcolm Lochhead and created under his direction by the Stirling Embroiderers' Guild, its theme 'Stella Maris' – Star of the Sea. Before it had been completed, seventeen stars had been added to the original design, in memory of Gwen and the children.

## 13 MARCH 1997

'Will the Prime Minister join me in recalling that it is a year to the day since the terrible event in Dunblane? We remember the little ones who died and we grieve with their parents and their friends. They will not be lost to the nation's memory'

(OPPOSITION LEADER TONY BLAIR)

By the time of the first anniversary it would have been all too easy to withdraw entirely to find peace and quiet. But it was naïve to think that 'Dunblane' would go away, and we wanted the public to know how we were getting on and what their help and love had meant to us. They'd supported us and we thought it would be good for them to know how much they'd helped us through the darkest times. Our children's deaths had been a national tragedy, indeed the more I travel the more I know it was something that affected people worldwide.

To try to make sure that the anniversary passed quietly in Dunblane itself, something we ourselves needed and the town wanted, the parents issued a press statement a few weeks before. We thought that the request was more likely to be respected if it came directly from us. We contacted the *Stirling Observer* and the Press Association:

> Thursday 13th March will mark the first anniversary of the deaths of our children and their teacher at Dunblane Primary School. This will be a very emotional day for us and for the rest of Dunblane. We have decided that this ought to be a day free from media attention, during which we will remember our loved ones in our own personal way. We do not wish there to be any public event on the anniversary.
>
> In a statement to be released through the Press Association we are requesting that the media stay away from Dunblane on 13th March and that they refrain from asking for comments from ourselves or any other members of the community on the day. We hope we will have everyone's co-operation in this.
>
> We do wish, however, to invite our fellow residents to mark the anniversary with one simple gesture. At 7 o'clock in the evening on 13th March we would ask you to place, with due care, a lighted candle in your front window. In this way you can show how much the memories of our children and Gwen Mayor shine on in Dunblane.

The idea of lighting candles was taken up by a number of newspapers. The *Daily Record* immediately announced that it would give away candles for the anniversary.

A year after such a horrendous event there was bound to be media interest and journalists would want to revisit the story, if not the town. It was not inappropriate for us to say something, and some of us willingly participated in the making of a television film and in the production of a book. It was almost inevitable that these would appear around the time of the first anniversary.

The making of the film *Dunblane: Remembering our Children* had evolved from a conversation I'd had with Anna Hall in the summer. Anna is Olwen's cousin and had been brought up in Dunblane before moving to England. She now worked for Chameleon, a television production company based in Leeds. She arranged to meet me and asked about the possibility of making a film. She was not the only television person approaching us at the time, but given her local connections, there was something particularly important about giving Anna's request serious consideration. The topic of gun control was suggested but was not developed, as there were too many other programmes about guns. The subject of the documentary remained open until Anna and her colleague Allen Jewhurst came to one of our Thursday meetings. Having listened to us talk, Allen commented that there really was only one possible subject for the film – us, the bereaved parents, our friendship and what we had given one another. By the beginning of November we agreed to go ahead.

Individual families were interviewed during the next two months and Chameleon's cameras came to some of our meetings and social functions. These included our pre-Christmas get-together in Auchterarder and a Christmas Day party at Karen and David Scott's. The cameras were also allowed to record more personal family occasions, the dedication of a tree for Abigail McLennan, a visit to the Wallace Monument by the Dunns and the Turners' trip to Ireland at the invitation of RTE, when Kareen braved her way through a reading of 'Little Child Lost' at a Christmas service in Galway Cathedral.

We had plenty of control over the content of the film. Some of the parents went to Leeds for a preview. They suggested very few changes. The producers had done a brilliant job, dove-tailing the individual family pieces together to make a programme that was so much more than a sum of the parts, a tale of friendship in adversity and of mutual support that had helped us come to terms, at least in part, with what had happened. Our children's spirits shone through as their mums and dads talked about them and shared some of their lives with those who watched.

Some people prejudged the programme. The letter published

anonymously in the *Stirling Observer*, the day before the first anniversary, provided a reminder of how some in Dunblane felt. Its author represented that small group of people who were either bitter at being reminded about an event they were trying to forget, or, worse still, jealous of the attention a small group of their fellow citizens was receiving. This person wrote:

> Millions sympathised with the parents of the dead and injured children — and many still do. But recent events have cast a shadow over any pity we can have for them.
>
> And now tonight, on Scottish Television, there is a programme which is said to be the most moving ever made. I for one won't be watching it. I've had my fill of heartache this month already, thanks to the saturation coverage in the nationals.

The wider public took a different view. We received hundreds of letters saying how much people had appreciated the programme. Even that hardened bunch, the TV reviewers, were full of praise. In *The Observer* Will Self described it as 'austere, uncomplicated and intolerably moving': it 'was dignified by simplicity, rendered unsensational by its no-frills camerawork and in no way exploited the feeling of the cruelly bereaved'. The film was later nominated for awards, but these positive reactions and reviews meant more than any prizes.

There were other resenting voices, not least one bitter gun owner who wrote to Pam and Kenny Ross accusing us of laughing while he and his fellow shooters stood to lose everything they enjoyed. It never ceased to amaze us how attached some men were to these lumps of metal. It was scary how crucial guns appeared to be to their lives. Even the film, a dramatic reminder of the damage their guns could do to others' lives, failed to move them.

The book *Dunblane: Our Year of Tears* was the suggestion of two *Sunday Mail* journalists, Peter Samson, whom we already knew, and deputy news editor Alan Crow. There were twelve chapters, each one telling the story of an individual affected by the Dunblane massacre. There was a shopkeeper, the Dunblane florist Irene Flaws; a politician,

George Robertson; a TV presenter, Lorraine Kelly; a journalist, Melanie Reid of the *Sunday Mail*; a churchman, Colin McIntosh; and a musician, Chris de Burgh. Those most directly affected were represented by a child, Col Austin, who had survived horrendous gunshot wounds; a teacher, Eileen Harrild; Pam Ross, included as the campaigner; a husband, Rod Mayor; a mum, Kareen Turner; and a dad, myself. My contribution was based on a long taped interview that was translated into text and gives only a snapshot view of what I was feeling and thinking at that particular time. The book didn't set out to describe the whole story, nor analyse all the whys and wherefores. Thomas Hamilton's name was never mentioned.

I thought that the structure of the book might make it too disjointed and that it would read like a series of newspaper articles. But it worked well, showing how a group of real but diverse people had been affected by the atrocity that Hamilton had committed. Like the film, it gave those who had written to us and helped us an opportunity to find out how we were one year later. No profit was made from the book. By the autumn its sales had raised £50,000 for the Save the Children Fund.

The media didn't ignore Dunblane on the day of the anniversary. Papers printed stories and the television news included sensitive reports. But not one reporter came to Dunblane. The families were able to go to the school, to visit the Cemetery and to gather together at Churches House for a meal in the evening without any interference from the press. We had learnt a lot about dealing with the media, and although it wouldn't always be so, our relationship with them worked well. Candles were lit in Dunblane that evening, hundreds of them. Everywhere I went candlelight flickered in windows, memories shining out. News reports recalling 'Scotland's blackest day' described candles being lit across the country.

We weren't forgotten elsewhere. In the House of Commons Tony Blair's first question to the Prime Minister invited John Major to join him in recalling the anniversary: 'We say to all the people of Dunblane our thoughts and prayers are with them today and in the years to come.' John Major responded that the Leader of the Opposition had spoken for everyone in the House and millions beyond it. 'Clearly this will be a very difficult and emotional time for the bereaved and the entire community of Dunblane.'

## SPRING 1998

'You can almost hear the chatter of children in the sound of the fountain'

Although there was some immediate community comment about the need for a memorial, nothing happened until after the families had been consulted. Because it was within the grounds of a working school, the site of the gym was not an appropriate place for the main memorial. After the gym was demolished the site was cleared and marked with tubs of flowers. Now it is planted out as a small garden, and at one corner there is a cairn bearing a simple plaque with the names of those who died. For those unaware of its history it would be impossible to imagine this as a place of mass murder. I hope, however, that those who do know will never forget.

One of the first suggestions for a memorial was a stained-glass window at the Cathedral. It was something that the bereaved families endorsed, something particularly fitting as the Cathedral had been such a focus after the shootings. For many outside the town the Cathedral had been one of their main images of Dunblane. Obstacles were raised to this and I never understood why, especially as there were no such difficulties in three other local churches, which now have beautiful new windows. St Blane's, near the centre of Dunblane, has a window whose design includes seventeen doves released from the hands of a young girl and boy. The window at Lecropt Kirk, which stands on a hillside between Dunblane and Bridge of Allan, is based on the words of 'All Things Bright and Beautiful'. The Church of the Holy Family in Dunblane has three windows called 'Lead, Kindly and Light' in which seventeen doves carry seventeen different flowers; each one linked in some way to one of the victims. Sophie's flower is a Pelargonium, Sophie Cascade.

Four years after the massacre a memorial was finally erected in the Cathedral, a two-metre high Clashach standing stone. On the stone are various inscriptions. The sculptor, London-based Richard Kindersley, believes the inscriptions give the stone a voice: 'The stone, with its inscriptions, is placed to heal that man-made chasm [the shocking and violent intrusion of the adult world into the children of Dunblane].' The only direct reference to the shootings is the inscription, 'The Tragedy of Dunblane 1996' on the Caithness flagstone base.

It was decided by the bereaved families that the main memorial would in fact be sited at Dunblane Cemetery in the form of a Memorial Garden. Headstones for the children and Gwen Mayor had been erected during the months following the massacre. Each one is unique in its shape, design and wording. I took my time with Sophie's. It was important to get the words for her exactly right. I wanted her mum to be remembered, too. It was always Sophie's smile that shone through the sadness and I thought of this, more than anything else, as I struggled to compose an appropriate inscription. I sketched out a design with a snowdrop for Sophie, the Breakthrough crocus for Barbara and between them a radiant golden sun: 'Still Smiling Somewhere'. I ordered the stone just before Christmas 1996, and the stonemasons ensured that it was in place in time for the first anniversary.

Planning the Memorial Garden began during the summer of 1996. From the autumn onwards a small group of us that included Kenny Ross, Les Morton, Charlie Clydesdale and myself held regular meetings with Stirling Council officials. We discussed all aspects of the work, the design, development and construction. The other families were given regular updates. The plans were co-ordinated by Stuart McKenzie until he left the Council, and then by Dougal Thornton. We were grateful to both of them for the time they took and the care they showed in helping us with the project. The construction of the Garden was funded by donations made to the Dunblane Fund and the *Stirling Observer* Help Fund. Money has also been set aside to ensure that it is a lasting memorial that is always cared for and maintained.

The families saw photographs of many types of memorial to help us decide on the design of the main feature. We agreed unanimously on a water feature that incorporated coloured pebble mosaics designed by

Manchester artist Maggie Howarth. Maggie sent plans for a fountain in which her mosaics formed the base of two intersecting circular pools, the upper one with a fountain at its centre for Gwen Mayor, the lower one for the children. Water flows gently from the upper to the lower pool. The children's pool has pebble images of the sun, the moon, a rainbow, flowers, fish and sea creatures – things that would appeal to everyone who is young at heart. The upper pool has a ring of pebble flowers around the fountain. Each pool is edged in granite in which the names are carved. The words 'Forever Remembered' are also carved into the upper pool. The Portuguese granite was shipped to Scotland for cutting and carving. Indeed as much as possible of the work was carried out by Scottish contractors. Watsons Stonecraft was responsible for the construction of the memorial pools and fountain.

The planning of the Memorial Garden was an example of what could be achieved when we worked together quietly and carefully with the Council, uninfluenced by publicity or the so-called needs of the community. The families were more than equal partners. It wasn't necessary to have projects carried out on our behalf in our absence. We were, after all, still competent human beings. Tragedy sets you back, but doesn't deprive you of basic abilities.

The Garden is an integral part of the Cemetery. Anyone entering the Cemetery and walking up the sloped roadway can easily spot it. Around a slight curve there is an area, bright with the colour of flowers and alive with the movement of windmills. The air is filled with the gentle tinkle of wind chimes and, in the background, the bubbling of the fountain. Surrounded by birch trees and beech hedges, the Garden's entrance is marked by a stone wall on which a bronze plaque is mounted in the form of an open book. On the right-hand page are the names and dates of birth of the seventeen victims, surrounding a burning candle. On the left-hand page are the following words:

This garden is dedicated to the
Memory of our Beloved Children
And their Dear Teacher
Whose Lives were Taken
So Tragically on 13th March 1996
At Dunblane Primary School

We Treasure Them for all They were
And Remember that They Hold a
Unique and Precious Place in the
Hearts of Those who Love Them

May all who Visit this Garden find
Peace and Hope for the Future

To the left, on a hill, is a curved bench beside another of Maggie Howarth's mosaics in the form of a snowdrop that looks especially beautiful when the pebbles are wet after a rain shower. This is a quiet place to sit if the Cemetery is busy. A path leads down the hillside from the snowdrop mosaic, crosses the cobbled roadway and enters a circular seating area, protected by a sandstone wall. At its centre is a spring-flowering cherry, which blossoms shortly after each anniversary. A daisy-chain pebble mosaic encircles the tree. Beds surrounding the tree and outside the wall are planted out with flowers throughout the year. The Garden has a number of benches donated by well-wishers to Dunblane. The path leads on to the fountain, passing through the heart of the Memorial Garden. On either side of the path are the two rows of headstones and the lairs they mark, the reason why a beautiful garden is here.

The construction of the Garden was a time-consuming project, but it was ready by the second anniversary when two dedication ceremonies were held. On 13 March the families held a simple ceremony on our own. Four of us read a few lines, some prose or poetry, and then the fountain was switched on. Watching the water gurgling out for the first time, Alison Ross squealed with delight, her joy captured on a video recording that our friends from Chameleon TV made. For the rest of us the joy was diluted by thoughts of Alison's sister Joanna and of Joanna's classmates and teacher.

The official dedication ceremony took place on Saturday, 14 March. We invited as many as possible of the people who had been involved in the project: the fund trustees, the planners, the craftsmen and the gardeners, people such as David Wilson, who built the garden's walls, and the artist Doug Cocker, who designed the bronze book. We had asked the media not to come, but gave them details of what was happening and told them that video footage would be available through Chameleon TV. We'd invited the Revd Maxwell Craig from Scottish Churches House to dedicate the Garden. Scottish Churches House had been generous in their provision of facilities for us, and Maxwell's involvement was one way of acknowledging our gratitude to them. On a beautiful sunny spring day he provided the appropriate words about remembrance. He added:

What the parents have done is to share something of themselves with all of us in a positive, life-changing way. One of those changes is that handguns are now outwith the law. More importantly they have shown us an aspect of God's truth that despair can give way to hope.

After Maxwell's speech it was my turn to say thank you:

During the last two years there have been many events we have approached with mixed emotions. Today is certainly no exception. For myself, the emotions have never been so mixed; there is a feeling of satisfaction at what has been created here, but there is, as always, immense sadness.

This Garden is a beautiful place in which we can all remember the loved ones we lost. The cheerfulness and brightness of a Primary One classroom is evoked by each one of the pebbles in the pools; you can almost hear the chatter of children in the sound of the fountain. The flowers have always been here to brighten our darkest mood, the benches have provided somewhere to rest when we have wanted to stay for a while. The stone walls reflect the strength and permanence of our love for Gwen and the children. And through the words of the plaque and the names carved on the memorial we know that they will not be forgotten.

The links between us and those we lost can never be broken. There is no indelible line we can draw to separate us from what happened in March 1996. We shall never forget. No one should ever forget.

Without each other and without the kindness, love and generosity shown to us by so many people from around the world, it is difficult to know how we would have stumbled into the future. We have gained great comfort from all this support, and we thank everyone who has helped us, in whatever way. This Garden was created, first and foremost, in memory of Gwen Mayor and our children, but there is no doubt that it is also a symbol of the love and support we have been given.

To those of you who are here today may I say how much we have appreciated the skill, labour and devotion you have put into creating the Garden and Memorial. We thank you for everything that you have done. The Memorial Garden is something that you and the families can be very proud of, that Dunblane can be proud of. It is a fitting tribute to a wonderful teacher and sixteen wonderful children, Forever Remembered.

Throughout the year one or other lair is brightened by the arrival of dozens of extra flowers as each child's birthday is lovingly remembered. Each Thirteenth of March, and at Christmas, more flowers and messages arrive and candles are lit. Even little Christmas trees have a place.

We probably know of only a fraction of the other memorials that people worldwide have set up since March 1996. A group of us drove to Skye on 2 May 1997 to visit Carbost Primary School where the children had created a new garden. A cairn had been built in the garden and was dedicated to the children of Carbost and to Gwen Mayor and the children of Dunblane. Our children's names are inscribed in brass and mounted on the stones of the cairn. In a simple ceremony Donnie Munro, for many years the lead singer with Runrig, performed the dedication. I've been back to Carbost twice, and on two rainy September Sunday mornings have stood amongst the fuchsias, montbretia and roses of the garden and appreciated this reminder of how much the deaths of our children had affected a wider community beyond Dunblane.

There have been many trees planted in memory of the Dunblane victims. Many are growing in peace parks in Israel, some on Holy Island off Arran. I especially like the oak trees planted at Edwinstowe in Sherwood Forest. Sophie and I had visited the Visitor Centre there in April 1995. With the help of Fran, who was visiting me from Australia, and the local vicar, I found these young oaks growing on the edge of the Forest in December 1999.

In April 1998 a number of us travelled to Leicester for the dedication of another Dunblane memorial. I drove on my own on a journey that brought back memories of another journey I'd made in June 1996. I drove back down the M74 and M6, past Lockerbie, the Lake District and

Forton Services, but this time I didn't keep checking the radio news. I'd lived in Leicester 25 years before and the last time I'd been there was in 1995 when Sophie and I had eaten at McDonalds. The families met up together at a quirky hotel on the outskirts of Leicester, my 'extended family' having a weekend away. We were there to be part of the naming ceremony for the 'Flame for Dunblane'.

In response to the shootings at Dunblane, The National Association for Primary Education (NAPE) had been donated £12,000 by primary schools and individuals from all over England. NAPE had contacted Dunblane Primary School about their idea of using the money for a memorial, and, assuming that the idea had the blessing of the families, NAPE had gone ahead with commissioning a sculpture. The sculpture was to be placed in The National Forest, a major new project on the borders of Leicestershire, Derbyshire and Staffordshire where trees were being planted on reclaimed industrial land. Sculptor Walter Bailey had presented his idea for a ten-foot wooden flame carved from a yew tree. It wasn't until NAPE made a press announcement about Walter's sculpture, in October 1997, that the families first became aware of the memorial. Karen Scott immediately made contact with Chris Davies, then Chair of NAPE, who was horrified that we'd been told nothing about their plans. We weren't surprised. It wasn't the first time that information hadn't reached us. Chris and Walter came to Dunblane straight away. Everyone was relieved that the sculpture met with our support and that the preparations could go ahead.

George Robertson was invited to perform the naming ceremony. We met him at the National Forest as an old friend. Chris Davies read a poem he'd composed especially for the occasion and David Scott gave a speech on our behalf. A piper played and local schoolchildren placed tributes. It was good to know that the children and Gwen would be remembered here too, in the heart of England. I visited the Flame again in December 1999. Standing proudly within a grove of rapidly growing birch trees, it will soon be surrounded by new forest.

These memorials have been made possible because of the generosity of many thousands of people who care, those who understand the importance of remembering what happened in March 1996.

# PART FOUR

## 1997 ONWARDS

Candles lit for a third time,
Brighten your name for a while.
Leaves turning gold, for the third time,
Unlit by your golden smile.
So many know that smile now,
But for most too late.
Today you should have been eight
WRITTEN FOR SOPHIE'S BIRTHDAY, OCTOBER 1998

# CHAPTER ELEVEN

# Learning from Experiences

## 1997 onwards

'No event in recent Scottish history has caused more horror and revulsion'
(*TWENTIETH-CENTURY SCOTLAND*)

Almost four and a half years have passed since that terrible day in March 1996. We are into another decade, a different century and a new millennium. In 1999 a number of books were published that attempted to squeeze the whole of the twentieth century between their covers, recording its key events at home and abroad. There is no doubt that history judges what happened in Dunblane as a major event. Turn to March 1996 in many of the books and you'll find a photograph of an infant class, its pupils' eager faces beaming out from the page. These Dunblane children were supposed to become young citizens of the third millennium, but sixteen of them never got there. As the years go by, the issues raised by their deaths should not be ignored.

The last four and a half years have provided me with many experiences I wish I'd never had to have, but ones that have also taught me a lot. My academic career is over. I tried to get it going again. When I finally went back to the university and to lecturing at the beginning of 1997, it was always a struggle. After a single hour's lecture, I'd be left with a splitting headache: the strain of staying focused for even that short time was too much. I staggered through tutorials, a form of teaching I once thrived on, never feeling on top of what I was doing. During all-day practical classes I wasn't able to give the students anything like the attention they deserved. My powers of thought and concentration had been decimated. I found it difficult to be with people and couldn't deal with the humdrum of departmental meetings whose politics now seemed trivial. And even if I could deal with the teaching, the zest for research had gone. The frontiers of science wouldn't stand still and wait for me to get going again. I felt more and more out of touch and less and less capable of catching up.

I had a number of meetings with representatives of my union, the Association of University Teachers. They'd been supportive throughout, both of me personally and of the gun-control campaign. I wanted to be sure that I made the right decisions. The university's Principal had been encouraging about my getting back to work but knew that things would be difficult. I was disappointed, however, with the response from elsewhere. Retirement looked like the only option open to me. I'd considered working part time, but even that would have been too much. I was on medication, anti-depressants and sleeping pills and still wasn't coping well enough. After long discussions with my union representative, my GP and my head of department, I conceded that I couldn't continue working full time. I took early retirement through ill health in September 1997. I've tried to reflect on how I might have fared if I'd defied medical advice, ignored how I was feeling and carried on working. I am confident that I made the right decision.

My departure was low key. I slipped away from so many of the things that had dominated my life since I started my undergraduate studies in Oxford in 1966. I'd had over thirty years of experience that I now thought I'd never use again. Yet that experience has, I think, allowed me to bring a measure of objectivity to those other issues in which I've become involved. Although I wouldn't be publishing or editing any more scientific papers, I could use my skills in other ways. Sophie did get her name on a research paper, however. When we'd visited San Diego again in 1995, she'd sat with me as I discussed research work with an American colleague, Hud. She'd interrupted us rather a lot, but had made such an impression on Hud that he dedicated one of his papers in the *Journal of Cell Science* to Sophie's memory.

I left Dunblane in July 1997. The town had too many painful associations. I was searching for some peace and quiet. The move away from Sophie's home was always going to be emotional, but was made worse by the intrusion of the tabloid press into my private life. It was the first, but wouldn't be the last time that I found the press had overstepped the mark. I didn't sell Willowbank House immediately. It was still full of Sophie's things. In the end I gave a lot of them away, but I've kept many of the clothes, toys and books, poignant reminders of those five and a half years we'd shared together. I finally sold the house to friends who allow me to go back and visit whenever I want to.

Since Sophie's death there were some good things Dunblane had given me which I didn't give up. I drove down for the Thursday meetings to maintain those vital links with the other parents, and I played my part in the group's tasks. For a while there were a few problems with leaks from the meetings, one member of the group talking to the press about confidential matters. This was upsetting for all of us who regarded the meetings as private opportunities to get things off our chests. If there were anything to tell the media, we'd agree to release a press statement that we all approved. Once the Memorial Garden had been dedicated in March 1998, there was less formal business and the weekly meetings eventually came to an end a year or so later. The strength among the families continues and we see each other a lot, still among the few who can really understand exactly how we're feeling.

From the outside our togetherness and strength may have been difficult to understand, but it served us well when we could have been cowed by the aftermath. The togetherness was something we shared with others we met, others who'd also been deeply affected by tragedy. When I first met Judith and Tony Hill there was an immediate and mutual understanding between us, parents who had lost daughters to gunmen in Dunblane and Hungerford. The understanding helped us to cope with all the pressures of setting up a new gun-control movement. The Dunblane families have forged close links with some of the families who had lost loved ones at Port Arthur in Tasmania. John Crozier and Les Morton visited the site in April 1997. Back in Scotland, on the first anniversary, the Dunblane families held a memorial service for the Port

Arthur victims in Scottish Churches House Chapel. A month later, Walter Mikac, whose wife and two daughters were among those killed by Martin Bryant, was a welcome visitor to Dunblane. Some of us had corresponded with him and he included generous references to his Dunblane friends in the book he wrote after the Port Arthur tragedy. I was able to meet him in Melbourne in December 1998. Later that month, with my Australian friends Fran and Michael, I went to Tasmania and visited Port Arthur where I was warmly greeted by John and Sue Burgess, whose daughter Nicole had been killed there. They, too, have now visited Dunblane.

On 13 March 2000 the families welcomed a group of students from Columbine High School in Colorado to Dunblane. Eleven months before, they'd experienced the horror of being in the school when two of their colleagues had opened fire on fellow students, killing twelve of them, a teacher and then themselves. I've had the opportunity to speak to survivors of gun incidents (victims and members of victims' families) through the Bell Campaign, a survivor-based organisation with chapters across the USA. I stay in contact with the Miller family in Phoenix, Arizona, whose teenage son was shot dead, and went with Beckie and Don to a meeting of their support group, Parents of Murdered Children. We are a group of people who are able to reassure one another that there are sources of comfort, and even meaning, after such adversity.

The Dunblane families had learnt the value of the support we'd received and tried to give something back. Through the combination of the book, *Dunblane: Our Year of Tears*, to which a number of us had contributed, the Dunblane single and the Dunblane Tartan Ribbon campaign, we helped to raise around half a million pounds for the Save the Children Fund. The ribbon campaign in the autumn of 1997 was inspired by the ribbons we'd worn at the Memorial Service. Save the Children expressed their appreciation by inviting a group of us to their reception on board the Royal Yacht *Britannia* in Glasgow attended by its president, Princess Anne. The sale of the two roses has been making steady contributions to the Gwen Mayor Trust and the Children's Hospice Association of Scotland (CHAS). CHAS and Childline had also benefited from the sale of the Dunblane record.

I still do things for Breakthrough Breast Cancer, though less than I'd like to. I've recently written an article for their magazine, *Purple*, explaining why I consider it important to continue doing something positive. By late 1999 Breakthrough had achieved its original aim. I was pleased to be a guest when the new laboratory facilities at the Institute for Cancer Research in London were officially opened by Prince Charles.

Out of all the things that had happened in the aftermath of Dunblane, the handgun ban was undoubtedly the most widely publicised. The deaths of the children and their teacher didn't alter the logic of the argument against the private possession of handguns. That was strong enough before. What the tragedy did was to concentrate minds, shake people into taking notice of the argument and doing something about it. Britain now has some of the toughest gun laws in the world. I hope it is never thought, however, that gun control, while fashionable in the late 1990s, is no longer an issue in the new millennium. Guns have started reappearing in advertisements, in promotions and in celebrity photographs. This is not acceptable. Guns were, are and always will be lethal weapons capable of producing appalling tragedies.

British gun enthusiasts believe that the handgun ban denied them a basic right. They continue to ask questions about Hamilton in the hope that by finding answers in procedural lapses they'll be able to deflect attention entirely away from his guns. As I've already argued, both the easy availability of guns and Central Scotland Police's firearms licensing procedures contributed to Hamilton's ability to prepare for a massacre. I've never shifted from the view that without his legal guns, Hamilton would never have planned, let alone committed, his outrage. He probably went through a series of fantasy preparations, imagining what he might do, then what he could do, until one day, weighed down by financial problems, a sense of isolation and a grievance against society, he turned fantasy into reality. His murder tools were readily available and he turned the guns he kept at home on his innocent victims. He also needed his guns to ensure his own death. It would be heartening to think that all of the parliamentary questions and other probing by the gun lobby reflect a quest for the whole truth. It appears to be part of a campaign to restore handgun shooting as a legal activity.

There is no doubt that the gun lobby, unwilling to accept the wishes of the people, will continue to look for ways to reverse the 1997 legislation. As I am writing this chapter, a report has appeared in *Scotland on Sunday* about the exemption that will allow pistol shooting to be part of the 2002 Commonwealth Games, to be held in England. In the article John Leighton-Dyson, the chief coach for the [UK] National Rifle Association, is quoted as saying that the move to allow pistol shooting at the games was the first part of a long-term strategy aimed at allowing the sport back into Britain full time:

> From day one there has been an understated, quiet attempt to get the sport back on the national agenda. We know that it will be a hard slog but we are hopeful that we can get there. Allowing pistol shooting at the Commonwealth Games was seen as an encouraging first step.

This is the thin end of the wedge. In 1997 Parliament threw out an amendment that would have allowed exemptions to the ban on .22 pistols for international competition. There should be no exemptions now. The British public will be told that we've lost the chance of gaining medals in a sport in which the home countries have always done well. After Dunblane, Hungerford and other incidents, what do most people think that handguns have given Britain — medals or murder?

Newspaper stories have been raising the spectre of increasing gun crime since the handgun ban was introduced. The stories focus very selectively on gang shootings and drug-related murders. The gun lobby emphasises that the ban hasn't stopped these. This, of course, is true, but it is ludicrous to think that these types of crime were previously committed with legally held weapons. Gun-control advocates never predicted that the ban would immediately rid the country of all gun crime. Gun control must be complemented by tougher law enforcement. Now, at least, the police and public don't have to worry about rogue gun club members using their handguns to commit crimes or about legal handguns falling into criminal hands through theft.

There is no hint from official statistics that the handgun ban has had anything but a positive effect. Gun crime in Scotland had increased until 1992 and was still at a high plateau in 1995. Since then there has been a significant decrease. In 1998, the year following the change to the law, Scotland recorded a 17 per cent reduction in all firearm-related offences. The Home Office reported that in the nine months following the handgun ban, firearm-related offences in England and Wales also dropped, by 13 per cent.

Continued vigilance and further tightening of gun legislation are essential. The Government recognised the need to listen to additional voices by broadening the expertise on the Firearms Consultative Committee. Gun Control Network (GCN) is now represented. The Parliament's Home Affairs Committee revisited the issue of 'Controls over Firearms' in 1999. In contrast to their predecessors, who had reviewed the 'Possession of Handguns' in 1996, the committee members took oral evidence from a broad spectrum of groups and individuals, including gun control advocates. No longer was the 'expert' opinion biased towards those who shoot. In GCN's written submission and oral evidence, we were able to express our concerns over a number of issues.

The first of these issues is the age at which children may start shooting. GCN is committed to the age of eighteen, matching the age of majority when people can lawfully buy alcohol, vote or enter into a mortgage contract. This is an appropriate minimum age for someone to have a lethal weapon in his hands. We must get away from the idea that it is okay for guns to be considered as toys.

A second concern is over small, rapid-fire weapons that had escaped prohibition, ones which shooters had acquired in a bid to flout the spirit of the new law. This was a situation that concerned police and politicians alike. Firearms should be regulated according to their degree of dangerousness and appropriateness, not on how they might be classified. There is no reason why these other small guns should not be treated the same as handguns.

There are also concerns about other types of gun. Shotgun owners are able to hold an unspecified number of guns on a single licence, for example. Replica, lookalike and deactivated guns can be as threatening as the real thing. Indeed in the wrong hands some deactivated weapons can be reactivated, creating another source of dangerous weapons. All categories should be outlawed. Air weapons cause damage, injury and sometimes death, but most don't have to be licensed. The danger posed by these weapons should be countered by bringing them into the licensing system.

The Home Affairs Committee's Report was published in April 2000 and made over forty recommendations, many concerned with tightening controls over gun use and ownership. GCN responded that 'this report is well-intentioned and good in parts, but it will please the gun lobby and do little to discourage future generations of shooters'. It had, however, recommended changes to shotgun licensing and the licensing of all air weapons powerful enough to be lethal. The Government's response is still awaited.

We in Dunblane are not alone in having to deal with the aftermath of a gun outrage. In the last two decades there have been too many incidents in which shooters have gunned down innocent victims because of grudges held against workmates, fellow pupils or students, a community or society in general. In other countries besides Britain, gun-control movements have grown out of personal tragedy. This timing is a sad reflection on western society's inability to face up to the problem of guns until after the event, yet we all share the blame. Where was my interest in gun control before Sophie was murdered? The strength within the gun-control movements has allowed them to achieve significant successes. The Coalition for Gun Control in Canada, for example, was set up after the shooting dead of fourteen women at the University of Montreal's Ecole Polytechnique on 6 December 1989. It has pushed for major changes in Canada's gun laws, and in spite of fierce opposition right up to the level of some of the provincial governments, a federal gun registration scheme has been introduced. The number of Canadians who have died of gunshots in suicides, homicides and accidents fell from 1,367 in 1989 to 1,131 in 1996. Firearms robberies also decreased significantly. As the Coalition says, 'While other factors influence gun-related crime and injury, progressive strengthening of gun control has had an effect.'

The National Coalition for Gun Control in Australia helped

strengthen their government's arm in the wake of the Port Arthur massacre. In their country, too, there has been a fall in gun crime since one seventh of its estimated stock of firearms was destroyed in 1996. The 1997 figure for the number of firearm-related deaths was the lowest for eighteen years. I have links with the Austrian gun-control group *Waffen Weg* (Weapons Out), whose organiser Maria Navarro, a lawyer, was shot twice in a courtroom incident in which five others were killed. Her organisation is trying to get Austrian gun laws tightened. From South Africa to Brazil, from France to New Zealand, governments have introduced, or are working on, tougher gun legislation that will make it less easy for anyone to kill with guns. Because of cultural differences and the ways in which guns have been traditionally used, each country requires its own solutions, but there is no doubt that the more guns there are in private ownership the higher the incidence of gun deaths. Gun control does make countries safer for the vast majority who are not shooters.

Whenever a government moves to introduce stricter gun laws, wherever it might be, the opposition's arguments are much the same. The lead voice has been that of America's National Rifle Association (NRA), which is very touchy about outside interference with the USA's own lax gun laws, but doesn't hold back from offering its pro-gun message to other countries. The Dunblane families and campaigners were told by Charlton Heston, the NRA's president since 1997, that we'd got it wrong. To him the Dunblane massacre had demonstrated that tough gun laws don't work. The NRA would have had armed teachers at Dunblane Primary School because in their world you have to match gun with gun, increasing the possibility of lethal shoot-outs.

What if there weren't any guns at all?

Robert Scheer in the *Los Angeles Times* recently described, accurately and succinctly, the NRA's position on the need for citizens to be armed:

> What makes the NRA position so loony is the organization's and
> its supporters' fundamental assumption that representative
> democracy is not to be trusted, and that an armed citizenry is a
> necessary check on the power of our three branches of

government on both the federal and state level. The NRA's insistence that gun-toting citizens are central to the checks and balances of a modern democracy is a paranoid response to the realities of modern governance and mocks this country's commitment to the rule of law in the eyes of the world.

The NRA has misleadingly been telling America's television viewers that the new gun laws in Australia, Canada and Great Britain haven't worked and that the basic rights of these countries' citizens have been undermined by the new firearms controls. The American gun lobby places the right to bear arms above everything else, failing to concede that it compromises other more precious rights. In a civil society we have to prioritise our rights and any sane observer cannot help but be shocked by how many Americans' right to life has been ended through gunfire. In 1997 guns were used to commit 13,522 homicides. From this side of the Atlantic the litany of massacres, including a sickening series of outrages in America's schools, highlights one common factor, the easy availability of guns. Not so, says the gun lobby and many prominent politicians, often the recipients of campaign funds from the NRA. Even a significant proportion of the population defend gun ownership as a fundamental feature of American life. There's a collective denial, which flies in the face of America's experience. Some argue that shooting atrocities can be blamed, as did presidential candidate George W. Bush, on a 'wave of evil'. If a wave of evil is flooding the USA then surely one way to minimise the damage it can do is to remove its main weapon, the gun.

A number of the world's shooting organisations and gun manufacturers have joined together to form the World Forum for Shooting Sports to try to promote shooting throughout the world. Its first meeting was held on 13 March 1997, the first anniversary of the Dunblane massacre.

The possession and use of guns is a global issue. Gun-control organisations in different countries have themselves linked up to exchange experiences and share advice. GCN organised the first get-together in London on 14 February 1997, when representatives from six countries met. The success of the British campaign has encouraged others abroad. Whether it is through personal stories, as told in some of the Dunblane families' interviews, details of the campaigns, or reporters' accounts of the changes to the UK legislation, a message has been sent out from this country that changes are possible and that the gun lobby can be resisted.

The people of America have stirred, shocked by the horror of recent shootings. More than twenty municipalities, frustrated by the toll of death and injury that has cost them dear in lives and resources, have taken out law suits against the gun manufacturers. The editorials of some of the most influential newspapers have adopted a strong stance, some advocating the unthinkable – a handgun ban in the USA. Gun control is a political issue, although in sharp contrast to Britain and Australia, a single atrocity in America fails to shift the majority of legislators. But step by step, city by city or state by state, something will happen.

On 14 May 2000 over 700,000 Americans showed how they were feeling about the gun culture in their country when they joined the Million Mom March on the Mall in Washington, DC. The moms, and many dads, were calling for tighter gun laws. Three of the Dunblane mums, Karen Scott, Kareen Turner and Alison Crozier had been invited to participate and, with the Capitol behind her, Karen gave one of the first speeches of the day. A passionate crowd sang along when Ted Christopher and his band performed their anti-gun songs, written for Dunblane, but also making sense in the land of the free. 'Throw these guns away'. My mum and I were there too, invited by the Bell Campaign. Only time will tell whether this huge protest will have an effect. Too many in America still talk about the freedom to own guns, which they believe is enshrined in the Second Amendment to their Constitution. What sort of freedom has the highest rate of gun death in the world?

Should we in Britain concern ourselves with the situation in the USA? We certainly should, for not only is slaughter offensive wherever it occurs in the world, but there are knock-on effects on other countries. The gun culture is infectious and pernicious. It spreads if left unchallenged. Through the advertisements and articles in gun magazines that glorified guns, their power and ease of concealment, Britain was being influenced by the American way of shooting. Slack gun laws in one country make it easier for firearms to be obtained by those who wish to use them illegally in another. America's numerous and notorious gun shows provide an easy source of weaponry for people who might otherwise be prevented from purchasing them. The guns used by the two schoolboy killers at Columbine High School were bought for them at a gun show. One example of relevance to Britain is an IRA gun-running scheme in which a Florida gun show was used for the purchase of handguns.

The destructive contribution to the world's problems of the widespread availability of guns has been recognised at the highest levels. I've been able to play a role, albeit a very small one, in the current moves to ensure that the global dimensions are addressed. The UN Crime Commission has been discussing the illicit small arms trade and GCN and other gun-control organisations have been invited to participate at some of their sessions. GCN has emphasised four basic tenets:

- •Gun violence in any country or community is directly related to the level of gun ownership and the availability of illegal guns;
- •Gun ownership is a privilege and not a right;
- •A gun culture will grow and threaten public safety in any society unless positive measures are taken by governments to limit it;
- •Gun control will be most effective when countries work together.

In May 1999 I was privileged to share the platform with Nobel peace laureate José Ramos-Horta and Bethuel Kiplagat, the representative of the International Resource Group in Kenya, at the launch of the International Action Network on Small Arms (IANSA) in The Hague. IANSA's activities are modelled on the successful campaign to outlaw anti-personnel landmines. The two hundred or more groups that make up IANSA, including large charities such as Oxfam and Amnesty International, peace and conflict resolution organisations and gun-control groups like GCN, are working together to try to reduce the damage that guns inflict on the lives of millions of people. Since 1990 small arms have been responsible for the deaths of more than three million civilians worldwide.

After the changes to Britain's gun laws and the Labour Government's commitment to an ethical foreign policy, I had hoped that this country would look more carefully at its involvement in the small arms trade. I'd had the opportunity to say so at a press conference organised before the European Summit in May 1998. In *Hidden Agendas* John Pilger noted what Home Secretary Jack Straw had said about the Dunblane massacre shortly after Labour's election victory.

> We cannot take risks with public safety in the interests of sport. Allowing .22 calibre weapons to remain legal would be fraught with difficulty . . . Such guns have no place in a decent society. If there is any doubt, remember the children of Dunblane.

Pilger contrasted Straw's words with the Government's approval of handgun sales to most of Europe, the United States, the Far East, Algeria, Sri Lanka and Colombia. As the situation in East Timor worsened in 1999, John Pilger commented:

> Indeed it is no exaggeration to say that British-supplied small arms have caused in East Timor the equivalent of the Dunblane massacre many times over. The grotesque hypocrisy of Tony Blair weeping for the children of Dunblane, then sending machine-guns that mow down children in East Timor, was ignored.

British governments have operated double standards in other respects. In 1998 it selected the cyber character Lara Croft as an 'ambassador' for Britain. Lara Croft is usually portrayed wielding handguns, hardly a suitable reflection on Britain's tough anti-gun policy. The families wrote to the then Secretary of State for Trade and Industry, Peter Mandelson, expressing disquiet. However when it comes to films, videos and computer games, one point must be emphasised. Obnoxious as some of the images they portray might be, no one has been killed or maimed by a video alone, no one has been shot with a computer game. The images are seen all over the world, they go into homes in America, Britain and

Japan, yet the incidences of gun deaths in these countries are vastly different. Gun violence requires a gun and the easier it is to get a gun, the more likely it is that the fantasy can be turned into reality.

The changes in gun legislation have been positive, but is it possible to conclude the same about other post-Dunblane issues? With respect to the police, the short answer is 'No'. Some key players have now left the Central Scotland stage. John Ogg took early retirement from the force in 1998, William Wilson left in April 2000. At the time of Wilson's retirement, the *Stirling Observer* reported that he had described the Dunblane tragedy as the darkest day in his police career, 'in fact the darkest day in my life'. Editor Alan Rennie commented that the Chief Constable, whom he described as a good friend to his paper over the years, had been sensitive and sensible enough not to say more than that about the tragedy. Rennie added: 'This cannot be easy when others will fly to pass judgment, all armed with that incomparable benefit called hindsight'. Here we have an influential member of the community effectively suggesting that there should be no criticism because assessments and conclusions have been made after the event. Had Wilson's force behaved appropriately at the time, such criticism would never have been necessary. Police accountability to the community does not equate with friendship with, or approval from, the local newspaper editor. The families never did get an apology from the Chief Constable.

In the absence of any openness it's hard to know how many lessons the force has learnt. A new, tougher attitude towards guns was given a high profile when newspapers reported a number of cases in which firearms were confiscated by Central Scotland Police and licences revoked. But the experience of two of my friends suggests that some complacency persists. They had complained to the police about a local gamekeeper who'd been firing his shotgun in an intimidatory way. Rather than take their complaint seriously, the officer from Dunblane police station made every excuse for the gamekeeper, said he found him very helpful and failed to take a statement of their complaint. On the basis of the inaccurate report from the Dunblane police officer, the Deputy Chief Constable initially dismissed the complaint. Only after my friends persisted, and the Royal Society for the Protection of Birds had become involved, was he prompted to send in an officer from outside the area. It was then investigated thoroughly and my friends received an apology from the Deputy Chief Constable and thanked him for his persistence. It had taken months before the matter was taken seriously. The police did find that there was substance in what my friends had reported.

Discussions are currently under way as to whether Scotland should have an independent police complaints authority, similar to the one operating in England and Wales. The police are opposed to it, preferring self-regulation through Her Majesty's Inspectorate of Constabulary. When the discussions began in 1999, Les Morton and I wrote to *The Scotsman*:

> The current debate regarding the necessity of an independent Police Complaints Authority in Scotland is an issue that is important to all the people of Scotland. The supervision and regulation of our police service must be transparent and fulfil the requirements of democracy. The argument for change is a powerful one and it is problematic that the people who decide on these issues are the least likely ever to be affected by the decisions they make. Public opinion must carry significant weight with politicians elected to represent the people and not the 'establishment'.
>
> As parents who lost children in the Dunblane Tragedy we were (and remain) deeply unhappy with the conduct and performance of the Chief Constable of Central Scotland Police. Following the existing regulations, described as 'fair and impartial' by Jim Wallace, the deputy first minister and justice minister, resulted in nothing but frustration and anger owing entirely to the unwillingness of Central Scotland Joint Police Board to answer perfectly reasonable questions and to explain their decisions. We saw no evidence of fair and impartial treatment and certainly no independence.
>
> 'Fair and impartial' is a matter of opinion. We suggest the

opinion should be based on the views of a body comprising more than those with vested interests. Democracy and accountability must be delivered and be seen to be delivered. Only an independent body has any chance of achieving this.

The experience of Dunblane suggests that an independent body is essential. I hope that the Scottish Executive and Parliament set one up.

With respect to treatment of the victims' families on 13 March 1996, some agencies are listening. The Emergency Planning Society has taken a keen interest in how victims and their families are dealt with immediately after disasters, a crucial time when mistakes can have lasting effects. The Society invited a number of people who'd been involved in disasters, including three of us from Dunblane, to talk about our experiences. The talks revealed shortcomings common to a number of different disaster situations. I had been asked to speak about the police and made the suggestion that the task of dealing with victims' families was not an appropriate one for the police and should be immediately handed over to another agency. I've since said the same at meetings of local authority emergency planners and the Red Cross. There is a willingness on the part of some agencies to take on board the real concerns of those who've been at the receiving end when their emergency plans are put into effect.

Past tragedies, not least the one at Dunblane, prompt the expression of learned opinions on a variety of issues. No issue appears more muddled than the role of debriefing and counselling in the post-disaster response. It is a topic beset by prejudices on both sides and by writing about this I may stir up already muddled waters. From my experience, no two people and no two situations have the same requirements. I know plenty of people in Dunblane who benefited from formal counselling that the Support Centre staff and others were able to provide, but after Sophie was killed I avoided having any counselling. Yet that's not entirely true, for in some of my conversations with friends, my liaison team or medical staff, I was going through the equivalent, explaining to them how I was feeling and how I was reacting. As I was doing it I was also explaining everything to myself.

In March 1999 a storm blew up over two women police officers who'd been involved at Dunblane. They were taking legal action against Central Scotland Police. The vast majority of the responses had been hostile to the women, but I thought that there was another side to this story. It was not absolutely clear from the news stories what their precise roles had been, but they claimed to be suffering from post-traumatic stress disorder as a result of what they experienced. However, they were not claiming compensation for post-traumatic stress, rather they were suing the Chief Constable for failure to provide adequate counselling after the massacre. To my mind that was an entirely different matter. *Scotland on Sunday* invited me to write an article, which I used to comment on a number of things that had been concerning me:

> It has been disappointing to see a number of commentators criticise and in some cases vilify the two women for using the law for redress because of the harm they believe has been caused by a lack of support from police management.

Referring to the way in which senior police officers behaved towards the victims' families, I added:

> It seems quite likely that they would have been dismissive of two junior officers who reacted badly to what they'd experienced . . . so it would be no surprise to me if the counselling arranged by the police left something to be desired . . .
>
> There have been a number of comments about the counselling (or Critical Incident Stress De-Briefing as the police appear to call it) that might have been available to the women. The parents had often heard rumours that the counselling offered was an empty room and a bottle of whisky. This seems to have been confirmed by comments in Friday's press from an unnamed officer who says he remembers there was whisky for everyone who wanted it 'even though it was God knows what time in the morning'. Tellingly he then questioned whether the debriefing did any good. I hardly think that the

availability of whisky demonstrates a professional approach to counselling.

The sensationalised reporting obscured the debates that should have been taking place on the value of counselling, the nature of post-traumatic stress disorder and the extent to which it affects a person's ability to work:

> There would appear to be a widespread aversion to people receiving money for mental trauma, indeed the accusation from a senior Central Scotland police inspector that the women 'were trying to profit because you're upset' sums up that attitude.

Unless stock is taken of what actually happened and what helped, it is impossible to establish the value of the various components of a post-disaster response. An evaluation involves the difficult task of asking individuals or a community about how they dealt with their trauma. There is no perfect time to do this: too soon and it is insensitive, as academics from the University of Wolverhampton found when they sent a postal survey to Dunblane in early 1997; wait too long and the recollections will be less sharp and therefore less useful. It is not wrong, however, for academics to attempt to identify the value of support care. Indeed it is essential if lessons are going to be learnt. If practice isn't based on the real experiences of those at the heart of a disaster, a lot of nonsense will continue to be talked.

As the needs in the community diminished so the role of the Dunblane Support Centre was downgraded. A part-time facility is still provided. The community of Dunblane has certainly survived. For a while the rumblings and mumblings about money continued, there was too much talk of the need for a 'Rolls-Royce' community centre or a swimming pool, but this was eventually stifled when the Youth Project was announced. Friends have told me of their embarrassment at having to stand and listen to conversations in shops when people were getting 'angry' over what had happened to their money. On the other hand there were conversations, possibly involving the same people, when the talk was of everyone being tired of Dunblane only being known for the massacre. Visitors, I believe, get a different impression. To them Dunblane would appear to be a relaxed and busy place. I am pleased that it doesn't have the appearance of a tragedy town. The vast majority of its citizens have been able to settle down again to a 'normal' life. What happened in March 1996 will never be far from their thoughts, they will be glad that they were able to help those of us who were so badly affected and they'll know that it's inevitable that the town will be linked with the tragedy for a long time to come. That is realistic. Only a minority prefer to pretend that it didn't happen.

How has Dunblane Primary School fared? In August 1996 some of its pupils and some staff transferred to the new Newton Primary School that had been under construction in March 1996. In Dunblane East we'd been asked whether we wanted our children to go there when it opened. Sophie would have stayed at Dunblane Primary, but some of the other children who died in the gym would have moved if the Newton School project, first discussed in the 1970s, had gone ahead earlier. For many of us the links with Dunblane Primary School effectively ended when our children died. From then on I thought of it as the place where Sophie had been killed.

The families had two enjoyable get-togethers with the school staff. I had great sympathy for them after the terrible experiences they'd been through on the day in their own classrooms, in the gym and in the staffroom with us when they'd been forced to keep silent about what had happened. It was always in the best interests of the children for school life to go back to normal as quickly as possible. This was reflected in the Director of Education's comment in early May 1996 that the school needed time and space to get on with teaching and learning, not special events. For those of us who were now on the outside, and no doubt for many who worked there, this was not without its difficulties, because we didn't want the school to forget what had happened.

Headteacher Ron Taylor eventually moved on, too. After a period of secondment at the Scottish Office, he left for an administrative post with

Stirling Council. A new headteacher was appointed in March 1999. The school was refurbished at a cost of £2.1 million, funded by the Scottish Office. A brand new games hall was constructed. When the refurbishment was complete in November 1998, Michael Forsyth and George Robertson returned to the school with Scottish Secretary Donald Dewar for a low-key visit. Agnes Morgan, then acting headteacher, said, 'It means we can now look ahead to the future, while at the same time never forgetting the reasons why the refurbishment was necessary.' Kids Club, too, has new premises, purpose-built following the award of £195,000 in lottery funding, part of a hand-out from the National Lottery Charities Board Scotland. The new office is graced with photographs of two of its former members, Emily Morton and Sophie North.

I only visit the school on 13 March, when a small group of us stand on the site of the old gym for a few quiet moments. The school remembers with special assemblies, but a handful of parents have objected to their children having to participate in any reminder of what happened in the school. Perhaps they believe children should not be told about such terrible events, although it seems highly unlikely that their children would not learn what happened. As a parent of one of the children killed, I feel hurt by this seeming denial of the tragedy.

Time has not made it any easier for me to imagine what happened in the Primary School gym. It remains the unthinkable. It was a brutal slaying, when a group of bright, happy children who were about to do gym exercises, were deliberately and violently attacked by a man firing bullets into their young bodies. Lord Cullen concluded that Hamilton 'was not mentally ill but had a paranoid personality with a desire to control others in which his firearms were the focus of his fantasies'. Have we learnt enough to be able to answer that ubiquitous question, 'Why'? What we can surmise is summed up well by Peter Barnard in *We Interrupt This Programme*:

> Psychologists, for once in agreement, said that in seeking to look after children, through his clubs and camps, Hamilton was seeking the parents' acceptance. He was saying that he could be

trusted, but his behaviour with the children meant that he could not be trusted. In Hamilton's mind, this had nothing to do with the children as such, it was the fault of the parents. And if there was one sure and savage way to punish parents, it was to take away their children. That is what Hamilton thought he was doing on 13 March 1996. He took the lives of 16 children, in order to take revenge on their parents.

For sixteen families this fails to answer that awful question, 'Why was it our children?', and for one husband, 'Why was it my wife?' They were, it appears, in the wrong place at the wrong time. Unlike others in the town, they had nothing to do with Hamilton and neither did those of us who lost them.

One complaint voiced during that shameful pre-Christmas period in 1996 was that our children's deaths were being treated as more important than others. In life the children had been ordinary kids, special to us, but no different from thousands of other children all over Scotland. They were set apart from those other children when they became victims of a mass murder. In death they became public figures. Out there in the world beyond my house in Dunblane, others now knew Sophie and her classmates. The country treated them as special.

However it is viewed, for a small community the scale of the carnage was horrendous. One sixth of Dunblane's five-year-olds were killed and more than half of that year's deaths among under-25s in the Stirling area occurred during those three minutes in the gym. But I know that in a world that repeatedly throws up horrific events, the scale of the Dunblane massacre was small. I've travelled a lot in the last two years and in the course of those travels I've visited other places stained by human atrocity. With Fran and Michael I stayed with an aboriginal community at Oombulgurri in the Kimberley region of Western Australia, where in June 1926 an unknown number of aborigines were shot by a police party and their bodies burnt. Local whites didn't want an inquiry and to this day some of the white population deny that it happened. In January 2000 I stood in the snow at the most awful place

I've ever visited, the site of the death camp at Auschwitz-Birkenau in Poland. Here over a million and a half people died between 1940 and 1945. I try to put the murders at Dunblane in a global and historical perspective. I'm even more aware than ever of the deep trauma experienced by others.

There are wider lessons. When tragedies like this happen, we want to recognise the warnings, face the implications of what has happened and draw out of them something new, something better than we've had. We must be honest. I've described many instances where words have not been matched by deeds, reports haven't equated with reality. My own courage has been tested to the limit. There are positive lessons, not least that survivors can and do still stand and face the world. This is especially so when they can find collective strength. There is no need to yield to the agendas of those who cannot face the consequences of what's happened. Those of us who have grieved are often told that we should have moved on, but to move on too far would be to forget. Indeed there is a constant tension between forgetting and remembering. If we forget we enter the dangerous realm of denial. To remember is to honour truth.

Dunblane is thriving, expanding, as popular a place to live as ever. As if to remind those of us who regularly visit the children's graves that the town has moved on, a new housing estate is being built on three sides of the Cemetery. Occupants of some of the new houses will have a view over the headstones towards the Memorial Garden. The town has evolved and will always be more than the tragedy, but I hope that those who died on 13 March 1996 will always remain at its heart and that Dunblane will never forget.

This story still has too many gaps and too many loose ends that may never be tied up. The greatest and most lasting gaps are among the family of a dedicated teacher and in those households where a lively nine- or ten-year-old child should have been today, where framed faces on the walls should never have been forever five. Although she's not here, Sophie seems ever present in my house. Her smile lights every place I visit. She has lived on through those positive achievements of the last four years, even though she knew nothing of them.

This book is as hard to finish as it has been to write. I have trouble finding an 'end'. For Sophie there was no proper ending and I have no wish to impose another one. Neither is there a need for one, because for me and countless others her memory lives on.

Sophie, on each of your last two birthdays I wrote you a poem. This year, with you in my thoughts throughout, I have written a book. You will always be remembered, never forgotten.

# Bibliography

Althea, *When Uncle Bob Died*. London: Dinosaur Publications, 1982

Barnard, Peter, *We Interrupt this Programme*. London: BBC Publications, 1999

Barty, Alexander (with additions by J.W. Barty and Elisabeth Okasha), *The History of Dunblane*. Stirling: Stirling District Libraries, 1994

Britton, Paul, *The Jigsaw Man*. London: Bantam, 1997

Chapman, Simon, *Over our Dead Bodies*. Annandale: Pluto Press, 1998

Clements, Alan, Farquharson, Kenny and Wark, Kirsty, *Restless Nation*. Edinburgh: Mainstream, 1996

Cullen, W. Douglas, *The Public Inquiry into the Shootings at Dunblane Primary School on 13 March* (the Cullen Report). London: The Stationery Office, 1996

Davis, Howard and Scraton, Phil, *Beyond Disaster – Identifying and Resolving Inter-Agency Conflict in the Immediate Aftermath of Disasters*. Report from the Home Office Emergency Planning Division, 1997

————, *Disaster, Trauma, Aftermath*. London: Lawrence and Wishart, 2000

Dunblane Community Council, *The Dunblane Community Council Survey Report*. Stirling: Stirling District Council, 1993

Dunblane Fund Trustees, *The Report of the Trustees*. Stirling, 1999

Dunblane Support Centre, *Three Years On*. Stirling: Stirling Council, 1999

Emergency Planning Society, 'People's Rights – Organisational Wrongs':

Transcript of Conference, 14 April 1999

Essler, Gavin, *The United States of Anger*. London: Michael Joseph, 1997

Hannan, Martin and MacLeod, Donald, *Twentieth-Century Scotland. A Pictorial Chronicle 1900–2000*. Edinburgh: Mainstream, 2000

Home Affairs Committee, *Fifth Report: 'Possession of Handguns'*. London: HMSO, 1996

————, *Second Report: 'Controls over Firearms'*. London: The Stationery Office, 2000

Keay, John and Keay, Judith (eds), *Collins Encyclopaedia of Scotland*. London: HarperCollins, 1994

Lewis, C.S., *A Grief Observed*. London: Faber and Faber, 1961

McKerrachar, Archie, *The Street and Place Names of Dunblane and District*. Stirling: Stirling Council Libraries, 1992

Mikac, Walter, *To Have and to Hold*. Sydney: Macmillan, 1997

Munn, Louis, 'Handling the Media at Dunblane'. *Civil Protection*, 42, 8–9, 1996

Pilger, John, *Hidden Agendas*. London: Vintage, 1998

Preston, Peter, *Dunblane: Reflecting Tragedy*. London: British Executive International Press Institute, 1996

Samson, Peter and Crow, Alan, *Dunblane: Our Year of Tears*. Edinburgh: Mainstream, 1997

Scraton, Phil, *The State of the Police*. London: Pluto Press, 1985

————, *Hillsborough: The Truth*. Edinburgh: Mainstream, 2000

Stevens, Evelyn, *Galanthus byzantinus* 'Sophie North'. *The Rock Garden* (Journal of the Scottish Rock Garden Club) xxv, 147–149, 1997

Sutherland, William, *Central Scotland Police 1996. A Report of Her Majesty's Chief Inspector of Constabulary*. 1996

Taylor, Ian, 'Respectable, Rural and English: the Lobby against the Regulation of Firearms in Great Britain'. In Carlen, Pat and Morgan, Rod (eds), *Crime Unlimited? Questions for the 21st Century*. London: Macmillan, 1999

Vulliamy, Ed, *Seasons in Hell: Understanding Bosnia's War*. New York: St Martin's Press, 1994

Wagner Shelly, *The Andrew Poems*. Lubbock: Texas Tech University Press, 1994

Whyte, Dave, 'Ladbroke Grove Inquiry: a Public Stitch-up?' *The Socio-Legal Newsletter*, 29 November, 1, 10–11, 1999

## ARTICLES AND LETTERS WRITTEN BY THE AUTHOR

North, Mick, 'Private Grief, Public Action'. Letter to *Scotland on Sunday*, 7 April 1996

————, 'Licence to Kill must be Revoked'. *Times Higher Educational Supplement*, 27 September 1996

————, 'Don't put Sport before Safety'. *Sunday Times*, 13 October 1996

————, 'The Father's Story'. *Scotland on Sunday*, 20 October 1996

————, 'The Pain and Sadness never go Away'. *Scotland on Sunday*, 22 December 1996

————, 'Dunblane: a Victim's Rights'. Letter to *The Guardian*, 2 June 1997

————, 'Take the "Toys" from the Boys'. *News of the World*, 9 November 1997

————, 'The Case against: Citizens should not be allowed to carry Guns for Defensive Purposes'. *International Journal of Risk, Security and Crime Prevention* 3, 313-318, 1998

————, 'Echoes of Dunblane Tragedy in Police Efforts to duck the Power Report'. Letter to *Scotland on Sunday*, 26 April 1998

————, 'God protect us from the Anti-grief Police'. Letter to *The Observer*, 6 September 1998

————, 'Storm clouds the Issues'. *Scotland on Sunday*, 6 April 1999

## ALL PROFITS FROM THIS BOOK WILL BE DONATED TO THE FOLLOWING:

Breakthrough Breast Cancer
6th Floor
Kingsway House
103 Kingsway
London WC2B 6QX
www.breakthrough.org.uk


Children's Hospice Association of Scotland (CHAS)
3 High Street
Kinross
KY13 8AW


Gun Control Network (GCN)
PO Box 11495
London N3 2FE
www.gun-control-network.org